# Mentors and Tormentors

*On the Journey to Self-Respect*

TIM JONES, M.D.

ISBN 978-1-63903-258-7 (paperback)
ISBN 978-1-63903-259-4 (digital)

Christian Faith Publishing
832 Park Avenue
Meadville, PA 16335
www.christianfaithpublishing.com

Printed in the United States of America

# Contents

Introduction.................................................................5

1. The Two Secrets of Happiness..............................9
2. Become a Bartender .........................................22
3. Running Interference ........................................36
4. Slick 'n' Greasy................................................51
5. The Three *B*s—Beg, Bargain, and Bully.............64
6. The One Person ...............................................82
7. How to Say No ................................................86
8. Prune Your Tree...............................................102
9. Great Expectations ..........................................112
10. The Luckiest Man Alive ....................................125
11. The Mule-Headed Formula................................141
12. Pure Evil........................................................157
13. Don't Peck on Me............................................174
14. The Con ........................................................194
15. Emotional Fatigue...........................................209
16. Respect Yourself .............................................226

About the Author.....................................................230

# Introduction

# Pay Attention and Ask Questions

"Where's my radio?" Wendall muttered to himself. He thought, *I know I had it here in my room this morning. It's not in my backpack or my desk. Did I take it somewhere and lay it down? No, I haven't left the house.* Then Wendall heard a static noise that could only be emitted by an electronic device, a TV or…his radio.

"Damon!"

Damon was Wendall's five-year-old little brother. He had plagued Wendall for the past three years. Wendall didn't count the first two years of Damon's life. Damon was fine when he was a baby. But he had grown into a little brat with two principal vices: no respect for other people's property and no boundaries to his manipulative behavior. So Wendall had to keep tolerating Damon's stealing, pilfering, borrowing, and otherwise destroying Wendall's "stuff," again and again. This day was no different from any of the previous thousand days of the past three years.

Wendall yelled from the hallway, "Damon! You little jerk! Where's my radio?"

He could hear soft static coming from somewhere in the house. As Wendall approached Damon's closed bedroom door, the sound suddenly stopped. Wendall burst in unannounced. "Where's my radio?"

Damon was sitting on his bed holding his pillow over something. He looked up and away from Wendall. "I don't know."

"What's under the pillow?"

"Uh, my GI Joe, Ranger Rick. I'm smothering him. So he can learn to take torture."

"I'm gonna torture *you* if you don't give me my radio. Right now!"

"Mom! Wendall's gonna torture me!"

"Give it to me, you little twerp."

"Momma! He called me a little twerp!"

Wendall lunged for the pillow and ripped it out of Damon's grubby little hands to reveal, sure enough, GI Joe, Ranger Rick, with his ear up to Wendall's transistor radio.

"Gimme that!" Wendall snapped up his stolen property.

"Wendull!" Damon whined. "Now Range Rick can't talk to his squad. He'll be captured and killed, and it'll *all be your fault*. I'm gonna tell Mom…"

Wendall was already out the door. "Stuff it!"

In 1974, Wendall was a fourteen-year-old, middle-class teenager in small town Benson, Kansas. To describe him as being naive, sheltered, privileged, envious, and insecure would be accurate. But Wendall's distorted opinion of himself was much more flattering. He was simply "oppressed." As proof, he recited his many "problems" during his daily pity party: not old enough to drive, no girlfriend, no spending money, not big enough to play football, not fast enough to play football, too short, not particularly good-looking, too skinny, occasional acne, nearsighted, unable to grow a mustache, and of course, he had a demon for a little brother.

Fate had blessed Wendall with two assets that he completely took for granted, his parents. Both worked. Max Nichols was a repairman with Monroe Calculator Company in the days when "adding machines" had rows of buttons and a large handle on the side to pull down and mechanically make each calculation. Money was his main stress. His goal was to save enough to put Wendall and Damon through college, then retire. Susan Nichols worked nights as a nurse's aide in the newborn nursery at Sisters of Mercy in Benson, and she held another full-time job during the day as a housewife. The Nichols home had a standard three bedrooms and two bathrooms. Thankfully, Wendall had his own room. But his mom and dad wouldn't let him put a lock on his door to keep out the family kleptomaniac. They had only one car, a '72 Olds Cutlass, which Max took to work every morning and drove Susan to the hospital in the evenings.

Yet despite all his blessings and overlooked advantages, Wendall was resentful. Other kids his age "had more," "had it easier," or at least, "didn't have Damon." Therefore, Wendall had convinced himself that he was unhappy and that his life mostly "sucked." But in reality, Wendall's many "problems" were just figments of his low self-esteem.

Fortunately, one spring morning, Wendall noticed an interesting fact. He felt best when he was outdoors. Wendall initially assumed it was because Damon almost never went outside. However, he began to realize that it had nothing to do with Damon. It had everything to do with talking to eighty-year-old Mrs. Brown next door. Unless it was raining, she was outside working in her garden. Her smile, the tone of her voice, her attitude, and her general happiness *always* cheered him up. But how? If Wendall possessed one admirable quality, it was curiosity. It's surprising what a person can learn by paying attention and asking questions. These two persistent habits would help Wendall learn lifelong lessons from an assorted cast of remarkable people. Some were mentors; others were tormentors. Together, they changed his life, starting with Mrs. Brown.

This is Wendall's four-year journey from ignorance to enlightenment and from insecurity to confidence. Please enjoy, and remember to always, pay attention and ask questions.

# 1

# The Two Secrets
# of Happiness

*I tell my babies, if you're not grateful for* everything,
*you ain't* never *gonna be completely happy.*

—Mrs. Brown

The happiest person Wendall had ever met was Mrs. Brown. She lived next door. Mrs. Brown was the only black person in their neighborhood. Wendall didn't know her first name. He never asked. She was always just "Mrs. Brown." She lived alone, but visiting grandchildren and great-grandchildren filled her house and garden most of the time. She had six children, five still living, and she had been widowed for ten years. The more Wendall learned about her, the more he realized what a difficult and tragic life she had lived. Her earliest memory was picking cotton in Mississippi around 1900. She lost two little sisters, one to pneumonia and the other to meningitis, both before the age of five because there was no money for doctors or medicine. Her parents died of tuberculosis shortly after she married in 1915, leaving Mrs. Brown and her husband, Edgar, to raise a younger brother and sister. Then she lost an older brother to a lynch mob in 1920, which finally convinced Edgar to move the family out of Mississippi and on to Kansas. She lost a son in the Pacific in World War II and, finally, her cherished Edgar in a car accident. Mrs. Brown worked every day of her married life as a seamstress while rearing children and maintaining a home and family. She finally "retired from paid work" when the arthritis in her hands made it nearly impossible to sew by hand. Yet despite all the hard work, sacrifice, and tragedy, she was happy. Happier than anyone Wendall ever knew. But how?

Mrs. Brown raised four things in her backyard garden: roses, apricots, dewberries, and children. The children received an education about life by helping her with the other three. Her roses decorated the many flower vases in her small, two-bedroom, wood-frame house. Her dewberry pies were county fair, blue-ribbon quality, and her apricot jam was prized by her many friends. Mrs. Brown's young grandkids would help her pick the dewberries, but she needed Wendall on a ladder to harvest the apricots. Bruised ones on the ground just didn't make the grade; therefore, her three trees had to be picked every four or five days during the two weeks that they were in season. It was rare for Mrs. Brown to actually take a break and sit down. So Wendall had to interview her while picking apricots from her ladder while she handed him small corn husk baskets. Mrs. Brown didn't mind all of his questions. Wendall went straight to the point.

"Why are you so happy all the time?"

"Why shouldn't I be?"

"Well, I mean, you've had so many bad things happen in your life. You know, lost family members and especially what happened to your brother."

She nodded solemnly. "That's true. Life's not perfect. Sometimes it's not even fair. But I'm not gonna let that keep me from being happy."

Wendall reached for a branch a little too far and nearly tipped the ladder over.

"Be careful up there. I don't want a bad thing to happen to you."

"Right. That was close." Wendall stepped off the ladder to move it a few feet in an arc around the tree. He still hadn't gotten the answer he wanted.

"But how can you be happy when so many horrible things have happened to you?" Wendall shook his head. "How do you do it?"

Mrs. Brown laughed. "I thought you already knew."

"Knew what?"

"That happiness comes from *inside of you*. It doesn't come from what happens on the outside."

Wendall climbed the four steps on her rather wobbly wooden ladder and resumed the harvest. "Okay. But how do you get happiness inside and keep it there?"

"My grandfather taught me that. He was a slave in Mississippi until he ran away to the north during the civil war when he was sixteen."

"No kidding."

"That's right. When I was a little girl, I asked him just like you're asking me right now, 'Papa, why are you so happy all the time?' And you know what he said? He said, "Cause I'm *free*. Free to live where I want, do what I want, and have the family I want.' He always said, 'There ain't no happiness in the heart of a slave. *Happiness comes from freedom.*'"

Wendall stopped picking apricots for a few seconds and thought about being owned like an animal, told what to do, and when to do it and being whipped if he didn't. He looked down at Mrs. Brown with all seriousness. "I wouldn't have made a good slave. They'd kill me the first day."

A broad smile showed her false teeth. "That's good!"

"What? Good? No! Good that I would die?"

Mrs. Brown got so tickled she nearly dropped the empty baskets in her hand. "No, child. Good that freedom is so strong inside you. You've never known anything else. Now, if someone tried to take it from you, then you'd say, 'No, I'm not gonna let you.'"

Wendall handed Mrs. Brown another basket of apricots and took an empty one. She looked over the full basket and picked out one apricot with a small blemish.

"We'll give this one to the little birds." She tossed it near the fence and continued, "Papa called me Little Miss Question 'cause I wanted to know everything. I asked him, 'Where does freedom come from, Papa?' And you know what he said?"

Half of Wendall's brain kept picking apricots while the other half was locked onto her voice.

"He told me, '*Freedom comes from courage*, the courage to demand freedom and to *fight for it* if need be.'"

Wendall stepped down two steps to hand her another full basket. "It took a lot of guts for your grandfather to run away. 'Cause if they caught you…"

Mrs. Brown looked down. "They whipped you without mercy or sometimes cut half your foot off. And if you didn't die from bleeding or infection, then you were crippled. Some of my Papa's friends had their foot cut off."

She handed Wendall another empty basket. He climbed up two steps and kept pressing the point.

"So where does the courage come from?"

She wagged her finger at him. "You know, that's the exact same thing I asked." Her constant smile widened. "I'm gonna start calling you Little *Mister* Question."

Wendall grinned and took that as a true compliment.

"Papa said, '*Courage comes from self-respect*. Can't have no courage if you don't respect yourself.'"

Wendall stopped and thought. Her grandfather was absolutely right. Even the scrawniest kid in school will fight back every time, if he respects himself.

"You okay up there?" Mrs. Brown had noticed Wendall's temporary trance. "You gettin' too hot out here?"

"Uh…no. No, I'm fine. Just thinkin' about what your Papa said. He was definitely right."

"Well, of course he was." She smiled. Mrs. Brown always enjoyed retorting back with a pretend scold to reinforce her point.

Wendall got back on track. "So where does self-respect…"

Mrs. Brown cut him off, "I *knew* you were gonna ask me that!" They both laughed.

"Papa said, '*Self-respect comes from me*, your Papa. Teachin' you to stand up for yourself and for what's right. Got to learn to tell people 'no' when somethin' ain't right and make no mind to what other people might think or say.'"

Wendall stopped picking apricots, again. He looked at Mrs. Brown and thought out loud, "That's what you teach your grandkids all day long."

"Yes, sir, and their mommas and daddies before them. It's the most important thing. Every chance I get, I tell them how special and important they are. Tell them to stand up for themselves and for each other. Always do what's fair and what's right, no matter what anyone else is gonna say or do. I got fourteen grandchildren and three great-grandchildren so far. It's a full-time job."

"And all this time, I thought you were just a doting grandmother."

"Why, of course I am!" Mrs. Brown did it again. She pretended to be angry, but her smile gave her away.

Wendall had to shake his head. How had he missed that? It was so obvious now.

"My grandchildren will all be able to say, 'No, that's not what I want.' 'No, you don't treat me that way.' 'No, that's not right.' 'No, that's not fair.'"

Her advanced philosophy lesson was slowing down Wendall's fruit-picking. He stopped again and contemplated the importance of that little two-letter rejection. "*No* is a powerful word."

Mrs. Brown's wide-brimmed straw hat flopped up and down. "Yes, it is. Probably the most powerful word in any language. I remember my Papa telling me that the *one thing* his master could *never* accept was a slave saying *no* to any white folk."

"Really."

"Oh yes. 'Cause the minute a slave says *no*, then that means he's got self-respect, making him an *uppity* n—. That self-respect gives him courage, making him a *dangerous* n—. That courage leads to freedom, making him a *runaway* n—. And that freedom leads to happiness, making him a *happy* n—."

Wendall's eyebrows went up each time she used the *n-word*, as if someone was poking his ribs with a stick. Perhaps Mrs. Brown used it because those were her grandfather's exact words. Wendall had to find out.

"I always thought...n—was a bad word."

13

Mrs. Brown nodded and appeared pleased that he had questioned her use of the word. "It is. But those are the words my Papa used many years ago, with *defiance*. It was his way of saying, 'No matter what you call me, I'm still gonna get my freedom and be happy.'" She glanced up at the clear blue sky. "From then on, anytime anyone called me a n—, I knew they were afraid of me. Just like Papa's master was afraid of him."

Wendall's astonished look prompted Mrs. Brown to specify, "They're afraid of me becoming their equal."

Wendall was stunned. Mrs. Brown had transformed a foul, racist label into a touchstone of strength. As for the name-calling racists, she wasn't their equal. She was their better, and they knew it by the dignity she maintained. All Wendall could think to say was, "I hope things are better today than in the past."

Mrs. Brown lifted her chin with confidence. "Yes. Yes, they are. No more WHITES ONLY and COLORED signs outside the restrooms, stores, and restaurants. Now I can shop and eat where I want."

Wendall carefully handed her another full basket of apricots. As he watched her place it on the ground and reach for an empty basket, he wondered aloud, "Why did it take so long to happen?"

Mrs. Brown paused and stared at the ground for a few seconds before looking up at him. "I reckon because white folks in the north didn't want to upset the white folks in the south. They looked the other way and allowed all the bad laws and hateful treatment."

Wendall reached down to accept another empty basket. "Basically, they took away a big chunk of your freedom."

Mrs. Brown nodded sadly. "Civil rights is all about people demanding a chance at *happiness*, free from being treated second-class. Just like Papa said, it starts with self-respect and saying 'no' to being pushed down. It's self-respect that gives people the courage to protest. Like you see on TV, even when they're beaten and arrested, their courage forces the truth to come out. Eventually, other people take notice, and then the laws change, and finally, there's more freedom and happiness for everyone."

Wendall shook his head. "But racism is still out there."

"Oh yes. And it will be until people stop teaching it to their children."

Just as they finished the third and final tree, Mrs. Brown ran out of baskets. Her picnic table was covered with thirty or more all filled to the brim.

She motioned Wendall to come down from the ladder. "Time to make a batch of jam, but I think I'll wait until tomorrow to start."

Wendall helped her carry the loaded baskets to her kitchen. She insisted that he take home one basket as payment for his help that day. Instead, Wendall felt like he should be paying her. But how could anyone put a price on her wisdom.

That next week, Wendall thought about happiness coming from "inside" of us, starting with our self-respect. But he kept hearing people say something completely different. They repeatedly said he or she "makes me happy" or some gift or event "made me happy." Wendall's friend, Toby, was "happy" to get twenty dollars for his birthday from his grandmother. Debbie Smith's senior high boyfriend gave her his class ring, and she was "so happy." Johnny Blake was "unbelievably happy" when Katherine said she would be his girlfriend. How could something or someone on the outside "make" you happy? Please explain that to me, Professor Brown.

It rained the next weekend, which meant none of Mrs. Brown's grandkids would be coming to visit. Her home was small and too full of breakables for them to be "cooped up." Therefore, Wendall invited himself over and presented his paradox as they sat in her living room.

Mrs. Brown laughed as if he had just told a joke. "It's all the same thing."

"But how?"

"Because they're boosting the other person's self-respect. That twenty dollars and that uh…"

"Class ring."

"Yes, that ring. You know, a ring is real special to a young girl. All those *things* say, 'You're important to me. I love you and care about you.' Lifts up their self-respect."

Mrs. Brown held up her index finger, as she always did when she wanted to make an important point. "But you've got to be careful. If most of your happiness comes from things and people, then one of these days, you might lose those things and people, and then…" She shook her head.

"Then you crash?"

She nodded. "Yes, it's sad. That's why your self-respect must come from *inside* of you. You've got to *know* that you're important and worthwhile, regardless of all the wonderful things and people in your life. That way, your happiness is always gonna be there."

"But it's nice when other people appreciate you."

"Sure! That's the way people are *supposed* to treat each other, all the time. My Edgar used to tell me every day that I was the most beautiful girl he ever saw." Mrs. Brown snickered. "And I would say, 'Even with all these wrinkles and false teeth?' And he would say, 'Yes, ma'am.'"

Wendall smiled. Edgar was right. His wife's inner beauty radiated through the gray hair and sagging skin.

"I'm sorry I never got to meet him."

"I am too. But you know, there's someone who will *always* love you and boost you up and never die. That's our Lord Savior, Jesus Christ. So we *all got good reason* to be full of self-respect and happiness, no matter what."

Wendall nodded in agreement, but he was secretly embarrassed by the depth of his own faith. His was as shallow as a mud puddle compared to her deep ocean.

Mrs. Brown slowly pushed herself up from her living room chair. "Would you like some lemonade?"

"Yeah, that would be great. Thanks."

She walked around the corner to her kitchen.

Wendall looked around the room for further clues to her life. Mrs. Brown's house was always immaculately clean. The furnishings were modest and old but well cared for with knitted quilts to cover the frayed spots on the upholstery. Dozens of photos, pictures, figurines, and other mementos lined the bookshelves, the mantle, and the top of her TV. Two framed cross-stitch pictures hanging over the couch caught his eye. The top one said RESPECT YOURSELF and the one underneath, BE GRATEFUL FOR EVERYTHING. Wendall recognized the first one about respect. But they had not talked about the concept of being grateful. Gratitude could have been Mrs. Brown's middle name. She was genuinely grateful for everything, from the blazing sun to the cold rain. It didn't matter. She never complained. For Mrs. Brown, everything in life had a purpose. The good was to be embraced, and the bad was to be opposed. When she came back with the lemonade, Wendall asked her about the two pictures.

"My daughter, Sheryl, stitched those for me. Guess she figured those were my mottos. I've repeated them so many times to my children and now all my grandchildren."

Wendall grimaced. "I can't say I'm grateful for everything. After all, I've got my little brother, Damon, to deal with."

Mrs. Brown smiled. "Be grateful for Damon more than *anyone else* in your life."

"But why? He is such a little…aggravation." Wendall had almost said "little shit" but caught himself just in time.

"Because he can make you a stronger person."

"Really?"

"Yes." She nodded with a teacher's confidence. "Damon can teach you to be patient and tolerant but firm about what's right. And you can teach him to be respectful and grateful. You see, the best way to learn something is to teach it to someone else." She grinned. "Besides, you'll need the practice for all the children you're gonna have some day."

Wendall shook his head. "I'm definitely not ready for that."

"But you'll be so grateful for them when you are. I tell my babies, if you're not grateful for *everything*, you ain't *never* gonna be completely happy."

"I guess you're right."

"Of course I'm right!" Mrs. Brown let out a wide smile. "That reminds me. I got a funny story to tell you about my grandson Leroy."

"What did he do?"

"Well, I'll tell ya. Leroy's about four years old, and he has a serious sweet tooth. One day, I didn't have any more candy in the house, so we walked down to the little grocery store around the corner."

"Oh yeah, Bishops."

"That's the one. Well, he decided he wanted a lollipop. He wanted one of those thick yellow-and-orange-striped ones."

Wendall had seen that type of lollipop before. He didn't particularly care for them since they were half an inch thick, hard as a rock, and became very sticky. "We call 'em rope lollipops. They're like a rope of hard candy coiled into a circle."

"Well, Leroy didn't know it, but I bought him the smaller size, which was still as big as a silver dollar, knowin' he couldn't eat it all."

"So he was grateful?"

"For all of five minutes."

Wendall chuckled. "What happened? Did he drop it?"

"No. On our way home, a little girl rode by on her bicycle licking on the bigger-sized lollipop, the one that's the size of a saucer."

"Uh-oh."

"He started…" Mrs. Brown couldn't keep from laughing. "He started cryin' and pointing at her lollipop. I said, 'What's wrong?' And he said, 'She got a bigger lollipop, Mema.' So I told him, 'Leroy, you got to be grateful for what *you've* got.'"

"But that didn't help?"

She shook her head. "Not a bit."

"That's when I told him, 'If you eat all of your lollipop, then I'll buy you a lollipop just as big as the one that little bicycle girl had.'"

"Did it make him sick?"

"Almost. He got about halfway done. He finally said, 'Mema, I think I got enough lollipop. I don't want anymore,' and he handed it to me. I told him we would wrap it up and save it for next time. And you know what he said? He said, 'Because I'm grateful for what I got.' I was so proud of him. Gave him a big hug."

Wendall understood Leroy's initial envy. "I'm not always grateful for what I've got when I see what some people have."

"What do some people have?"

It was the first time Mrs. Brown had actually asked Wendall a question. He was caught off guard and forced to think on his feet.

"Uh, well, like a backyard swimming pool or lots of new clothes. Oh, and…uh, new shoes and a bigger house with a game room and pinball machines."

Mrs. Brown nodded. "Those are all nice things, but instead of looking at what you don't have, why don't you tell me about all the things you do have?"

Wendall was starting to feel nervous. He could easily end up sounding more ungrateful than Leroy. "Uh, like what?"

"Oh, like a nice house in a safe neighborhood in the freest country in the world. You got clothes on your back, shoes on your feet, food on the table three times a day, and you get to go to school and get an education. And don't leave out, you got people who love you and take care of you."

Now Wendall was embarrassed. But he knew it was his own fault.

She smiled. "Anything you have…" She raised her index finger again. "There are millions of people in this world who don't have it." She nodded. "You've got to be *grateful for everything*."

She motioned to her Bible on the coffee table. "You know, there's a reason the Tenth Commandment says, 'Thou shalt not covet.' Yes, sir…like I always say, God wants us to be happy."

"I hadn't thought of it that way. Guess you're right."

"Of course I'm right! When are you gonna learn?"

Wendall smiled. He needed to stop admitting his pleasant surprise whenever she was right.

Mrs. Brown continued, "We often forget to be grateful for the people in our lives. So many people don't have anybody."

They both sat silent for a few seconds. Wendall wasn't certain of what to say, so he blurted out what he was thinking, "Sometimes it's hard to remember all the people and the times we've had together."

Mrs. Brown smiled. "Well, I need a little help with that. That's why I have reminders."

"Reminders?"

"Sure. Everybody needs reminders of all their blessings." She swept her hand toward the picture-packed shelves. "See all the pictures of my wonderful family. I've got all my children on the top shelf. That's when they were seniors in high school. And on the second and third shelves are my grandchildren. Of course, I have to get new pictures every couple of years. They grow up so fast. Then on the fourth shelf are my three great-grandbabies. I expect the bottom shelf will be needed before too long."

Wendall thought, *What a lucky group of people.*

She pointed to an old black-and-white photo on her mantle. "That's me and Edgar on our trip to Hawaii for our fortieth anniversary in 1955. And that doll next to us was given to me by a little girl who lived next door when I was a child. It was the only doll I had until I was ten."

Wendall thought of the wonderful and distant people behind the smiling faces and the worn-out doll. "But doesn't it make you sad that those people and times are gone?"

Mrs. Brown's mouth dropped open. "No. Of course not." This was no pretend scold, and just when Wendall thought he was finally getting a handle on this happiness business.

"Why should I feel sad about the joyful life I've lived? I am oh so grateful for all the people I've loved and all the times we spent together."

She looked down, and her voice turned soft. "So many people get cheated out of what I got. I think about my two little baby sisters that died. I *do* feel sad for them. Never having a chance to grow up, fall in love, and get married and have children. Yes, God has blessed me more than I ever deserved."

They sat silently as Wendall thought for a moment about her little sisters. "When you think about it that way, I should be grateful for every, single day I have."

Mrs. Brown looked at him with a pride that only a mother could give to her child. "*Now*, you're startin' to understand."

Wendall never forgot Mrs. Brown or her two secrets of happiness: *respect yourself* and *be grateful for everything.* Over the years, he formulated his own conclusion that he believed she would approve: *Although happiness starts with a solid core of self-respect, the essential requirement is gratitude.* No matter how much self-respect, courage, and freedom you possess. No matter how much other people love you. No matter how talented or successful you are. No matter how many homes, cars, or toys you own. No matter how much money you have. Unless you are grateful for *everything*, good and bad, in your life, you will *not* be completely happy. Mrs. Brown had it right. You might be happy some of the time but never all the time. An old adage is to "count your blessings." Better yet, *write them down or create a computer file*. List every person in your life, every talent and skill you possess, every possession, everything about your health, and every memorable experience. Include both the good and the bad. Listing the "bad" is difficult. But remember, the challenges in our lives can make us stronger and teach us important lessons. Review and add to your list of blessings every day. Understand clearly that for every "good" blessing you possess, there are millions, even billions, of people in this world who do not have that blessing. Finally, just like Mrs. Brown, use *reminders* to help you remember your many blessings and to *cherish every day* as a priceless gift. After all, you only get so many on this earth.

# 2

# Become a Bartender

*Only they know what is best for them, not me. They'll eventually figure out what they need to do.*

—Shorty Tull

Shorty's Bar and Grill was the local watering hole. It was the only surviving business on the east side of Twelfth Street between Elm and Cedar. The row of clapboard, single-story buildings had long since lost all their paint and stood gray and rough. The proprietor, Shorty Tull, often joked that he wanted to paint the front of his bar, but then, it wouldn't match the rest of the block. Shorty's was the only business Wendall ever saw with a screen door on the front "to keep the bugs out." Weather permitting, the inside wooden front door was always open. Shorty's greatest fear was that some "delinquent kid" would break into one of the adjacent buildings to smoke cigarettes and burn down the entire block. Never mind that Shorty himself smoked. His paranoia explained all the combination padlocks on the other buildings, even though he didn't own them. It was well-known that Shorty would "whip us like scrambled eggs" if he ever caught someone trespassing. So none of the teenagers ever did.

Shorty was everyone's friend despite his rough edges. Shorty was…well, short but also balding, fat, and he enjoyed a cologne of beer, sweat, and cigarette smoke. He always wore a white undershirt that stretched tight over his bulging belly. People called it a wife-beater shirt, but Wendall was certain that Shorty had never beaten his wife. Charlene was a foot taller, a hundred pounds heavier, and she was always doing the heavy lifting in the back. It would not be a pretty nor a fair fight. Shorty was always bragging that when it came to men, he was the "complete package." He was "everything every mother doesn't want for her daughter." Wendall never met Charlene's socialite mom, but he was certain Shorty's description came straight from her, but not as a joke.

Shorty's was a popular hang out with the teenage guys. They could play pool for free, and Shorty had vending machines with candy and sodas. But behind Shorty's back, they affectionately called the bar by a different name, The Greasy Spoon, for obvious reasons. Shorty and Charlene had only three items on their menu: hamburgers, fries, and chili. For ten cents extra, you could add a slice of cheese to your burger. The only utensils Wendall ever saw in the place were spoons. No knives or forks were needed. The burgers were always wrapped in white butcher paper with a toothpick stuck in the center. If you didn't eat your burger right away, the grease would soak through the lower bun and into the butcher paper making it translucent. Sometimes, you had to eat your burger upside down. A red woven plastic basket with the same white paper held the hot, dripping, greasy fries. You always got mustard, pickles, tomatoes, onions, and lettuce on your burger whether you wanted them or not. "Take off what ya don't want" was the standard reply to requests for no onions. You could add ketchup from the squeeze bottle on your table, but don't ask for mayo. Shorty's philosophy was "Mayonnaise spoils and can make ya sick." Wendall had to admit that despite the grease, The Greasy Spoon's burgers were not only bigger, but they also tasted better than McDonald's. He later learned the secret to the great taste. It was bacon. Wendall dropped by early one Saturday morning and found Charlene frying a full package of bacon to give to their old basset hound, Scooter. She said Scooter wouldn't eat anything else. Charlene always poured the bacon grease into an empty Folgers can and later mixed it with Crisco to fry the hamburgers in a skillet. Thus, unknowingly, Charlene had invented the bacon burger…but without the bacon.

The Greasy Spoon may not have looked like much, but Shorty and Charlene ran a successful small business despite the greasy food and the run-down exterior. Beer kept the business afloat, and Shorty certainly knew how to sell beer. More importantly, he knew why people came to his bar. It wasn't to pick up a woman. If fact, Wendall couldn't remember ever seeing a woman, other than Charlene, in the Greasy Spoon. Men came to Shorty's bar for what he called beer therapy.

"Beer therapy? Shorty, what do you mean by beer therapy? Do guys just get so drunk they forget about their problems?"

Shaking his head with a smile, Shorty replied, "No, no. I don't get people drunk. That's illegal."

"Really? I didn't know that."

"Oh yeah, you can't get people drunk and then let 'em go out on the street. They might hurt themselves." Shorty smiled with a hint of pride. "Nah, I just get them to open up and talk about all their problems. That's where the beer comes in. They feel better, I make a little money, and it's a win-win for everybody."

Wendall briefly grimaced at the thought of listening to other people's problems.

"What's the matter? Don't like it when other people tell ya their woes?"

"Uh…Well," Wendall stammered. "Yeah, it usually makes me feel uncomfortable."

Shorty laughed. "You're just not thinking about it right. I don't try to *fix* their problems. I just get them to talk about 'em, and most of the time, they figure out what to do all by themselves."

"Oh, okay" was all Wendall could think to say at that time.

However, Wendall's curiosity eventually got the better of him, as it always did. He wanted to see just how Shorty pulled it off. So he lied to his mom about a late baseball practice, braved the bar's fog of cigarette smoke, and waited for peak therapy time to begin at 7:00 p.m.

"Say there, Bill. What can I get for ya?" Shorty was already filling a mug of beer.

"Uh, yeah, that beer will be just fine, Shorty."

Bill had been an accountant in town for years. Thin and wiry, his heavy black plastic glasses dominated his face and complimented his well-oiled black hair that was parted on the left side.

"So how's life treatin' ya?"

"Oh…" Bill sighed. "Not so good. My wife thinks I'm having an affair."

"Well, you ole dog you!" Shorty slapped him on the shoulder.

Bill looked petrified. "No, no, don't…Don't even say that… please!"

"I'm just kidding." Shorty smiled. "I know you'd never do somethin' stupid like that. But what's got Edith all up in arms?"

"Well…" Bill took a gulp of beer. "There's this young woman the boss hired. I think he's sleeping with her because she does nothing at the office…nothing but put on lipstick and comb her hair all day."

"Ya don't say." Shorty had by now filled four mugs of beer for other nearby customers, but he was still in the loop. "So what's the problem?"

"Well, we're running out of paper because she's kissing all of it."

This made Shorty stop for a second. "Kissing the paper? What do you mean?"

"She puts on her lipstick, then she takes a perfectly good piece of typing paper and kisses it to get off the excess lipstick. Then she'll do it again with another piece of paper if she thinks there's still too much on her lips. She does it all day long."

"Really. Maybe she's just practicing for the boss." Shorty was now back in full stride. "Hey, Tom, this one's got your name on it."

Bill continued, "But she only kisses each page only once. Then she throws it away. And my department is always running out of paper."

"Man, that's a tough problem," Shorty said with a glance. "Good to see ya again, Johnny. Doin' okay?"

"Right." Bill nodded. "Don't want to get fired by upsetting the boss's girlfriend."

"So whadda ya think, Bill?" Shorty was still smiling and was now working the cash register.

"I went ahead and told her she was wasting too much paper, and you know what she did?"

"I have no idea." Shorty looked back over his shoulder from across the bar. "Tell me. 'Cause women can do anything."

"She just smiled, looked straight at me, and then before I could move, she kissed the collar of my white shirt with that bright-red lipstick."

Laughter erupted from surrounding beer drinkers who were eavesdropping.

"Laugh all you want, but my wife didn't find it very funny. And she still doesn't believe me."

Shorty quickly reassured him, "Bill, we're not laughing at you. We're laughing with you. What can ya do? Women are like mountain lions, dangerous and very territorial."

"Really?"

"Oh yeah, I understand what you're going through. Hell, remember that Johnson girl in those cut off shorts lookin' like Daisy Duke and always coming in here wantin' free beer?"

Bill nodded. "I thought she was a prostitute."

Another round of laughter. But this one made Bill smile.

"Believe it or not, that's exactly what Charlene thought." Shorty was shaking his head but continued to smile.

Bill still looked distressed. "But, Shorty, what should I do if she doesn't stop?"

"Don't worry," he said with confidence. "Your wife and your boss know you're a good guy. You'll win in the end."

Bill thought for a few seconds. "I appreciate that, Shorty." He reached out his right hand, and Shorty immediately gave him a reassuring handshake.

Wendall had no idea whether Bill's wife eventually believed him or not. But one thing was certain. When Bill left the bar, he was much better prepared to convince her of the truth.

Whenever he could, Wendall sat quietly in the corner of the bar pretending to read a book. He listened to Shorty work his magic. Wendall soon noticed a simple fact. Shorty did nothing more than repeatedly use the same worn-out one-liners. Wendall even jotted down a list. Then he had fun marking down how many times Shorty used each one. "I understand" was the clear winner. The runners up were as follows:

- "I know."
- "Tell me about it."
- "You're right."
- "What are ya supposed to do?"
- "I hear ya."
- "Isn't that the truth?"
- "Who knows?" And then throwing up his hands.
- "Same thing happened to me" or Charlie or Bill or John, etc.
- "Can't live with 'em and can't live without 'em."
- "Go figure."
- "Happens every time." And then nodding his head.
- "Ain't that the drizzles?"
- "Ya know, it's just a pain in the butt sometimes."
- "Been there, done that."

Shorty owned a broken record of reassuring responses. His message was simple but effective: "I'm listening, and I understand what you're saying." But Shorty *never* told his customers what to do or what not to do. Come to think of it, he never offered *any* advice. Not that a lot of guys didn't ask.

"Shorty, what do you think I should do?"

Shorty's response was always the same. "Oh man, that's a good question." Then he would rub his chin. "Hard to say, but I'm sure you'll figure it out." Then with a cheerleader's confidence, he would add, "Hang in there."

To Shorty, everything was a "good question," a "tough problem," a "sticky situation," or a "pain in the butt." Whenever Shorty was asked, "What should I do?" his responses were "Not sure," "Wish I knew," and "Hard to say." But he *always* immediately followed it up with "Hang in there," "Don't give up," and "You'll figure it out."

Wendall also noticed that Shorty never actually *did* anything for any of his customers. Well...other than serve them another beer, *even if,* they asked him specifically for his help.

27

"Shorty, could you loan me fifty bucks until I get paid next Friday? You know I'm good for it."

"I wish I could, but I'm not in the banking business. I can only afford to sell beer."

"Shorty, could I borrow your lawn mower this weekend?"

"Sorry, Ed, I was about to ask you if I could borry *your* mower. I think mine needs a new blade."

For everything else and for *all other requests*, Shorty's response was generally, "Wish I could, but I just can't. But I'm sure you'll find someone to help ya out."

Shorty never got involved in his customer's problems. It was a skill that Wendall came to admire. He later asked Shorty about it.

"Oh yeah. Just let 'em know that you're there for 'em. That you understand what's goin' on."

Wendall tried to imagine himself in that role. "But what if you don't understand?"

"Ya still say, 'I understand'…even if ya don't."

"So…you lie?"

"Sure!" Shorty bellowed with a chuckle. For a few seconds, he became a balding, beardless Santa with a belly full of jelly. "Why not? Not gonna hurt anybody." Shorty started to brag, "Believe me, I've heard some unbelievable shit that I'll never understand."

"Oh, and another thing…" He pointed his finger at Wendall for emphasis. "*Never*, and I mean never, take sides or badmouth anybody."

Wendall let Shorty's seriousness sink in. "Okay."

"Not their wife or boss or kids or mother-in-law, not anybody."

"But what if they're already trash-talking somebody?"

"*Especially* if they're trashin' somebody else. Don't get in the middle of things. Besides, you might insult their wife or kids *too* much. Now they're mad at you for insulting their family." Shorty looked down and shook his head. "I know it sounds messed up."

Shorty suddenly looked up. "Oh, and one more thing."

Wendall almost started laughing. "One more thing" was one of Shorty's favorite expressions.

Shorty leaned forward over the bar. "Don't offer any advice."

Wendall had to lean back a little to maintain some space and avoid Shorty's bad breath.

"What's wrong with advice? You could maybe help them." Wendall wasn't trying to provoke Shorty. He was just sincerely curious.

"Because if you do, one of three things is gonna happen." Shorty held up three stubby fingers. "And all three of 'em are bad."

Wendall nodded. "Okay."

"First, they'll come up with some lame excuse as to why they just couldn't do what you suggested or they already tried it, and it didn't work."

Wendall nodded. "I've heard that before."

Shorty paused then continued despite the unwelcome interruption, "Or second, they'll take your advice and come back later to complain that it made things a whole lot worse. So now it's your fault."

"That doesn't sound fair."

"Who cares about fair?" Shorty barked. "Or third, and this is the worst, they'll try your advice, and it'll actually help...a little. Then they expect you to help them even *more*. Now you can't get rid of 'em! They're like a stray mutt that you fed some table scraps. Hell, you just became their workin'-for-free shrink."

Shorty's face began to turn red, and Wendall could see the bulging veins in his neck. It was obvious that he had learned this lesson the hard way.

"Yuk," Wendall blurted out.

"Exactly. Like a bad beer. Nope, you let 'em figure it out for themselves."

"Really." Wendall was genuinely surprised.

"Of course. Only *they* know what's best for them, not me." Nodding confidently, he added, "They'll eventually figure out what they need to do. I just give 'em confidence to hang in there until that happens."

"So it's all about giving them confidence." Wendall couldn't resist parroting what Shorty was teaching. Somehow, he thought it would help him to remember.

It was a lesson that Wendall would soon experience again. The Greasy Spoon wasn't the only business establishment providing much-needed "therapy" in town. There was the dreaded hair salon, Lucy's Curl Up & Dye, which was exactly what Wendall felt like doing every time his mom dragged him in there.

"Oh, Mom! Do I have to go?"

"Yes. Get your shoes on." Susan headed back to the kitchen to pick up the grocery list.

"Why can't I just stay here at the house?"

"I told you." The irritation in her voice was now unmistakable. "You need to help me pick up that table from your grandmother's, and I won't have time to come back here to pick you up."

Bummer. Wendall would have to sit in a hair salon for an hour to save his mom twenty minutes of driving. The problem with the salon, besides the choking smell of hair spray and nail polish remover, was that Wendall would be the only male in the place, *and* he would be treated as if he were still six years old. He was a little rooster about to walk into a hen house.

"Oh, look how much little Wendy has grown!"

Wendall hated being called Wendy. Wendy was a girl's name. Little Wendy was even worse. Sometimes he envied Damon. You can't feminize the name Damon. You can only change it to "Demon."

"It seems like just yesterday, Susan, you had to carry a diaper bag and push a stroller in here."

"Goodness, Susan, is that some peach fuzz on his upper lip?"

"Wendall, darling, I'll have to introduce you to my little granddaughter, Lilly. You two could go to the soda shop for a malt sometime."

Wendall immediately began looking for a diversion. A small black-and-white TV was positioned in the corner of the tiny waiting area. The soap opera General Hospital was just starting. Drats! The Cincinnati Reds and the Oakland A's were playing game 3 of the World Series on Channel 5. Wendall glanced around to see if anyone would notice if he changed the channel when…

"Oh! Look! Our show is on! What happened to Phillip and Amanda yesterday? I missed it."

Several of the women started talking at once. "Just a minute, just a minute. Marge, you tell her."

"Well, we should find out more today. But yesterday they almost got caught…"

Wendall tuned them out. Angry at having to be there in the first place and for being cheated out of his inalienable right as an American male to watch the World Series. Wendall looked over the magazine rack. Nothing was there but dog-eared *Good Housekeeping* and *Southern Living* editions, not a single *Sports Illustrated* or *Field & Stream* in sight. Why didn't he bring a book? Of course, in today's modern world, Wendall would have a smart phone and the Internet to save him. But those inventions were thirty years in the future. So he pretended to read an article on the latest kitchen designs and stay as inconspicuous as possible. However, curiosity always got the best of Wendall. He started secretly listening to the women talk about all their problems. Wendall soon realized that he was hearing the feminine equivalent of Shorty's beer therapy.

"Oh, honey, they're all like that. They're never gonna change."

"Men can be really stupid. Well, not all of them…but sometimes."

"They never seem to understand."

"Boys will be boys."

"I can't explain it. It must be a man thing."

"Everyone knows you can't live with them. But at the same time, you can't live without them." (Wendall had to stifle a laugh, an exact duplicate from Shorty!)

"You just have to make them think that it was *their* idea."

"Some kids are just born rebellious. Nothing you can do about it. I blame it on my husband. You know, like Doberman's being naturally mean and aggressive."

Wendall heard a lot of "uh-huhs," and he saw knowing heads nodding. He recognized that the hairdressers were using Shorty's strategy and dialogue. First, listen, or at least pretend to listen. Then say, "I understand" or an equivalent, over and over again, but give *no* advice and do *nothing* for the customer. It definitely helped the women vent their frustrations and worries. Yet the hairdresser "therapists" weren't uncomfortable at all. They actually seemed to enjoy the interaction. No wonder his mom liked going to the beauty salon. She always seemed more pleasant and relaxed afterward. But the best was yet to come that afternoon. It was something Wendall had never witnessed at Shorty's Bar & Grill, group therapy.

Margaret was in her fifties and had lost her husband to a sudden heart attack three weeks before. It was apparent that most of the women knew her because they greeted her by name when she came in the door. No doubt, some of them had gone to the funeral. Fortunately, Margaret had an experienced hairdresser, Meg, who had worked at the Curl Up & Dye for years.

"How are you today, Margaret? Do you want a cut today or just have your hair done?"

Margaret sighed. "Oh…I don't know. Probably just a shampoo and curl."

Meg knew she had to tread lightly, so she chose what she thought would be a happy topic.

"How are the grandkids? Did Sarah have her baby yet?"

Meg was standing behind Margaret and couldn't see her eyes suddenly glisten with tears.

Wendall saw Margaret swallow hard. "Uh, yes. Last week." She tried to force a brave smile.

"Wonderful." Meg smiled. "What did she have? A boy or a girl?"

"Uh…A boy," stammered Margaret. "She named him Charles after…after his grandfather." Now Margaret's tears and sobs came flooding out.

Immediately, all the women, hairdressers and customers alike jumped to their feet and huddled around Margaret. Shampoo and suds were dripping off their heads and hands onto the floor and all over Margaret.

"I'm so sorry. You poor dear."

"It'll be okay."

"We're here for you."

"I'm sure he can see that baby now from heaven."

"It's okay, sweetie."

"Just let it out."

"We understand."

"You know we all love ya."

A literal whirlwind of overlapping expressions of condolence, understanding, sympathy, and love filled the room. This incredible scene went on for several minutes with hugs and tears all around. Margaret eventually regained her composure and gave a smile of genuine relief and gratitude. "Thank you all so much. You girls are the best. I'm just having a hard time accepting that he's really gone. I miss him so much."

"We understand, sweetheart." Meg leaned forward and gave her yet another hug. "After I lost my Roger, for two whole months, I kept waking up every hour to tell him to quit hogging the covers."

Better and faster than any drug or the best-trained psychiatrist, this beer therapy, hairdresser therapy, best friend therapy, or whatever you wanted to call it, really worked. Wendall supposed that it went all the way back to prehistoric times. Man is a social animal. We need each other, not just for food, protection, and shelter, but for emotional support as well. Also, Wendall couldn't help but be impressed at the explosion of emotion from Margaret. When she walked into the salon, she was so composed and quiet. Then the bomb went off. He later asked Shorty about it.

"Doesn't surprise me a bit. People can hold a lot of crap inside. They can get like a pressure cooker."

"No kidding."

"Oh yeah. Bad for 'em too. *Really* bad."

"How so?"

"Lots of ways. They either get some health problem like an ulcer or even a heart attack. Or they hit their wife or kids and get thrown in jail or worse..." Shorty paused with his index finger pointing at Wendall. "They shoot themselves in the head or take a bunch of pills or drive off a bridge."

A light went off in Wendall's head. "So some of the car accidents on the news—"

"Right. Ain't exactly accidents."

"Oh my gosh! But why would—"

Shorty cut him off again, "Why would they kill themselves? All the stress and upset got to be too much for 'em. Like a person jumpin' out of a burnin' skyscraper. Anything's better than the heat and the pain they're feelin' at the time."

"Wow." Wendall shook his head. "I had no idea."

"Yep. If they could just let that pressure out, they'd be okay. That's where I come in." Shorty smiled proudly.

"So they just need to talk about their problems."

"Yeah," Shorty let out a slow sigh. "But…people don't always wanna do that."

"Why not?"

"Well, mostly because they don't want to dump their problems on somebody else and make 'em feel *uncomfortable*."

"Really?"

Shorty shot Wendall a sideways look. "Are you kidding me? Don't you remember tellin' me how uncomfortable *you* get when other people tell ya their problems?"

"Oh yeah. That's right. I forgot."

Shorty reassured him, "Don't worry. You're like most people. You feel uncomfortable because you think it's *your job* to *solve* their problems. But it's *definitely* not."

Shorty added, "Oh, *and another thing*. People don't talk about their problems because they're afraid you'll *criticize* them or *judge* them."

"Criticize them?"

"Sure." Shorty flashed a wry smile. "It goes something like this: 'Why the hell did you do that for?'

'Didn't ya know that was gonna lead to trouble?'

'Well, I hate to tell ya, but it's your own damn fault.'"

Shorty laughed. His sarcastic, know-it-all tone made Wendall laugh as well.

Shorty shook his head. "Nothin' worse than being scolded for gettin' yourself into a pickle."

"I can understand that."

"Oh, *and another thing*. They don't believe anybody *can* help them. So why bother even talkin' about it."

"Then…how do you get them to talk to you?"

"Easy. I ask 'em straight up. How are ya doin'? How's life treatin' ya? You doin' okay? What's wrong? If they still won't open up, I tell 'em something really stupid and funny that I once did that caused me fits. That usually does the trick. Then all they need from me is a little reassurance. I let 'em know they've got lots of friends who understand and give a damn, and lots of other people have the same shitty problems they've got, and no matter what, they're gonna be okay."

On later reflection, Wendall realized that Shorty had just described what he did for Bill with his lipstick-stained collar. Meg and the other women at the beauty shop did the same thing for Margaret when she was grieving for her beloved husband.

As the years passed, Wendall learned to "become a bartender" to help others. He mastered the "I understand" responses. He gave no advice, bad-mouthed no one, and did nothing for anyone. Instead, he reassured them that a lot of other people have the same or similar problems, and he repeatedly encouraged them to "hang in there" because they would eventually "figure it out" and everything would "be okay." Wendall didn't try to solve their problems. He never forgot Shorty's warning: "Don't become their workin'-for-free shrink." But on a rare occasion, Wendall would slip up and give advice or do a favor. When he did, he was painfully reminded that *there are some people who love to be pitied and enjoy feeling miserable.* None of your advice, best efforts, or money will ever solve their endless problems to their satisfaction. Therefore, for these poor souls *be a bartender and nothing more.*

# 3

# Running Interference

When you see a friend or loved one being stressed out, the best thing you can do for 'em is to run interference. Be their blocker.
—Dalton Davis

Like many young mothers, Susan Nichols was one of the hardest working people on the planet. She literally worked all the time. The only sleep she could enjoy was during the two nights a week that she didn't work at the hospital and the few hours during the day when Damon and Wendall were in school. Susan's night job was the easier half of her routine. Her day job took real stamina. It included doing laundry, preparing meals, cleaning the house, ironing, refereeing Damon and Wendall, and shopping on weekends when she could use the family car. Susan's extra-curricular activities were volunteering at church, helping with school activities, counseling her "needy" friends, worrying about money, and keeping tabs on her mother and her thievish brother, Clarence. Her efforts were the equivalent of running a marathon every day with a backpack full of bricks labeled home, kids, husband, money, mom, friends, church, school, job, and miscellaneous.

Susan was starting to show "runner's fatigue." Wendall noticed that his mom was simultaneously angry and sad most of the time. One weekend, Wendall and his mother were in the grocery store checkout line when he saw her eyes start to tear up, and she got what he called her funeral face.

"What's wrong, Mom? Are you okay?"

She seemed startled that he had noticed and quickly regained her composure. "Nothing, nothing. Here, go ahead."

She motioned toward the store entrance. "Take the groceries to the car."

"But are you sure you're, okay? You look upset."

Susan suddenly became irritated. "Just do what I tell you."

Over the next few weeks, she had the same brush-with-a-breakdown more and more frequently with the sudden pause in her activity, the deep, forced sigh, teary eyes, distraught look, and the dash to the bedroom or bathroom. Her responses from behind a locked door were always the same.

"I'm fine. I just need a minute."

"Don't worry about me."

"Nothing's wrong."

"Just go on."

"You didn't do anything wrong."

Wendall started paying attention to his mom's stress levels. How could he help? And why did she keep rejecting his obvious attempts? Of course, Wendall assumed that most of his mother's stress was Damon's fault. He was the easy scapegoat. Wendall decided to talk to Damon with a seriousness that he hoped Damon would understand.

"Damon, I need to talk to you about Mom."

"Why? Because she's gonna die?"

"Die? No, no. Not gonna die."

"Good! Because the last time you said you needed to talk to me, the little gray kitty got run over."

"Uh...you're right. I forgot about that."

"You forgot about the little gray kitty! You *never* liked him, did you!"

Wendall was trying hard to control himself. "Damon...I liked the little gray kitty, and...I'm sorry he's dead. But this is about Mom. Okay?"

Damon pouted. "Okay."

"I think she's getting stressed out."

"What does that mean?"

"Well, it means she's really sad and tired all the time."

"Why doesn't she take a nap? That's what she makes me do."

The little bugger actually made some sense. "That's...a good idea. But she can't."

"Why not?"

"Because she has so much work to do. I mean, she works at the hospital and takes care of all of us and cooks the meals, everything."

"She's not gonna quit, is she?"

"No. Don't worry about that. But we need to help her."

"I'm too little to fix food."

"Right, but we can help her around the house. Keep our rooms clean, and, uh, take our dirty clothes to the laundry room and not argue or fight, at all."

"But what if you're mean to me? Like you always are!"

"I promise. I won't be mean to you, *if*..." Wendall held up one finger to slow Damon down. "You stay out of my room ..."

"But..."

"*And* you ask me *before* you borrow anything."

"So I can still borry your stuff?"

"*If* you ask first."

"Okay."

Their ceasefire agreement did end one battle, but the war dragged on for Susan Nichols as she continued to struggle. Wendall began to suspect his mom had bigger problems. Time to pay closer attention and ask more questions.

Dalton Davis was the richest young person Wendall knew. At thirty-three years of age, Dalton was "retired," meaning he didn't have to go to work every day. Wendall cut Dalton's grass every week from April to October. Using only a push mower, it took a long ten-hour Saturday to mow the two-acre estate. Mr. Davis was unmarried, but he wasn't without female companionship. Wendall noticed a different girlfriend step into his bright-red Jaguar sports car every Saturday evening. Wendall wondered, *How did he become rich?* One Saturday, as Wendall took his usual lunch break under a tree in the yard, Mr.

Davis brought him a bottle of Coke. Wendall's curiosity, naturally, could not be restrained.

"Mr. Davis…"

"Please, call me Dalton."

"Oh, sure. Dalton, I'm looking ahead to college in a few years, and I still haven't decided what I should study for a career. If you don't mind me asking, what did you study in college?"

Dalton smiled. "I don't mind you asking. Other than college girls, I majored in accounting and business."

"That's how you became so wealthy?"

Dalton shook his head. "No. But a business degree helped me save my family's money even before it became mine."

"Oh yeah?"

Dalton Davis told Wendall of his family's accounting firm founded seventy years before by his grandfather and a partner, Mr. Honeyman. Although they struggled in the early years and especially during the Great Depression, their business thrived during the 1940s and '50s when Dalton's dad, Frank, joined the firm. Some of Dalton's earliest memories were hanging around the office and meeting local business leaders and other clients. After his grandfather and old man Honeyman died, the business passed to Dalton's father (50 percent) and to Honeyman's two sons (25 percent each). Since the two brothers rarely agreed on anything, Frank Davis controlled the firm. However, about ten years ago, Frank began forgetting things.

"Dad was slipping. His doctor said he was developing dementia."

"That's too bad."

Dalton nodded. "Especially when the Honeyman brothers noticed it."

"What did they do?"

Dalton's expression tightened. "They started pocketing money. Then they convinced my dad that his long-time secretary, Estelle, was stealing from the firm. The hardest thing he ever did was fire her. With Estelle gone, my dad was completely lost. The Honeymans cooked the books. They didn't list most of the invoices being sent out or the payments received. They stole nearly all the payments."

Wendall had never heard of white-collar crime. "Whoa!"

"Yeah, right. I finally got wind of it when my dad started selling his stocks and bonds to cover the company payroll and pay the business utilities. He said the firm was going bankrupt, and the Honeymans offered to buy out his half. But…he couldn't remember the dollar amount they offered. That day was the only time I ever saw my dad cry."

"Oh, man, I'm sorry."

Dalton smiled. "But not as sorry as those Honeyman brothers were after I was finished with them."

Wendall smiled. "What did you do?"

"I ran interference for my dad."

"Ran interference?" Wendall hadn't heard that phrase before.

"Yeah, like in football, the offensive line blocks for the running back. They 'run interference' by 'interfering' with the other players trying to tackle him."

Dalton then told the bitter story of exposing and prosecuting the Honeyman brothers. First, he got a complete copy of the firm's fraudulent books. He told the brothers that he needed the records, "To make certain my father's buy out, at five cents on the dollar, is fair." Then he quietly visited every single client of the firm. Many of the businessmen had known Dalton since he was a child. They gladly gave him copies of the invoices they had received and the payments they had made to the firm over the previous three years. Dalton discovered that the Honeymans had embezzled over $800,000. The local district attorney had also known the Davis family for years. He charged the Honeyman brothers with fraud, embezzlement, and elder abuse. They took a plea deal to pay $500,000 in cash and relinquish their half of the firm to Frank Davis. After his dad passed away, Dalton inherited the firm outright, and he now employed ten full-time accountants.

Dalton punctuated his story with "When you see a friend or loved one being stressed out, the best thing you can do is to run interference for 'em. Be their blocker."

Wendall was grateful for the advice. He felt a new respect for a guy whom he had previously considered a lazy, rich playboy.

Wendall was determined to find out who or what was pressuring his mom and "run interference" for her. His first suspect had been Damon. But after their truce and Wendall's Herculean efforts to avoid any conflict with the little devil, his mom was still "worn out" and "tired all the time." Fortunately, a new suspect soon appeared.

Clarence Dent was Susan's younger brother. He was a man of many addictions: smoking, drinking, womanizing, gambling, and lying. Of these, gambling caused him the most trouble because he was a terrible gambler. One night, his poker *buddies* no longer wanted to play double or nothing. They just wanted their money, all two thousand dollars' worth. Clarence had already secretly pawned all of Granny Dent's jewelry, except for her wedding ring, and only because she never took it off. Desperate to avoid an ER visit for two broken legs, he committed what was later called the furniture heist, which led to his infamous nickname Clearance. The drama began with a phone call from Grandma Dent to Wendall's mom.

"Hello, Susan?"

"Hi, Mom. Are you doing okay?"

"Yes, but I need a little help loading my laundry."

"Into the washing machine?"

"No, into my car. I need to take it to the laundromat. Clarence didn't come home last night, so he's not here to help me load it."

"Why? Is your washing machine not working?"

"Oh, well, you see, Clarence had it picked up to be cleaned."

"Cleaned?"

"Yes, he said it would work much better after it was cleaned. They're also cleaning all my furniture too."

"Who is?"

"Some men. There were three of them with a big truck. They loaded all my furniture. I didn't want them to take my dining room table and chairs, but Clarence said they needed cleaning more than anything else."

"Daddy's table and chairs? Oh my god! I'll be right over."

"Daddy's table and chairs" was Grandmother Dent's prized mahogany dining set. Grandfather Dent bought it for their twenty-fifth wedding anniversary. He had secretly saved five dollars every

41

TIM JONES, M.D.

two weeks from each paycheck from the time they were married. After roughly 650 paychecks, he was able to pay the thirty-two hundred dollars for the ten-foot-long, hand-carved table and eight matching chairs with Italian upholstery. Wendall remembered that the table had grapes and leaves carved into the sides of the legs. It was always covered by a white lace table cloth. No one ever sat in the chairs or ate at the table. It was more like a big wooden sculpture than a piece of furniture. None of the grandchildren were allowed near it.

Wendall and his mom arrived at Grandma's in record time. Susan even ran a stop sign. The house was cleaned out except for two folding chairs in front of her old black-and-white RCA television. The new Magnavox color set that Susan gave her for Christmas was gone. Except for the refrigerator, everything else was gone: washer, dryer, couch, beds, dressers, kitchen dinette, and of course, "Daddy's table and chairs." Even the toaster was missing. Clarence had placed a canvas cot in Grandma's bedroom. Her clothes were all neatly stacked along the wall where her dresser once sat. Wendall had never seen his mother so upset.

"Where's that jackass?"

Grandma was shocked. "Oh my! What's wrong?"

"He sold all your furniture!"

"No. Clarence wouldn't do that, would he?"

"Momma, think. Who were the men? Was there a sign on the side of the truck?"

"I don't remember any signs. They seemed nice."

"I gotta call Betty!"

Aunt Betty was the oldest of the Dent children. Betty was a registered nurse and a force to be reckoned with in the family. She was working at the hospital but immediately came over and picked up Wendall. They drove off to track down her pilfering brother. Clarence wasn't hard to find. His Lincoln was parked behind the Longhorn Bar on Cleveland Street. He was passed out drunk in the back seat with his car unlocked.

Wendall commented, "Wish we had a bucket of ice water to throw in his face to wake him up."

Betty sneered, "I've got something better."

42

She pulled off his cowboy boots and removed his smelly socks to reveal a bad case of foot fungus. Taking the longest key on her key-chain, she raked the bottom of his right foot, hard, from heel to toes.

"Aah!" Clarence jerked his foot back and bolted upright. "What the f—!" Then he saw them.

"Betty, what did ya do that for? That *hurt*!"

In less than thirty seconds, Betty and Wendall were in her car and off to Harvey's New and Used Furniture. They had Clarence's boots, his keys, and $134 from his pockets.

As they pulled into the parking lot, Betty told Wendall, "You can come in, but I'll handle this."

They walked in quietly and *shopped* the entire store. Grandma's couch was against the wall on the right. Her bedroom set was on the left. The dining room table and chairs were the show piece in the center. A red CLEARANCE sign was propped up on the table with a $7,999 price tag. The deep red wood on the tabletop reminded Wendall that he had never seen his grandma's table without that white lace tablecloth. The only thing missing was her washing machine. Wendall was worried that it might have already been sold. But then, he peeked through the glass window of the showroom's back door. There it was, washing Harvey's laundry.

Betty methodically collected the tags from all of her mother's furniture and insisted to Harvey that she really needed the washer in the back as well. Even though it wasn't for sale, she would pay double for it. Finally, they were at the cash register to check out.

Harvey beamed. "This is the biggest purchase we've had all year. You're buying a complete houseful. Yes, ma'am, this is quality used furniture. Except for the mahogany table and chairs. We just got those in yesterday from Italy. To what address would you like all this fine furniture delivered?"

Betty said dryly, "401 East Lansing Street." (Grandma's place)

Harvey stopped writing. His smile disappeared but he didn't look up. Wendall could see his eyes look left, then back right.

"Uh, will, uh, that be cash or charge?"

Betty slowly folded the red "Clearance" sign that she had taken from the table. "That depends on the price. For zero dollars, there will be no charges from the district attorney against this shit hole that you call a furniture store. Otherwise, my *best* friend's husband is going to throw you in jail for *knowingly* receiving and selling stolen property from a little old lady who happens to be my mother!"

The return delivery that day was overseen by Betty. She barked out orders and obscenities like a drill sergeant. The toaster was never found. It was likely pawned weeks before. Brother "Clearance" was kicked out of the house. His few clothes and an extra pair of boots were thrown, literally, to the curb. A sincere sisterly death threat was promised if he ever returned to his mother's house.

Betty's banishment of Clarence helped, but Susan continued to struggle. Hmm? Maybe she wasn't getting enough sleep. She did work nights, and she had to sleep during the day. Or maybe his mom had some medical problem. Then, as luck would have it, Wendall developed a medical problem of his own, a bad head cold that forced him to miss two days of school. He solved the mystery of his mother's fatigue on the first day. It was the telephone. More specifically, it was Peggy Sanders calling and waking up Susan at all hours of the day.

Peggy wasn't a neighbor. She lived on the other side of town in an upscale "housing addition." She wasn't a relative. She wasn't a former classmate. She wasn't a nice person. Instead, she was a meddler, a neurotic, a fellow Methodist, a racist, and a problem. Although Peggy constantly demanded Susan's advice, she would reject all her suggestions, which allowed her to continue complaining. She griped nonstop about anything and everything. Peggy considered Wendall's mom to be on call twenty-four hours a day. Everyone else at church had long since distanced themselves from her. Unfortunately for Peggy, Wendall served as Susan's answering service during his two sick days at home. He immediately recognized Peggy's irritatingly arrogant voice over the phone.

"Hello."

"Let me talk to Susan."

Wendall said in a gruff voice, "Is there a Susan here? Wait. Harry, wait! That order was for two pepperonis pizzas *without* black olives. Pick all those off. Well…put some extra cheese on it to fill in the divots."

Wendall heard a *click*.

Exactly seven seconds later, the phone rang again. Wendall answered it with his nose pinched firmly between his thumb and index finger. "Larry's Pizza. Can I take your order?"

"Now...I *know* I dialed the right number. Is this not the number for Susan Nichols?"

"Bill! We got another one of them prank calls for a Susan Nichols! Do you want me to call the phone company or the police?"

Wendall heard "Damn it" just before the *click*.

Unplugging the phone ended Peggy's telephone consultations but not her in-person visits with Susan. Wendall got a front row seat to one of their "sessions" during the week of spring break.

"I am just beside myself, Susan. Jill [Peggy's daughter] is considering transferring from Kansas State to the University of Houston in the fall. *Because* get this. She met a Mexican boy at a Young Republicans conference."

Peggy was distraught. "It's a bad sign, Susan. A really bad sign."

"Why? Is Houston not a good school?"

"No! Susan, you're missing the point! What if they become friends? Or worse, start seeing each other?

"What's his name?"

"Carlos...something or other. I don't know his last name. It's probably Hernandez."

"That's nice."

"Nice! Did you even hear what I said? A Mexican!" Peggy put her hands to her rouge-covered cheeks and shook her head in disgust. "Can you imagine? A Mexican in the family? I'll have little brown brats for grandchildren! Tell me. What should I do? I'm counting on you to help me out of this mess."

Susan shifted nervously in her chair. "I'm really not sure. Have you met him?"

"Of course not! I'm not going to legitimize *anything*."

"Well, maybe he's a nice boy."

"Susan, he's a Mexican. Don't you know anything about those people?"

What Peggy *didn't* know is that Susan's first best friend was a little girl named Maria Gonzalez. Maria was now Mrs. Maria Martinez and still a best friend. In fact, the two families took turns having each other over for dinner. Maria would cook traditional fajitas and enchiladas, and Susan always fried chicken served with mashed potatoes and gravy. Maria's meals were so delicious that Wendall would no longer eat fast food from The Taco House or any of the other Mexican restaurants in town. They just didn't measure up.

Peggy's racism marched on. "Anyway, Susan, I have a plan. Jill is going to be home this weekend, and she'll be with me at church. You're going to meet us in the sanctuary before Sunday school and tell us all about the dirty Mexicans in this neighborhood and how they beat their wives and girlfriends."

"But we don't have any Mexican families in our neighborhood, and the ones I do know are really nice people."

"That's not the point. We have to convince Jill to end this misguided friendship with this Mexican before it's too late! Trust me. The end, clearly, justifies the means."

Wendall could feel his pulse pounding in his temples, and he was beginning to bite a hole through his tongue. What a racist! He wanted Peggy out of their living room and out of their house ASAP. He was desperate for any help to run interference. Therefore, Wendall decided to do the *unthinkable*. He offered to play army men with Damon, in the living room, where they could have a *big* battlefield. Surely, a major troop deployment would force Peggy to retreat to her own house. But Wendall was wrong. She declared that the living room was a demilitarized zone. "Go play somewhere else."

Damon's mouth flew open. "What? This is Ranger Rick's country! He fights for America!"

"Little boy…"

"My name is General Damon!"

Then Damon did what he does best. He used psychological warfare to demoralize the enemy.

"You smell like my grandma." "You wear too much makeup." "You have hair in your nose."

Then Damon started his enemy interrogation.

"Why are you so fat?" "Can I see what's in your purse?" "Did Jill marry a Mexican?"

He had apparently overheard Peggy complaining about "the Mexican."

Peggy was thoroughly offended. "Well! I never!" She stormed out the door.

Victory! The enemy had withdrawn from the field.

The rest of that week, Wendall could tell that the "Mexican conspiracy" was weighing on his mom. On Saturday evening, the Nichols family enjoyed what Max Nichols described as "an incredible spread" of Mexican cuisine at the Martinez's home. Wendall noticed, that for at least one evening, his mom appeared relaxed. But as he anticipated, she looked particularly distraught early Sunday morning.

"Mom, are you feeling okay?"

"Uh…yeah, I'm okay."

Wendall knew better. "You don't *look* okay."

"You're right. I got roped into meeting Peggy and her daughter, Jill, at church."

"Oh that's right. You've got to warn Jill about all the horrible Mexicans in our neighborhood."

"You overheard that?"

"Oh yeah. Peggy is plenty loud."

Susan scowled. "I think it's terrible."

"I agree. The desired end *never* justifies the deceitful means."

"So you heard that too? What am I going to tell Peggy?"

Wendall decided it was time to run interference for his maternal running back. "I can shut down Peggy."

"How?"

"I'll tell her the truth. You didn't feel good about today and decided to stay home and rest."

Susan looked down. "I'm sorry I haven't been able to stand up to her."

Wendall gave her a hug. "You'll get there. In the meantime, I'm gonna enjoy blocking for ya."

On the way to church, Wendall decided to have a little fun with Peggy's future family genetics. On their arrival, his dad took

Damon to the preschool class, and Wendall went to the sanctuary where everyone milled around and socialized before Sunday school. Peggy and an innocent-looking young college brunette were waiting there. Poor Jill. She had a racist for a mother and an invisible red and white bull's-eye painted on her forehead.

"Hi, Peggy."

"Oh, hello…uh…"

"Wendall."

"Right. Where is your mother?"

"She's at home. She just felt terrible this morning and decided to stay home."

"What?"

"Yeah, the Martinez family had us over last night. We usually have dinner together once or twice a month. And Maria, oh my gosh, made authentic Mexican food for us."

Peggy panicked. "Oh no! The Mexicans poisoned her?"

"No, no. The food was fantastic. For some reason, she has just felt sick since your last visit."

"Huh, well…"

Wendall extended his hand to Jill. "Hi, I'm Wendall."

"Hello, I'm Jill."

"Hi, Jill."

Wendall leaned slightly forward and looked at Jill with a serious face. "Have you ever had real Mexican food? I mean, like they cook in Mexico. Not this Tex-Mex stuff we have around here."

"Yes, when I was in Houston."

"Isn't authentic Mexican the best! Maria made chicken and beef fajitas last night that *still* make my mouth water, just thinking about it. And the cheese enchiladas…"

Jill perked up. "With the four cheeses inside?"

"Yes! And she covered them with homemade chili sauce with the red and green peppers."

"The enchiladas in Houston just melted in my mouth. They were to die for!"

Out of the corner of his eye, Wendall could see Peggy looking back and forth between the two of them with a horrified expression.

Their ping-pong match of Mexican food compliments was freaking her out.

Wendall stepped up the pressure. "And of course, for dessert…"

"Sopapillas!" Jill and Wendall said in unison.

Jill sighed. "I love those with honey, mixing with the sugar and cinnamon."

"You should try them with chocolate syrup."

"Really?"

Wendall was on a roll. "Oh my gosh! They're delicious! Forget French pastries. These are *so* much better. You know what? Maria's son made the sopapillas. He's *my* age. He's one of my best friends. His name is Carlos."

Jill pressed her hand against her heart. "That's my boyfriend's name!"

Peggy exploded, "*Boyfriend!*"

Her fog horn echoed twice in the sanctuary. First, off the choir seating in the front, and then, off the stained-glass window in the rear.

"How long has he been your boyfriend?"

The huge room was as quiet as a funeral service. Wendall could feel every eyeball staring at him, mistakenly believing that *he* was the objectionable boyfriend.

In a hushed voice, Jill stood her ground. "Mom! We've been dating since Christmas."

Peggy could barely control herself. "But…he's a Mexican!"

"No, he's not. He was born in Houston."

"But his parents were born in Mexico!"

"Well…Daddy's parents were born in England."

Peggy sputtered, "But…they're not…Catholic!"

Satisfied that his mission was a success, Wendall glanced at his watch.

"Oh, look at the time. Got to get to Sunday school. It was very nice to meet you, Jill. Good luck to you and Carlos. Oh, and…when he comes to visit Benson, please give us a call. Maria knows a lot of people in Houston. I can guarantee you. She'll want all of us over for dinner."

Jill smiled while Peggy was speechless. "I definitely will."

"Just remember, my dad's name is Max Nichols. We're in the phone book."

Wendall slapped his forehead. "Silly me, of course, your mom has our number. But remember, Max Nichols."

After church, Wendall couldn't wait to get home to inform his mom of Jill's new romance. Wendall hadn't heard his mother laugh like that in a long time. He was determined to "run interference" and block out Peggy until his mom learned to say no to her. Wendall hoped that day would come soon.

Running interference is sometimes necessary to protect the elderly and the disabled from fraud and abuse. However, the majority of people who need help are not elderly or disabled. They are the kind hearts like Susan Nichols, people who simply never learned to block for themselves, or in other words, to effectively say no. Running interference is all about saying no. No, you do not treat my mother, father, child, or friend that way. No, you will not talk to them that way. No, you will not take their money, property, or time. No, you will not cheat them, lie to them, or manipulate them anymore. Obviously, being the knight in shining armor can be very satisfying. But the most satisfaction comes from training the oppressed person to say no for themselves. (More on that skill set later in this book.)

A word of caution: Before you start trying to be a hero, make certain that the person you are rescuing actually wants your help and doesn't mind if you "run interference." It's twisted, but some people actually enjoy the attention they receive from being repeatedly abused.

Finally, it's also the duty of all parents to "run interference" for their children. Parents must protect them from anyone who would cheat, abuse, deceive, or abduct them until they are mature enough to fend for themselves. Of course, most children and young adults, at some point, believe that their parents are simply "interfering" in their lives. But instead, those caring parents are blocking and steering their children away from the many pitfalls and manipulative people in our world.

# 4

# Slick 'n' Greasy

Never worry about what other people think. If you do,
then you start doubting yourself, bending the rules,
and promising stupid things you can't deliver.
—Billy Hayworth, a.k.a. Slick 'n' Greasy

Slick 'n' Greasy, or "Slick" for short, was the best mechanic in Benson. If it had a motor and a transmission, he could make it run down the highway. Only his family knew him by his real name, Bill Hayworth. He got his start at the age of five in his father's garage, then apprenticed in some of the finest back-alley, jalopy factories in Kansas. From the time he was twenty years old, Slick 'n' Greasy could change a five-lug tire faster than anyone in town. However, after forty, his tire-changing championship title was vulnerable due to advancing age and irritating arthritis. Slick 'n' Greasy did what he usually does with a worn-out vehicle and discontinued parts. He improvised. At Slick's next title bout, an upstart kid from the Ford dealership was a worthy opponent. Slick was noticeably slower at twirling off the lug nuts, and he began to fall behind. But he had devised a short cut. Slick didn't toss the nuts into the upside-down hub cap as everyone expected. Instead, he popped them into his mouth like jawbreakers. Then, as he put on the new tire, he spit them into his hand, one at a time. The maneuver shaved ten seconds off his time, more than enough to win. Afterward, Slick 'n' Greasy commented, "Best thing about losing all my teeth was it sped up my tire changing."

Bill Hayworth was Wendall's great uncle, one of three brothers of his grandmother, Ruby Nichols. Slick's nickname was purely descriptive. He was usually covered with oil and grease. His coveralls weren't stiff because of starch. They were rigid from a dried paste of axil grease, oil, dirt, and sand. It was a waterproof, machine-shop stucco, not unlike the original, oil-impregnated canvas "slickers" in nineteenth century England. Slick was wiry thin but surprisingly strong when unscrewing rusted bolts and hoisting engines out of vehicles. Slick 'n' Greasy always had a cigarette in his mouth. His wife, Linda, joked that he smoked like an engine needing an overhaul. Wendall was amazed at how Slick could roll a cigarette with one hand while talking on the phone, then continue the conversation with it bobbing up and down between his lips. He would have none of those expensive "packaged smokes." At fifty cents a pack, "that's just too damn much…paying for all those jingles on TV." After the government banned cigarette commercials on television, Wendall asked Slick if he ever worried about lung cancer. "Nah, I'm not worried. It's all those *chemicals* the cigarette companies are putting in their smokes that cause cancer." By rolling his own smokes with "natural tobacco," he was gonna live to be a hundred.

Slick 'n' Greasy's shop was a twenty-by-thirty-foot metal building on the lot next to his house. There was no sign out front. He didn't need one. Everyone knew Slick's Garage. His "waiting list" was the nine or ten cars parked outside. The shop featured two ten-foot-tall sliding panel doors in the front and two squares of plate glass windows on each side. The concrete floor was stained black from oil and grease. The smell of solvent soaking some auto or truck part was always present. The car lift in the center was the only equipment that distinguished the place as an auto repair shop.

Although his personal hygiene was oily and aromatic, Slick 'n' Greasy's tools were pristine and polished. He kept them organized in large red rolling tool boxes with rows of pull-out drawers. Every tool had its place, and he knew exactly where each was located. Slick owned every type of mechanic's tool known to man, or so it seemed.

Wendall never saw so many different wrenches, sockets, screwdrivers, gear pullers, jacks, hammers, punches, and chisels. When it came to tools, Slick lived by three simple, steadfast rules:

"Use the right tool for each job. Only a fool hammers on a screwdriver or a wrench."

"Organize your tools if you wanna work fast. No sense in wasting time looking for a tool."

"Keep your tools clean and always carry a grease rag in your pocket. Dirty tools are dangerous. They can slip in your hand."

Speaking of grease rags, Slick had two laundry baskets in the shop. One contained dozens of neatly folded, faded red rags that Linda had washed the day before. The other was piled high with oily rags that Slick had tossed in that general direction. Linda had to launder a full load of grease rags every day just to keep up with him.

Although Slick worked fast and for long hours, he couldn't please all his customers all the time. But that never bothered him. He had a confident, often profane, but never troubled view of his business. His demeanor was in stark contrast to some of his customers who were frantic to get their cars back on the road as soon as possible.

Wendall arrived at the shop one afternoon as a man in a business suit was whining, "But, Slick, you don't understand. I gotta have my car tomorrow! I'm desperate. You have to help me out here."

"Yesterday, I told you it would be three days. Nothing's changed. It'll be the three days, even with the extra help I got." Slick motioned toward Wendall standing a few feet away. A surprised Wendall glanced around to see if a real mechanic had walked in the shop unnoticed.

"But…"

"No buts. I'm runnin' in high gear as it is. You're just slowing me down by arguing with me."

"Okay. I guess I'll have to just wait!" Disappointed and angry, the customer stomped off.

Wendall asked Slick about unhappy customers, "Don't you ever worry about people getting upset?"

"No, I don't worry."

Slick 'n' Greasy always described everyone and everything with automotive metaphors, "Yeah, I see a lot of people blow a gasket.

They can throw a rod if they want. But I'm not gonna get overheated worrying about their *other* problems."

"What other problems?"

"You name it. They likely got it."

Wendall hadn't even considered that many of the irritated, impatient customers might be struggling with other issues.

Slick continued, "Most of the time, they're just lettin' off steam. I don't take it personal, unless they're blowin' their smoke at me."

Wendall began to feel some sympathy for the previous customer. "Who knows what other problems he may have."

Slick smiled. "Who knows? Usually, *I'm* the one who knows. *Because* people pour out their problems to me while I'm trying to get their vehicle out the door."

Wendall chuckled. "Really."

"Every day."

Slick recounted the pathetic tale of Ronald, a portly middle-aged dentist. The poor guy had been married to his second, much younger wife for only six months. They already had a one-year-old baby girl as proof of his extra-marital affair, which, of course, destroyed his first marriage of thirty years. The new wife now decided she needed the nightly attention of her personal trainer. Therefore, she filed for divorce and convinced a judge to toss Ronald out of his own home. Next, his first ex-wife demanded more money to pay for their daughter's college expenses. Then his dental partner complained that Ronald was missing too much time from their dental practice because of the divorce proceedings. But by far, his most distressing problem was his broken-down Bentley. It was hard to start, and according to Slick, "it knocked like a kid outside a locked bathroom door."

Slick shook his head with pity. "I never saw anyone so depressed. He looked like he was outta gas and running on fumes."

"He told you all those problems?"

"Oh yeah." Slick stuck his nose in the air. "Must have thought I was Dr. Freud."

"But he caused his own problems."

"You got that right. Thing was, he just kept spinning his tires. Not going anywhere or getting anything done to *fix* his problems. It was sad."

"So what did you tell him?"

Slick looked up from the carburetor he was dismantling. "Told him to be a man. Do what he knows is right and quit trying to please everyone, especially his ex-wives."

Slick grinned and shook his head. "And you know what?"

"What."

"He got all out of alignment. Started getting mad at me!"

Wendall remembered Shorty's warning about giving advice.

"Yeah, but I knew he was just revvin' his motor. One look from me, and he shut it down pretty quick. He knew I was right. He just didn't have the horsepower to admit it."

"What was wrong with his car?"

"Wouldn't ya know. Some jerk switched a couple of his spark plug wires to throw off the timing, probably his slutty wife's new boyfriend. Hell, I had his car fixed and the bill filled out before he was even finished with his sob story."

Slick 'n' Greasy smoked too much, and he swore too much. But these vices complemented his defining personality trait, a complete disregard for the feelings and opinions of others. Oh, he wasn't intentionally rude. He just didn't "give a damn about what other people think." Despite repeated, well-intentioned pleas from family and friends to consider the consequences of his insensitivity, Slick was unmoved. His practical response was this:

"There are only two kinds of people in this world who have to care about what other people think, politicians and salesmen. And I'm never gonna be either one."

Wendall was trying to comprehend it all. "But, Slick, what about your wife, Linda? Don't you care about what she thinks?"

He paused for two seconds. "Yeah. Dammit! I guess you're right. But don't tell her I said that."

Slick was no hypocrite. He lived what he preached. Wendall witnessed it firsthand one Saturday morning when the biggest cheapskate in town, Doug Beasley, dropped by to check on his '51 Chrysler.

"Doug, I'll give it to you straight up. The engine is shot. The block is busted. There's no fixing it. You'll need a new engine."

Beasley was on the verge of a panic attack. "I don't have that kind of money! Can't you weld it or something?"

"No. It's cracked through two cylinders. No way to weld it perfect. And even if you could, you'd have to machine out the cylinders afterward, and that would cost more than a new engine."

Beasley's eyes were darting around the shop. "How did this happen?" He pointed at Slick. "*You*! You were the last mechanic to work on my car!"

Slick nodded once. "Damn right, five years ago, which is also the *last time* you had the oil changed. Hell, you didn't have oil in the engine. It was *glue*."

"You should have told me."

"I did better than that. I wrote it down." Slick pointed to the driver's side of the windshield. "See that sticker? What does it say?"

Beasley pouted like a four-year-old being scolded. "I don't know."

"Well, goddammit, read it."

"I don't have to put up with this."

Wendall had to look for himself. It read, "Next oil change: 87,000 miles." Beasley's odometer showed 111,536.

Beasley pointed his finger at Slick. "I know what you're trying to do. You're trying to rip me off! You mechanics are all the same. I'm gonna to take my car to Paceman's [the Chevy dealership]. They'll treat me right."

Slick picked up the phone hanging on the wall and started dialing. "That's the best damned idea I've heard all day." He winked at Beasley. "Gonna help you out here."

From three feet away, Wendall heard a woman's loud voice answer the phone, "Paceman's Chevrolet."

"Yeah, Dorothy, this is …I'm doin' just fine, thank you much. Say, is Jimmy around?"

Slick strummed his fingers on the work bench while he waited. It reminded Wendall of a galloping horse.

"Jimmy? This is Slick. Can you send a tow truck over to my place? Got a customer for ya. It's Doug Beasley and his '51 Chrysler. You won't?" Slick chuckled. "Can I tell him why? All right. I'll pass it on to him. Talk to ya later."

Slick hung up the phone. Then he turned around shaking his head with a wide smile that displayed his coffee-and-cigarette-stained dentures. "They'll be glad to send a tow truck, right *after* you pay your bill from six months ago."

Beasley bristled. "Well I'm not doin' that! I'll just have my brother-in-law come pick up my car."

Slick nodded. "That sounds like a good idea to me. I'll push it out front, and he can come by anytime."

To Wendall's surprise, Beasley blurted out, "Thanks for nothin'! I'm gonna tell everyone you're the worst mechanic in town!"

"You go right ahead. *If*…you can get out of my garage in one piece."

Beasley lost most of the color in his face. Then he tripped and nearly fell as he ran toward the door.

Slick wrinkled his nose. "Did he shit his pants?"

"He might have. He did let out a huge fart."

They both busted out laughing, which made them breathe in even more of the stench.

"Damn!" Slick started coughing. "We better step outside. He *was* full of shit!"

It was one of the few times in his life that Wendall laughed so hard that his sides hurt. After regaining their composures, they pushed Beasley's car out the front door and to the side of Slick's lot.

Afterward, Wendall asked Slick if he ever worried what people might think or say about him.

"Of course not! I can't control what other people think…or say. So why worry?"

"But isn't it bad for business?"

Without hesitation, Slick replied, "No. It's *good* for business. You run off all the deadbeats that don't wanna pay their bills."

But Wendall was still clinging to the philosophy that you had to be nice to everyone. "But what if they think you're being rude?"

Slick fixed his eyes on Wendall and lectured him with an oil-stained finger. "Listen…*the rudest thing you can do to a person is mislead them or lie to them.* You've got to be completely honest even if it pisses them off. "

Wendall had never thought of it that way. Now it made sense. All he could say was, "I guess you're right."

Slick smiled. "So you're just *now* figuring that out?"

Wendall had to smile.

Slick continued, "Never worry about what other people think. If you do, then you start doubting yourself, bending the rules, and promising stupid things you can't deliver. Basically, getting yourself over a barrel. Why even put yourself in that awful position?"

Slick paused and then grimaced with disgust. "You know the worst part? Most of them end up blaming *me* when things don't turn out *perfect,* even though I'm working my ass off for 'em."

Slick leaned under the hood of a '64 Dodge and inspected its carburetor. "Could you hand me a 9/16$^{th}$ end wrench?"

"Sure." By now, Wendall was familiar with Slick's organized tool boxes and made quick work of his request.

"Thanks. Yeah, I used to worry about what other people thought or wanted. It almost cost me my business."

Wendall's curiosity was piqued. "What happened?"

"Years ago, when I was starting out, I borrowed money from the bank to build this shop. Linda and I had just gotten married, and we had a mortgage on the house too. But business was slow because I was just a new kid and hadn't built my reputation yet."

"Did you advertise in the paper?"

Slick looked up from the carburetor. "Can you hand me that Phillips-head?"

Wendall quickly complied.

"Thanks. No, I didn't advertise. I thought about it but didn't have the money. I had to rely on word of mouth. And the more desperate I got for business, the more I tried to please everybody."

"What's wrong with that?"

"Nothing. Until…you start giving them what they want, instead of what they need. Like I said, bending the rules and getting yourself over a barrel."

Wendall could sense a disaster on the way. "So what went wrong?"

"I guy named Bud Boone died."

"What? Oh my gosh!"

Slick stopped working and leaned against the Dodge. "He bought a '61 Corvette and brought it in because the transmission was shot. Teenagers had been street racing it. The entire body on those early Vettes is fiberglass, so they're real lightweight. Before a race, drivers would put sandbags in the trunk to give the back wheels some traction. Well, the transmission wasn't designed for that. Anyway, the gears were stripped, the clutch plate was worn out, and the damn thing kept poppin' out of gear, especially first gear."

"Let me guess, he didn't want to replace the transmission."

"That's right. Cost too much. Would take too long. He told me to, 'Just patch it up. I need to save money for a new paint job.'"

"What good's a new paint job on a car if you can't drive it?"

"Right. But Bud didn't see it that way. He planned to sell that Vette and turn a quick profit."

Slick cleared his throat. "You know the shame of it? Bud had plenty of money. He could easily afford a new transmission. But it was all just a game for him."

Slick paused and looked over at the car lift. Wendall imagined that Slick could still see the Corvette. "I tried to convince him, but he had already made up his mind. I should have told him I wouldn't touch it. But I was bending over backward trying to please everyone. I tightened the plate the best I could and put in the heaviest transmission fluid they make."

"So it worked?"

"For about two weeks. After he hot rodded it around town, the car started poppin' out of first gear again, and the rest of the gears were grinding."

"Did Bud bring it back?"

"Oh yeah. He was all upset at me. Like an idiot, I tightened the plate some more, but I knew it was the wrong thing to do."

A cloud came over Slick's face that Wendall had never seen before.

"Two days later, Bud and the Corvette were hit by a train at a railroad crossing. The driver behind Bud said the Vette started slowing down and coasting. He thought it ran out of gas until he heard Bud grinding the gears. The Vette came to a stop on the tracks. Bud kept trying to force it into gear. Then a train appeared. The other guy jumped out of his pickup to help Bud push the Vette off the tracks. But the train was coming too fast, and Bud didn't get away from the car quick enough."

"I am so sorry, Slick."

Slick sighed. "Not nearly as sorry as I was. Bud's widow sued me for a million dollars."

"What! Why?"

"Well, she knew I had worked on the car, and she just assumed it was my fault. And they had the testimony of the guy who tried to help him. You know, he heard Bud 'grinding the gears.'"

"What happened?"

"Lucky for me, I gave Bud two written estimates, one for a new transmission and the other for a rebuilt one. And because he was so stubborn, I wrote 'strongly recommended' on them. Those two pieces of paper saved my ass."

"Thank goodness for that."

Slick shook his head. "Yeah, well, it still cost me. I got a lot of bad publicity, and I had to pay an attorney to defend me."

Slick ducked under the Dodge's hood and resumed working on the carburetor. "You remember that. You can try *too hard* to please people. So don't ever care about what they think of you or what they want. Don't bend the rules."

On another Saturday afternoon, Wendall witnessed the pinnacle of Slick's anger. Wendall always knew Slick had a temper. He usually showed it when some noble car or truck had been neglected. But today was different. A steady stream of curse words filled the shop.

Wendall found Slick looking up at the transmission of '67 Ford high on the lift.

"What's got your blood up, Slick?"

He glanced over at Wendall. "Come over here. Wanna show you something."

Slick stuck his index finger into the drain hole of the transmission. When he pulled it out, his finger was covered with transmission fluid. "Feel that between your fingers."

Wendall obediently swiped off some of the thick amber fluid and rubbed it between his thumb and index finger. It had a gritty texture. "What is that?"

"Goddamn sawdust!"

Wendall's confused look prompted an outburst from Slick.

"Some sonovabitch mixed sawdust with the transmission fluid so the gears wouldn't slip."

Wendall always knew Slick treated vehicles as if they were human. This vehicular atrocity was equivalent to a parent giving their baby a bottle of milk laced with drugs.

"Sawdust is poison to a transmission!"

Wendall volunteered, "Wonder if the owner might know who did it?"

Slick snapped, "He's the one who did it. He's planning to sell this Ford."

Slick's tone now changed to mocking sarcasm. "It's running great, Slick. I just dropped it off so you could check it over before I sell it.'"

Wendall naively blurted out, "Good thing he did."

Slick looked at him dryly. "No! Bad thing he did. Trying to slip something by me and get my stamp of approval so he can get a better price when he dumps this lemon on some sucker."

"Maybe that sawdust was in there when he bought the car."

Slick coughed and shook his head. "Nope, it's a one owner. He bought it new, and I'm pretty damn sure the Ford assembly plant has never dumped sawdust into a transmission.

"Oops" is all Wendall could say.

Slick motioned to him. "Let me show ya another thing."

Slick bent down to a locked file drawer under his work bench. Using a small brass key, he opened it and removed a large roll of two-inch-by-three-inch plastic stickers. Slick handed one to Wendall. "Read that."

Wendall mumbled, "Inspected and approved by Slick 'n' Greasy for one year. Date:_____."

With an air of pride, Slick declared, "I take my reputation seriously. Those stickers of approval go inside the windshield next to the state inspection sticker, which doesn't mean a tenth as much as mine."

Wendall thought for a minute. Something "didn't thread right" as Slick would say. "But…I thought you didn't care what other people think?"

"I don't. But I *do* care about my reputation."

"But isn't your reputation what other people think of you?"

"Sure it is. But I control my reputation. I don't control what other people think or say."

Wendall was still not seeing the difference. "Uh…"

"Listen, if your honest and do excellent work at a fair price, then your reputation will be solid, no matter what some people might think or say. So *I* determine my own reputation."

Slick gave a slight snort. "A lot of people believe that *they* can ruin a man's reputation by bad-mouthing him. But they're stupid. The truth is in a man's character and the quality of his work."

Wendall hadn't visited Slick in several months. Slick had more cars than usual parked in the yard. Why? Surprisingly, he and Linda had travelled to Kansas City for a one-week vacation. It was their first time off in over ten years. Wendall noticed a new calendar hanging on the peg board over Slick's work bench. The month of April featured a topless redhead with a come-hither smile. Slick noticed that Wendall was mesmerized by it. He grinned. "Like my new calendar?"

Wendall broke off his stare. "Uh…sure."

"Keeps my drive shaft straight. An old army buddy of mine gave me that for my birthday. Linda hates it."

Wendall laughed. "I bet she does. But uh, Slick, today is June 15. Why do you still have it on April?"

Slick glanced back at the bare-breasted beauty. "Well hell! You have to ask?"

Wendall hadn't been exposed to any nudity before that day. In fact, Miss April was the first topless woman he had ever seen. Therefore, he really couldn't give Slick a comparative analysis. So Wendall took his word for it. "Yeah, she looks nice."

"Lots better than May or June. If July is sexier, then I'll switch her out. Besides, I don't need a calendar to tell me what day it is."

Slick didn't change that calendar until October. A blue-eyed brunette finally dethroned Miss April. Every single customer, including the little old church ladies, couldn't avoid seeing the prominently displayed calendar. But Slick didn't care at all. It was a symbol of his philosophy. The calendar beauties were all whispering, "*I don't care what you think.*"

Over the years, Wendall thought about Slick 'n' Greasy's motto. He *almost* had it right. What other people think *is* important because *being considerate* can win respect, create many friendships, and enhance a good reputation. *But* what other people think is not *as important* as what *you* think. Slick learned this lesson the hard way with the tragic death of Bud, the Corvette owner. Never go against your better judgment because you fear what other people may think or say or want you to do. Otherwise, *you become a slave to other people's opinions and desires.* Then you begin "doubting yourself, bending the rules, and promising stupid things you can't deliver." Ironically, this uncomfortable position *destroys your self-respect* and the respect of the very people you are trying so desperately to please. Instead, be "straight up" with them. Because like Slick said, "*The rudest thing you can do to a person is mislead them or lie to them.* You've got to be completely honest even if it pisses them off."

# 5

# The Three *B*s—Beg, Bargain, and Bully

I'm a professional. I can get *anything* I want.
So you might as well just give up.
—Mona Lisa Barnett

Damon was a bona fide genius. No, he wasn't destined to become a rocket scientist or win the Nobel prize for physics. But he was a genius nevertheless at acquiring exactly what he wanted. His bedroom looked like a toy store that had just been hit by a tornado. A fleet of Tonka trucks, yoyos of every color and style, and an entire division of army men littered his floor. Damon had so many GI Joes he could have formed his own clone army. Wendall never had so many toys. What was Damon's secret? Wendall decided to study the little devil and find out. A trip to the grocery store revealed a distinct pattern of "Damonly" behavior.

"Momma, *please* can I have some lemon drops? I said *please* like I'm supposed to. Please?"

Damon was jumping up and down with his head bobbing a subliminal *yes*. His mother was only temporarily distracted by his pleading. "Uh, we'll see. I've got to find…"

"Mahm" was the whining reply. "C'mon, Momma. I need some lemon drops, please?"

"If you're going to act that way, then you're not going to get anything."

Of course, this was a hollow threat, and Damon knew it. "Mom! Pretty please?"

Wendall thought, *What a beggar.*

Begging wasn't working. Instinctively, Damon changed strategies. He'd make a deal with his mother. Promise her *anything* for those lemon drops.

"Okay, okay, I promise I'll be good. I'll wait till after lunch to eat my lemon drops, and I'll...uh, clean my room, and I...I won't fight with Wendall. Promise...okay?"

Wendall couldn't hold his tongue any longer. "Yeah, right. You promised all of that last time and..."

"Shut up, Wendall."

"You ate all your candy before we got home..."

"I said shut up!"

"And you never cleaned your room. Then you threw a superball at me when I reminded you of it."

"That's because you wouldn't help me. It was your fault!"

To Wendall's surprise, their mother was actually listening. "So is that why you threw Wendall's tape recorder against the wall?"

"That was an accident."

Wendall scowled. "Of course it was, you little liar."

"Well, Damon." Susan sighed. "I'll have to think about it."

In the Damon dialect, the English phrase, *I'll have to think about it*, translates as *no*. Time to change strategies again. No more begging and saying "please." Give up on bargaining and promising to be good. Damon reached for the *bully* stick.

"I hate you. You never give me anything!" Damon stomped his foot and shouted, "You *always* got candy for Wendall!"

Wendall smiled, another stab-in-the-dark lie.

"It's not fair! You're the worst mom ever! I'm gonna run away! You'll be sorry!"

Susan shook her finger at him. "You better straighten up right this minute or you'll never get any candy."

"See! You're so mean to me!"

Now Damon started the monsoon of tears with a wailing cry that could be heard throughout the store. People started staring at them down the cereal aisle.

"Okay, okay, just stop your squalling!" Susan was frazzled.

Instantly, an Oscar-winning transformation occurred. The crying disappeared, tears stopped flowing, and a satisfied smile of sweet victory emerged triumphant. Bad behavior had been rewarded. Damon won the dance around the lemon drops with a stepwise strategy. Wendall later described it as *the three Bs: beg, bargain, and bully*.

During the following week, Wendall noted that Damon used different Bs or "buttons" on specific people. For Grandma Dent, begging always worked. For his mom, each button worked about a third of the time; therefore, Damon would follow the protocol. But for Wendall, Damon went straight to bully because Wendall always laughed at his begging and bargaining. So why waste time? The only person who was completely immune to Damon's manipulations was his father, Max. Damon knew better than to even try. But despite his successes with the three Bs, Damon was only an amateur. With more experience and a slightly expanded vocabulary, he could become an apprentice of the three Bs, like his Uncle Clarence.

Given his sordid track record, Clarence was a scoundrel. But he was also overweight, smelled like sweat, and never clean-shaven. His wardrobe was limited to stained T-shirts, grungy blue jeans, and cowboy boots. He had shifty brown eyes, rotten, crooked teeth, and too much grease in his hair. But Clarence had "good taste" because he drove a Lincoln Continental, a ten-year-old Lincoln. Wendall was playing in his grandma Dent's backyard when Clarence pulled into her front driveway for the first time to "show it off." Wendall thought out loud, "Is someone mowing the front yard?" He walked around the house to see the smoking behemoth instead. It belonged in a junkyard. The old Continental Mark III sported faded gold paint, a cracked windshield, four bald tires, and a molting vinyl top. Wendall didn't dare get in it. It looked diseased.

Clarence was in constant debt. He would work at odd jobs just long enough to earn a little money for beer and poker night. After Betty threw him out of grandma Dent's house and took control of her monthly social security check, Clarence's finances became desperate. His backup source of much-needed funds was his sister Susan. Not surprisingly, he showed up at her doorstep when he learned that Max Nichols was out of town at a training seminar. Clarence demonstrated his well-practiced skill with the three Bs.

"Sis, before you say no, just realize that this is not for me. It's for Lucille. She's in bad trouble, and it's not her fault." (Begging.)

"What kind of trouble is she in?"

"Well…Uh…She…Uh…Let's see. Oh yeah, she went to Bartlesville, Oklahoma, for a bartender job interview and she got, uh, arrested 'cause the police thought she was a prostitute." (Obvious lie.)

"Why would they think that?"

"Well, she had to wear, you know, some clothes to show off her body. You know, if you want to work in a bar. Anyway, she's sittin' in that cold, dark jail, and my Lincoln is in the shop, and I know it's a lot to ask, and I really appreciate you so much…" (Begging.)

"You want to borrow our car." Susan frowned.

"Could I? Please. You don't know how much it would mean to me. Lucille is…the love of my life. You're such a wonderful sister. Thank you so much." (Begging.)

"I haven't said yes."

Wendall couldn't listen to Clarence's begging any longer. "Why don't we call Dad and ask him what he thinks?"

Susan was flustered. "His plane won't land in San Antonio until five o'clock."

Clarence knew that he couldn't manipulate Wendall. "Yeah, so Wendy, maybe you should go look after your little brother and let your mom and me talk."

Wendall snapped, "I don't need to go anywhere. And the name is Wendall."

Susan intervened, "Wendall, maybe you should go on. I can take care of this."

Shaking his head, Wendall walked around the corner to the hallway. He wanted to overhear everything.

"Please, sis. I'm really beggin' ya. You're my *last* hope. (Begging.)

"You know, Clarence, Wendall's right…"

"Wait, wait, wait! I'll have it back to you tomorrow, with uh… uh…a full tank of gas, and I'll wash it for you too, and uh…and I won't smoke in it." (Bargaining.)

"What time tomorrow?"

"By the afternoon." (Bargaining.)

"Well…that won't work. Tomorrow's Sunday, and we have to be at church for the bake sale by nine, so I'm sorry."

"Wait! I can get it back by seven in the morning. I promise." (Bargaining.)

"Clarence, it's just that…Bartlesville is a long way off. I'm sorry but…"

"But what about Lucille? She's there all alone. And…And you don't know what jailers do to young women at night." (Bullying: guilt induction, an innocent woman will suffer.)

"Surely not…"

"She was crying and terrified on the phone." (Bullying: guilt induction, an innocent woman is suffering.)

Clarence started to sniffle. (Bullying: crying, guilt induction.)

"It's just that…"

"You don't care about anybody but yourself. You girls always got everything growin' up." (Bullying: accusations.)

"Clarence, that's not true."

"Yes, it is." Now actively bawling. "You all got bicycles for Christmas, and I didn't." (Bullying: guilt induction.)

"What? Clarence, you got a motorcycle. Remember?"

"Uh…No, I don't. But that doesn't matter. If my car was running and you needed it, I'd loan it to you. But if brother, Clarence, needs a car, *no*!" (Bullying: accusation.)

"Clarence, it's not that."

"Lucille is there in Bartlesville, right now, thinkin' about killin' herself." (Bullying: a threat.)

"Oh, well…Don't worry, she won't do that."

"That's what she said! She'll do it! She's knows they'll gang rape her!" (Bullying: a threat.)

"Clarence, I would if I could."

More sobbing. "You can! You just *won't*! Fine! Be that way! Just keep your precious car!" (Bullying: accusation, guilt induction.)

"Okay. All right! Just stop bawling. You're embarrassing yourself."

"Thank you so much, sis." (Victory)

"Yeah, yeah. Uh…don't."

Wendall imagined Clearance was trying to give his mother a hug, and she was repulsed by him.

"I really appreciate it, sis."

"Okay. But it's the only transportation I have, and I've got to have it back in the morning, early."

"Oh, sure, sure. But, uh, there's just one other thing."

"What?" Susan sounded testy.

"I kinda need some money for her bail. I mean, it doesn't make much sense to drive down there if I can't bail her out." (Piggy back request: manipulates for the first request, then quickly hits her with a second.)

"How much is it?"

"Two hundred and fifty dollars."

"How much of that do you have?"

"I ain't got no money. And I'll need extra gas money too. So I really need three hundred. I promise I'll pay you back." (Bargaining.)

A smiling Clarence drove off in their '72 Oldsmobile Cutlass with three hundred bucks in his pocket. Seventy-five dollars of that came from Wendall's lawn mowing money. His mom promised to pay him back even if Clarence stiffed them, "Just, please don't tell your father."

Seven o'clock Sunday morning came and went with no Clarence in sight. At 7:30 a.m., the phone rang. Wendall answered it.

"Nichols residence."

A woman's voice came back, "Is Clarence there?"

"No. May I ask who's calling?"

"This is Lucille. I was just checking 'cause he didn't come in last night. He said he was going over to your place."

"Well, Lucille, he picked up our car and three hundred dollars in cash yesterday to bail you out of the Bartlesville jail."

Wendall heard her laugh. "He's such a liar. I've never been in jail. He went to bail out Bubba."

"Who's Bubba?"

"His drinkin' buddy. Bubba got in a fight and got arrested. Clarence wanted to borry my car and a hundred bucks, but I told him no. Bubba's no friend of mine."

"So Bubba's bail was a hundred dollars?"

"No, I think it was fifty. But Clarence was gonna need gas and beer money. Anyway, if ya see him, tell him to call me. Bye."

Before Wendall could explain the "real story" to his mom, it became even more colorful. The Bartlesville Police Department called looking for the owner of a 1972 Oldsmobile Cutlass, Kansas license plate: GR 3986. Their car was impounded after it was wrecked following a police chase. Clarence was in jail for DUI, reckless driving, resisting arrest, and assaulting a police officer. His passenger, Bubba Burns, was also jailed for resisting arrest in addition to public intoxication and indecent exposure. Allegedly, after Clarence hit a telephone pole, a drunken Bubba took off all his clothes and ran into a convenience store.

Despite his mom's promise to pay him back, Wendall wrote off his seventy-five dollars. He remembered the famous words of Benjamin Franklin, "Neither a borrower nor a lender be." Ben must have known a Clarence or two in his day. Clarence was forbidden to call, set foot on the property, or be within eyeshot of the Nichols's house. In the words of Max Nichols, "Until hell freezes over."

As effective as Clarence was at using the three *B*s, he was still just a journeyman. Wendall was about to meet a true three B master.

The Mona Lisa is the most famous painting in the world. Housed behind bulletproof glass in the Louvre in Paris, it is a masterpiece. Benson, Kansas, also had a Mona Lisa, but she was no masterpiece. Instead, Mona Lisa Barnett was a master of the three *B*s. Unfortunately, she got her hooks into the richest kid in school, Danny Bullock, who happened to be one of Wendall's best friends. Mona could wrap Danny around her little finger, if her little finger wasn't already sporting one of the dozen or more rings he had bought for her. But her haul didn't stop with rings. Necklaces, bracelets, charms, cards, flowers, chocolates, shoes, clothes, concerts, movies, and dinners were all required to keep Mona happy. Danny's one-hundred-dollar-a-week allowance from his parents, payable on Fridays, was always spent by Sunday morning. Wendall secretly referred to her as "Mona Leech." It was disgusting the way she manipulated Danny. Yet Wendall had to admire Mona's skill with the three *B*s. She was subtle, unrelenting, ruthless, and definitely worth observing.

Begging was a delicate art for Mona. She would never ask for anything directly. In fact, the word "please" had not crossed her lips in at least three years. Instead, Mona would "make it known" that she desired or deserved something.

(Sighing.) "I wish I had a ring like that."

(Pouting.) "Everyone else has a braided gold necklace."

(Smiling.) "Danny, you know what would make me happy? Another…"

Danny was then expected to "*volunteer*" to buy everything her heart desired. Because according to Mona, "I shouldn't have to ask… if you really love me." Danny quickly became properly "trained." Also, buttering up Danny was a clear signal that a volunteer opportunity was approaching. "You're just the best boyfriend in the whole world. Did you know that Barkley's has diamond earrings on sale this weekend?"

Mona also begged by using the "*favor setup*." Before hitting Danny with a big request, she would ask for a "favor."

"Danny, could you do me a little bitsy favor?"

"Yeah, sure."

"I need sixty dollars."

By agreeing to do her a "favor," Danny had already said *yes*. Now it was much harder to say *no* to the real request. If he tried, Mona would shame him. "But you said you'd do me a favor! Why do you lie to me all the time?"

Mona bargained by using subtle forms of extortion. She would never humiliate herself by "making a deal" that involved a clear exchange of goods or services. Mona preferred the "implied bargain." When she wanted something, Mona would imply a reward, usually sexual, *if* she got what she wanted.

"I want to go to a fancy French restaurant tonight. And you know, Danny, a happy girlfriend means a happy boyfriend."

Or flirting at the jewelry store. "Sometimes you have to pay if you wanna play."

Mona also collected "bargaining points." She would give Danny some poorly constructed mittens sewn in home economics class and dozens of cheesy love notes written on scraps of notebook paper. Mona always kept score of everything she gave to Danny, but she never tallied all the jewelry, clothes, and dinners he bought for her. Therefore, Danny was always in *her* debt. Mona would periodically "cash in" her accumulated bargaining points by reminding Danny, "Remember all the letters I've written and how I slaved to make those mittens for you? So you owe me."

Bullying was Mona Lisa's forte. She effortlessly wielded four "bully tactics": accusations, insults, guilt induction, and threats. All of them shared one purpose: to make Danny regret *ever* saying *no*. Mona used the four in progression. First, she would become violently angry and spew insults and accusations: "You're lying. You never loved me!" Then induce guilt: "Just leave me alone. I want to cry." Finally, make terrorizing threats of violence, abandonment, or even death: "You'll be sorry. I'll just kill myself!" Wendall jotted down some of her favorites. But keep in mind, this is only a partial list.

*Accusations: (You are so mean to me.)*
- "You don't love me anymore!"
- "You never loved me!"
- "You never buy me anything."
- "You like Julie, don't you! Admit it!"
- "It's *all your fault!*"
- "You're lying."

*Insults: (You're such a horrible, uncaring person.)*
- "How could you be so stupid?"
- "What's wrong with you?"
- "You're just a male chauvinist pig!"
- "Why are you such a Scrooge?"

*Guilt Induction: (I'm going to suffer because you won't say yes.)*
- "I'm so upset. I hope you're happy!"
- "I've never been so [humiliated, hurt, cheated] in my life."
- "Just leave me alone. I can't take it anymore."
- "Thank you very much. Now my head is killing me."
- "I just want to cry." Note: Crying is always guilt induction. Mona wouldn't just *tell* Danny how much he hurt her. She would *show* him by sobbing with flowing tears, on demand.

*Threats: (You deserve to be punished for hurting me.)*
- "You'll be sorry!"
- "I'm going to tell everyone."
- "You better. Or I'll tell my daddy."
- "I'll dump you."
- "I'll go out with someone else."
- "I'll never speak to you again."
- "I'll just *kill myself!*" The ultimate threat.

Mona's arsenal of three *B*s was impressive, but it was her ability to use them in rapid combinations that distinguished her as a master. She reminded Wendall of a professional boxer throwing flurries of devastating blows. Poor Danny was a helpless punching bag every Saturday morning at Barkley's jewelry store:

"I really like that necklace." (Beg: Danny must volunteer.)

"You *know* why you wanna keep me happy." (Implied: Bargain for sex.)

"Otherwise, I might have to go out with Jimmy Perry. I'm sure he likes me." (Bully: threaten to be unfaithful.)

However, on this particular day, for some unknown reason, Mona's triple combination did *not* produce the expected first-round knockout. Instead, Danny offered to purchase a slightly less expensive necklace. Stupid boy. Mona then pummeled him with a vicious combination from of *all four* bully tactics:

"Why are you being so mean to me? (Accusation.)

"You're such a cheapskate!" (Insult.)

(Sobbing.) "It hurts so...so bad." (Guilt induction.)

"We should just break up!" (Threat.)

In the virtual boxing ring, Danny staggered then dropped to the canvas. "I'm sorry, I'm sorry. Look, I'll buy you the longer necklace with the gold heart. Okay? Please don't cry."

The ringside announcer shouted, "It's a *second-round* knockout for Mona 'The Leeeeeeech' Barnett! Undefeated and still the Three B Champion of the World!"

Mona was fascinating to watch, but Wendall was careful to keep his distance. However, he eventually got sucked in. His Mona nightmare began when Danny asked him to help her write a midterm English paper. The little voice inside Wendall's gut screamed, "Don't do it!" But Danny was a best friend.

"I can *only* help her after school in the library."

Danny looked nervous. "I already talked to Mona, and she hates the library. And…she doesn't want anyone else to know she needs help."

"So where does she expect me to help her?"

"At her house?"

"Her house! Are *you* going to be there? 'Cause if you're not…"

"It's okay, it's okay. Her parents will be there. I've got football practice every day after school and on Saturdays. She said you two can work from the kitchen table."

"Do her parents smoke? You know I can't stand smoke."

"No, no. They don't. So you'll call her?"

Danny wrote down Mona's home phone number and address. He looked as if a thousand pounds had been lifted off his shoulders.

Right after school, Wendall decided, *Let's get this over with.* He called her number.

After three rings, a man answered, "Yeah what!" No doubt, it was dear old dad.

Wendall was startled for a second but quickly recovered. "Yes, is Mona there?"

"*Mona!*"

In the background, dogs were barking.

"Shut up, dogs! *Mona!*"

"I'm coming…*Jesus!*" Then very sweetly she murmured, "Hello, Danny."

"No, this is Wendall Nichols. Danny asked me to call you to schedule a time to help you with your paper. What day and time will work for you?"

"Uh, can you come by at two o'clock on Saturday?"

"Okay. That'll work for me. By the way, what's the topic of your paper?"

Mona cleared her throat with disgust. "Just a minute."

Wendall waited. Then he waited some more. Now he was sorry he had even asked.

"It says, 'Discuss the historical signif…'"

"Significance."

"Oh, that's what that word is! Okay…'Of the novel, Huckleberry Fine.'"

"Finn."

"Yeah, that's what I said."

"No, you said…Forget it. Two o'clock on Saturday."

"Okay…Byyyyyye."

The tone in her parting "byyyyye" gave Wendall a creepy feeling, the same one you get when you find a large spider crawling in your bed. He wouldn't put anything past Mona. He would need some protection. No, not condoms. Wendall needed a secret weapon, one he had already used in his skirmishing civil war with Damon, his new tape recorder.

Mona's family lived about a mile away in a double-wide trailer house so Wendall rode his ten-speed bicycle. A chain-link fence surrounded their dirt yard that was home to four large dogs. Fortunately, they didn't bite. Mona answered the door, and Marlboro smoke punched him in the nose. Thanks a lot, Danny, for lying about the cigarettes. The "kitchen table" was more of a workbench for motorcycle repairs. Wendall recognized a two-barrel carburetor, two cylinders, dozens of oil rings, and the guts of a transmission, along with scattered nuts, bolts, and washers of every size.

"Don't touch anything on the table," warned Mona. "Daddy gets real upset if anything gets moved."

The table matched the rest of the living room décor. Empty beer cans, Coke bottles, pizza boxes, assorted food containers, and dirty laundry covered most of the furniture and the stained shag carpet. Wendall thought, *I guess some people don't mind living in filth.*

"We'll have to go to my room."

Wendall looked around and noticed that *no one else* was home.

"Where are your parents? Danny said they were going to be here."

"Oh, they took my little brother to his flag football game. They won't be back for hours."

Mona's mischievous little smile and slow swaying hips signaled that Wendall was in trouble. He needed to turn on his tape recorder.

"Do you mind if I use your bathroom before we start?"

"Not at all. It's over there." She pointed down the hall.

Wendall started walking that direction.

Mona laughed. "You take your backpack into the bathroom?"

"Well, you take your purse into the bathroom."

Smiling, she said, flirting, "Did you bring some toys with you?"

Her hips swayed even wider, and she began running her hands through her hair.

"Not exactly. I'll be right back."

Wendall had to admit. He was surprised that Mona's room was not a total mess like the rest of the house. And although she was acting slutty, Mona was dressed…appropriately. Her white blouse had only the top button undone and her pink terry cloth shorts were loose and not too short. Mona plopped chest down onto her bed and bent her legs up over her bottom.

She patted the covers. "Sit here beside me."

Wendall ignored her request and scanned the room. "Where's your English notebook?"

"My notebook?"

"Yeah, your notes."

"What notes?"

"The notes you took in class."

"Oh, I don't bother with those. Mr. Gibson talks too fast."

Mona could see Wendall's disappointment. "What's wrong?"

No sense in explaining it to her.

"Nothing. Let's work on the outline first. It's the skeleton of the paper. Then you can flesh it out in the rough draft."

Mona wiggled. "Ooh, 'flesh it out.' That sounds naughty."

Wendall rubbed his temples and thought out loud, "Historical significance…"

Somehow, Wendall formulated a three-page outline that he hoped would be remotely related to what Mr. Gibson had discussed in Mona's English class. It was not without a struggle. Mona kept tossing her hair from side to side. She repeatedly wagged her hips, rolled over onto her back, stretched out her arms, and tried to touch Wendall's arm. At some point, she must have undone the next two buttons on her blouse. He brushed aside her repeated requests to sit down on the bed. Instead, Wendall stood the entire time and wrote on a clipboard.

"Okay, good! The real work is done. Now all you have to do is follow the outline to write the rough draft."

"Can't you do that for me?" (Begging.)

"No, it has to be in your words, not mine."

Mona stuck out her lower lip in a pout. "Danny said you were going to help me." (Begging.)

"I am helping you. I have helped you."

She looked up at him with well-practiced puppy dog eyes. (Begging.)

"Okay, I'll get you started."

Mona smiled. "But first, I need to give you a kiss for all your help." (Bargaining.)

"No. That's not necessary."

She smiled seductively. "But I *owe* it to you. You *know* you deserve it." (Bargaining.)

"I'm not going to kiss you."

"Danny wouldn't have to know. I won't tell if you don't." (Bargaining.)

"I just can't, okay."

She sulked. "Why not? Don't you think I'm pretty?" (Bully: guilt induction.)

"Oh sure. You're pretty enough."

"Pretty enough!" (Bully: guilt induction.)

"Sorry, I didn't mean it that way."

Looking perturbed, Mona rolled onto her back, completely unbuttoned her blouse, and pulled it open to reveal her bare breasts.

"Pretty enough for you now?" (Bully: insult.)

For about three seconds, Wendall stood, eyes staring, with his mouth open. Thankfully, he caught a glimpse of Danny's framed picture on the nightstand. It snapped him out of his trance.

Wendall shook his head. "Can't do that to Danny."

Mona jumped to her feet and buttoned her blouse furiously. "What's wrong with you?" (Bully: insult.)

"There's nothing wrong with me."

"You don't like girls?" (Bully: accusation.)

"Of course I do."

Mona looked down with a slow tear rolling down her cheek. "You just don't like *me*." (Bully: guilt induction.)

"Mona, you're Danny's girl."

Pouting again. "You don't even have a girl." (Bully: insult.)

"Sure I do."

"Do not! If you did, I'd know. I know who everyone is dating." (Bully: accusation of lying.)

"Her name is Carol."

Wendall didn't have a lot of imaginary people in his world. But they can come in handy at times, especially if you dress them up with enough believable details.

"There's no Carol at our school." (Bully: accusation of lying.)

"I didn't say she went to our school. She lives in Wichita. She's the class president, plays the violin, and runs track, cross country."

Mona began strumming her nails on the nightstand next to Danny's picture.

"You got a picture of her?" (Bully: accusation of lying.)

"Of course." Wendall fumbled through his wallet. "This is her." He handed Mona a picture of his cousin, Denise, when she was in junior high ten years before.

Mona glanced at it and handed it back. "She has a horse face." (Bully: insult.)

"Don't be fooled. She's wonderful."

Mona snapped, "You can leave now!" (Bully: insult.)

Wendall took a deep breath and let it out, relieved. He started gathering his clipboard and backpack.

"I'm going to tell Danny you made a pass at me." (Bully: threat.)

Sure enough. Just as he anticipated, she would lie.

"Go ahead. He won't believe you. He *will* believe me."

"I'm his girlfriend. He'll believe *anything* I want him to believe. (Bully: threat.)

Wendall growled, "*Not this time.*"

"Oh my! Wendy darling! Getting feisty, are we? I *like* that." (Bully: insult.)

"I'm out of here."

Wendall was almost to her bedroom door when Mona blurted out, "I'll tell Danny you attacked me." (Bully: threat.)

He stopped and turned around.

"You don't have any proof. So good luck with that."

She snarled, "You want proof. I'll give you proof." (Bully: threat.)

Mona wheeled around and stomped into her walk-in closet.

Wendall quickly unzipped his backpack to check the recorder. Good! Still recording.

She reappeared holding a pink "Church Camp" T-shirt.

"Danny gave this to me. It's his favorite."

She held it up by the collar with both hands, arms outstretched. "This is my proof."

With that, Mona ripped the shirt down the front. (Bully: threat completed.)

Whether it was from disbelief or just dumb luck, Wendall gasped. "Why did you rip that shirt apart?"

He later realized that the recorder would document the sound of the rip, but it couldn't prove who did the ripping. Fortunately, Mona made that crystal clear.

"So everyone will believe that *you* did it of course. Then you tried to rip off my shorts, and I had to kick you. (Bully: threat.)

Mona bent forward and started to cry and sob like a widow at a funeral. (Bully: threat.)

Now Wendall was scared. "You little witch."

She then slowly stood up straight and began laughing at him. "I'm a professional. I can get *anything* I want. So you might as well just give up." (Bragging.)

Wendall turned and started walking fast, through the living room, over the dirty clothes and empty potato chip bags, toward the front door. Behind him, he heard, "You'll be sorry! I'll tell my daddy, and he'll beat the hell out of you! The police are gonna throw you in jail!" (Bully: threat.)

Wendall flew out the door, past the dogs, and through the gate to his bicycle. Mona didn't follow him outside, thank God. He didn't stop pedaling until he got home. Once Wendall calmed down, he nervously rewound the tape to the torn-shirt segment. It was on there. Yes! In order to stay healthy and out of jail, Wendall knew that he had to stop Mona from spewing her lies to her parents before they returned from her little brother's flag football game.

He called her immediately.

"Hello."

Wendall tried to sound sarcastically cheerful. "Mona! This is Wendy darling."

"Have you finally come to your senses?" (Bully: insult.) "It's not too late. I haven't told anyone yet. (Bargain.) We still have time, if you come back right *now*!" (Bully: threat.)

"You're so sweet. That means so much to me, but no thanks. I just wanted to let you know that I recorded our *entire* time together. So if you lie...well, you're going to sound pretty stupid." (Bully: threat.)

"You're lying! I can tell when someone is lying and you suck at it!" (Bully: accusation and insult.)

"Oh really?"

Wendall pushed the play button. "So everyone will believe that *you* did it of course."

"Recognize any of that?"

"Nichols! You *bastard*! You tricked me!" Mona screamed so loudly that Wendall had to extend the phone away from his ear.

He heard a sudden *click*.

"Mona? Are you there? Hello?" He laughed for a full minute. Thank goodness for modern technology.

It was difficult, but Wendall played the tape for Danny. The truth was that Danny had wanted to dump Mona for weeks, but it was impossible to get rid of her. She just had too many terrifying threats at her disposal. Mona would have to dump him. There was only one way to make that happen. Cut off the money supply. At Danny's request, his parents withheld his allowance "until I can learn to handle money." His father was so proud of him and told Danny that he was becoming a man. Mona was so ashamed of him and told Danny that he was becoming a wimp for allowing his father to cut him off. In less than a week, Mona Lisa dropped Danny and latched onto Steve Ingall. Wendall didn't know him. But he did feel sorry for him.

The three Bs: *beg, bargain, and bully are the roots of all manipulation.* But they are not necessarily unethical or evil although dishonest bargaining and violent bullying are. The Bs are simply tools that everyone uses when attempting to change an unwelcome *no* into a reluctant *yes*. We learn the three Bs at an early age and use them our entire lives. We also learn very quickly which of the Bs works best on different people, in other words, which "button to push" for maximum effect.

A person's mastery of the three Bs determines their skill in the art of "persuasion." True masters can use their skills to become diplomats, top-notch salesmen or saleswomen, successful parents, business owners, or community leaders. *But be warned*: con men, sociopaths, and the Mona Lisa(s) of our world are also masters of the three Bs. They can use rapid combinations (particularly the bully tactics) to their advantage and to your detriment. Recognizing the three Bs is the *first* step. Defending against them is the topic of a later chapter: "How to Say No."

# 6

# The One Person

If I were not Alexander, I would wish to be Diogenes.

—Alexander the Great

Wendall thought that *everyone* used the three *B*s. But Wendall was wrong. In history class, he discovered *one person* who did *not* to use the three *B*s. Granted, the guy lived twenty-three-hundred years ago. No, he wasn't Jesus Christ. Jesus was born only 1,974 years ago, and he used all three of the *B*s. It's true. Jesus did use them. Jesus asked us to believe in him (beg). Then he made everyone an incredible deal: Do it, and we will live in heaven forever (What a bargain). But he gave us a solemn warning. If we don't believe in him, we will be lost forever (bully: a burn-in-hell threat). However, Wendall never thought of Jesus Christ as being a manipulator. Instead, Jesus was just trying to help everyone, like the friendly highway patrolman giving directions to an out-of-state couple on vacation.

"I'll have to ask you, folks, to please take a right onto Highway 7 (beg). It's brand-new and a smooth highway to heaven that leads to the prettiest resort in Kansas [bargain]. But if you decide to go left onto Route 666, then you're certain to drive into a big prairie fire, and there's nobody out there to help you [Bully: threat]."

No, the eccentric, enlightened, hippie-before-his-time who learned to *never* again use the three *B*s was the Greek philosopher, Diogenes. Among other things, he became famous in the ancient world for having only *one* possession, a cup for drinking water. Wendall's ninth-grade history teacher, Mr. Spence, never mentioned whether Diogenes had any clothes on his back. Wendall didn't dare ask because Mr. Spence always spoke Diogenes's name slowly, precisely, and with reverence. As the story goes, one day, Diogenes saw a boy cup his hands to drink water from a stream. Diogenes immediately threw his cup away. Now, he didn't need *any* possessions or anything from anyone. Therefore, Diogenes certainly didn't need to use the three *B*s. Meanwhile, the most powerful and wealthy man in the world was Alexander the Great. When he heard of Diogenes, he insisted on meeting this unusual man. Alexander wasn't quite convinced that the old cynic philosopher was legit. He couldn't believe that Diogenes had nothing and wanted nothing. Time to test Diogenes.

"Ask anything in the world, and I will give it to you."

Diogenes was lying on the ground, resting. Without opening his eyes, he softly motioned. "Could you move? You're blocking my light from the sun."

Are you kidding me? He asked Alexander the Great to move so he could sunbathe! That's it? Diogenes was such an idiot, or was he? Mr. Spence closed the history book and asked everyone in the class what *they* would have asked for if they had been in Diogenes's position. Many of the girls said they would have asked to be Alexander's queen. The guys had many more *material* requests in mind. David Starkley was determined not to be outdone.

"I would want ten *big* palaces with at least a hundred—no, a *thousand*, beautiful girls and uh, a million gold coins."

"Is that all, David?" A slightly devious smile came across Mr. Spence's face.

Wendall could smell a trap.

"Well, what else do ya need? I got my cribs, my babes, and tons of money."

"Oh, I don't know, say, maybe, your freedom and your *life*."

"My freedom?"

Starkley was suddenly blindsided. "Wait a minute. What do you mean my life?"

83

"Well, David Diogenes, you're supposed to be above desiring *any* worldly goods, and now at the first opportunity, you ask for a boatload of riches."

"So."

"So don't you think that Alexander the Great might, just might, think you played him for a fool?"

David shook his head nervously. "No. No, he said to ask for anything."

"Do you know, philosopher David, what Alexander valued most in the world?"

"Uh, money?"

"No!" Mr. Spence's explosive laugh surprised the entire class. "Class, who can tell me?"

Shout-outs came from all over the room.

"Power."

"Military conquests."

"His empire."

"His army."

Mr. Spence looked annoyed. "Think personal values. Anybody!"

"Loyalty."

"Honor."

"Devotion."

Mr. Spence barked out, "That's it! I heard it. Honor. Alexander the Great valued honor above all else." He then looked right through David. "So, people. We have the fiercest warrior who is the greatest conqueror of all time. And you, Mr. Starkley, have managed to hustle him." Mr. Spence turned to the other students. "Class? What is Alexander going to do to this fraud?" An index finger of condemnation was pointing at David.

"Throw him in prison," someone called out from the back.

"Castrate him." Debbie Betts sneered. She *detested* David.

David shot her a dirty look.

"Kill him."

Mr. Spence wheeled around. "Who said that? *That* would be correct. No doubt, Alexander of Macedonia would have run you through with his sword on the spot." Mr. Spence touched the eraser end of his pencil to David's chest to make his point.

David looked deflated. "May I go to the bathroom?"

Of course, in the annuls of history, Diogenes was spared, and Alexander paid him the highest compliment possible. "If I were not Alexander, I would wish to be Diogenes."

The history class exercise proved one thing. *All the ninth graders in Wendall's class were three B addicts.* But Wendall was correct in his previous analysis. Using the three *B*s doesn't make us evil. It makes us *normal.* Diogenes was not normal.

# 7

# How to Say No

He cares more about himself than he does about
anybody else. That's the key to saying no."
—Jerry Haley

"We are investing in the future of our children!" declared mayor,
William "Bill" White, at the ground breaking ceremony of the
Benson High School expansion. A growing student population, a
bond issue, and a fortunate oil and gas boom converged to make it
all possible. School was finally out for the summer of 1974, and the
construction of twenty classrooms, a new gymnasium, and a five-
hundred-seat theater were entrusted to the capable skills of Clarkson
Construction Company. Thurman Clarkson founded the company
forty years before, and he ran it with an iron fist. His uncompromis-
ing attention to detail, quality, and deadlines earned his company a
stellar reputation. No one doubted that the project would be completed on time and below budget before the beginning of fall classes
in August.

Thurman's only grandson, Rodney, attended Benson High
with Wendall. Rodney constantly complained that his "crusty old
grandpa" was a penny-pinching miser. However, several local char-
ities and the First Baptist Church of Benson would have strongly
disagreed. Mr. Clarkson was generous enough to allow Wendall and
Rodney to watch the construction, "As long as you wear hard hats

and stay out of the way." Wendall had never worn a hard hat before. He discovered that it was a lot cooler in the summer heat than a baseball cap.

Thurman Clarkson was at the construction site every day, every hour. He dealt with his workers, subcontractors, and suppliers with the same clear confidence and efficiency. Nothing escaped his attention. Wendall also noticed that the "crusty old grandpa" said *no* dozens of times a day. But it was more than that. It was the *way* he said *no* that made it so memorable and effective. A few examples of Mr. Clarkson's "charm":

The Athen's Lumbar delivery truck arrived with three bundles of two-by-four boards.

"Take 'em back. That's not what I ordered."

The driver was puzzled. "Didn't you order three bundles of ten-foot-long two-by-fours?"

"No. I ordered three bundles of ten-foot-long *number 2* two-by-fours. You tell me. Why am I rejecting this lumber? Do you think I don't know what number 2 grade lumber looks like? Do you think I can't see all the knots and the bark on some of these boards? Well, do you?"

Wendall thought, *How do you argue with that rejection?*

When one of his own workers asked a question, Thurman's response was even more blistering.

"Mr. Clarkson, we ran a little short on steel for the stem wall of the west side foundation. Jean accidently backed a truck over the rebar and bent a couple of pieces. We're only short about twenty feet. That'll be okay, won't it?"

Thurman scowled. "I can't believe you're asking me that. Why would you even dare ask me that? How long have you worked for my company? Why do you think we got this contract? Do you think it's because we cut corners? Have we *ever* cut corners on *any* project? *No!* Of course not! Call and order the steel you need *now!* Do it right!"

But the most memorable encounter occurred between Thurman and the school's superintendent, Mr. Jones.

"Yes, sir, Mr. Clarkson. You know, uh, if it wouldn't be too much trouble, I'd like an extra room connected to my office, maybe twelve-by-twelve-foot. It could be part of the same slab that you're pouring for the classrooms. And maybe add one sink, so I can put in a wet bar? Uh…by the way, have you ever vacationed in Florida? My brother owns a couple of condos in Miami."

Old man Thurman stared right through Jones's nervous bribe. "Do you realize what you just asked me to do? Think about it. Do you know what construction fraud is? Have you ever heard of bribery? Do you think I would ever do anything illegal? Seriously? Trust me. You do *not* want to ask me *anything* like that *ever* again."

Mr. Clarkson didn't just say *no*. He demanded explanations. Why are you asking me? Is your request reasonable? Why can't you do it yourself? What have you tried? What else can you try? Why haven't you tried? Who else have you asked? Why should I help you? He challenged people to *think* about their request which then *trained them* to be more responsible and self-sufficient. As a result, his workers, subcontractors, and suppliers quickly learned his standards. Therefore, they didn't need to ask him nearly as many questions. However, everyone knew that if they were uncertain of *anything* they were doing, they had better ask the boss first. Thurman accepted no excuses for "winging it."

Thurman's wife, Mable, brought him the same lunch every day at 12:30 sharp, a tuna salad sandwich, potato chips, and a Pepsi. Wendall and Rodney had already spent several days at the construction site when Rodney introduced his grandmother to Wendall. She promptly invited them to Sunday dinner. Rodney later explained that Clarkson Construction never worked on Sundays, even if they were approaching a deadline. Sunday was always a day of rest.

Wendall was surprised when he arrived at the Clarkson home. Thurman was one of the wealthiest men in town. Yet he and Mable lived in a small two-bedroom red-brick home with a covered porch and a one-car garage built in the popular style of the 1940s. Back then, everyone had a porch outside because no one had air-conditioning inside. But the Clarkson home did have a full basement, which served as a tornado shelter and a game room. Perhaps Thurman and Mable didn't need much room because they only had one son, Richard.

Wendall met Rodney's father and immediately realized that Richard was nothing like Thurman. Richard appeared nervous throughout dinner as if he were looking for something. He sold insurance for State Farm, but he didn't own the agency where he worked. Naturally, Richard had once worked for his father's company when he couldn't find a job after four years of college partying. But that employment only lasted a few months. Richard never could accept Thurman's method of saying *no*. It was too demeaning for a spoiled only child. Their strained relationship was held together by Mable and by Richard's fear that his father would leave all his inheritance to the church or some "bleeding heart charity." Well, at least that's what Rodney told Wendall.

After serving a delicious dinner of pot roast with potatoes and carrots, buttered corn, and rolls, Mable and Rodney's mother, June, took a cherry pie out of the oven to cool. Meanwhile, Rodney and Wendall escaped to the basement to play shuffleboard. The painted concrete floor was perfect with no cracks or ridges. Wendall wasn't surprised when Rodney mentioned that "crusty old grandpa" had built the home right after the war (World War II). The basement ceiling was open with the floor joists and hardwood flooring of the upstairs visible, which made the basement less than soundproof. Rodney and Wendall could clearly hear Thurman and Richard's dialogue when their "discussion" became heated. They stopped their shuffleboard game to listen:

"You already know *why* I'm telling you *no*. Think about it. What have you done to prepare yourself?"

"Dad! Anybody can run a car dealership. All they need is the financing. That's all I need, okay?" (Begging.)

"So you think I'm your banker? Do I look like a banker? Do I loan money to *anybody*? *No!*"

"Look, uh...we can be partners. You can own the controlling share of the business until I can buy you out. That's reasonable." (Bargaining.)

"Do I look like a car salesman? Do I have *time* to manage another business? Do you think I would even consider that?"

"I'm your only son, and you won't help me! You want me to fail in life so you can brag about how successful you are." (Bully, guilt induction.)

"I see. Your failure in life is *my* fault because I won't help you." Thurman laughed. "You sound like a toddler throwin' a fit. Time to grow up. Take some responsibility and learn to support yourself. You need to understand something. I have helped you! Make no mistake about it. I've given you advice, which is much more valuable than any check I could ever hand you no matter how many extra zeros I scribbled on it."

"Yeah, right! Great advice, get a part-time job at Paceman's Chevrolet as a car salesman. Do you know how humiliating that is?" (Bully, guilt induction.)

"What do you think a car dealership does? Sell cars! You want to talk about humiliation? Think about how humiliating it is to fail in a business because you didn't prepare yourself by learning the business *first.*"

"You're just selfish. You only care about yourself." (Bully, accusation.)

"You're half right. I do care about myself. I don't want to go bankrupt. I also care about you, which is why I want you to learn how to run a business *before* you jump into one."

Richard opened the basement door. "Rodney! Get up here! We're leaving. Now!"

Rodney bounded up the stairs. "Sorry, Wendall, gotta go."

Wendall stood awkwardly in the basement as he heard the front door slam. He decided to wait a few minutes to let things cool off upstairs before exiting. He waited too long.

The basement door opened, and Thurman called down, "Son, are you still down there?"

"Yes, sir. I'm just getting ready to leave." He started up the wood stairs.

"No need to leave just yet. We still have cherry pie and ice cream for dessert."

Wendall was surprised at Mr. Clarkson's relaxed, untroubled demeanor. It was as if the argument never occurred. Mable was her usual pleasant self, smiling as she cut the cherry pie while Thurman scooped vanilla ice cream into three bowls.

Once they were settled at the dining table and enjoying dessert, Thurman acknowledged the elephant in the room. "I must apologize for the training session that you no doubt overheard. But I have to handle such important things on the spot."

A "training session?" Wendall couldn't stop himself. "What were you training Richard to do?"

Thurman swallowed a mouthful of pie and smiled. He was clearly pleased to talk about it. "I was training him to become self-sufficient. Handle his own problems. Make his own dream a reality instead of expecting me to hand it to him. Richard still hasn't learned to think for himself and find his own way." Thurman shook his head with disappointment. "He just keeps asking for money, again and again."

"My little brother is that way. No matter how many times you tell him *no*, he never learns."

"How old is he?"

"He's five."

Thurman laughed. "That's normal for a five-year-old. But Richard's forty-five."

Wendall felt relaxed enough to tell Thurman and Mable about his recent discovery, the three *B*s: beg, bargain, and bully.

"Yes, yes." Thurman pointed his spoon at Wendall. "I thought I was the only one who recognized that 'progression.' But I don't call 'em the three *B*s. To me, they're the three *W*s." He counted with his fingers. "Whining, wheeling and dealing, and waging war."

Wendall laughed and pointed right back. "Right, right."

Thurman had found an eager student. Therefore, he poured out his knowledge and experience. There are only *six things* other people will ever want from you. Remember these because you're going to see them the rest of your life. They want *money*. Or they want *property*. Or they want to *borrow* something, which usually they try to keep. Or they want you to do something for them, either *work* or a favor. Or they want your *permission*. Or finally, they want you to *accept* something, usually their bad behavior."

Wendall mumbled and counted the six in his mind: money, property, borrow, work, permission, acceptance.

Mr. Clarkson continued, "I ignore the three *W*s, or as you call them, the three *B*s. I want people to think. Why are they asking me? What have they done so far? What else can they try? Who else can they ask for help? I sincerely want to know. I'm not being mean, although I can be."

Mable nodded. "Yes, dear, sometimes you are."

"Well, not very often. Unless they don't even *try*. My point is, instead of just *giving* them a fish to eat, I want them to *think* of how they can catch their own fish. After all, I'm not going to live forever."

Unfortunately, Thurman was right. He didn't live forever. One week after the high school addition was completed, he suffered a massive heart attack. Richard quickly manipulated Mable into signing over financial and medical power of attorney to him, "To take care of you, Mom." By Labor Day, Mable was being taken care of by a nursing home. Richard then sold her house and Clarkson Construction and bought expensive homes in Vale and Honolulu. Poor Mable. She never learned to say no.

On December 24, 1974, Mable Clarkson died in the Country Estates Nursing Home. Her funeral was four days later on the twenty-eighth. It was a cold and blustering Saturday afternoon. The First Baptist Church was overflowing with half the town of Benson in attendance. Noticeably missing from the crowd was Richard and his family. They were rumored to have been "delayed out of state because of bad weather." But Wendall knew better. He had just received a postcard from Rodney in Vale. Rodney's entire family was upset. Due to unseasonably warm weather and lack of snow, most of the ski lifts were shut down.

Haley's Gold, Silver, and Pawn Shop had the best used sporting goods in town. Wendall would often stop by and inspect Jerry Haley's merchandise. Since Wendall was a habitual eavesdropper, he overheard Jerry say no to his customers dozens of times a day. They would bring in everything under the sun to sell or pawn, and the haggling would commence. Customers routinely used the three *B*s in their quest to get a better price. But they were wasting their time.

Jerry had no sympathy for begging. Wendall was rummaging through the football bin when two men with stringy, long hair and short, wispy beards walked in. They were carrying pillow cases with clanging metal pieces inside. Wendall had never seen these guys before. The taller of the two wore a black long sleeves shirt with faded blue jeans. The shorter one wore a white T-shirt with cut off jean shorts and gray sandals. They both looked greasy.

Jerry greeted them at the counter. "I don't know ya, so I'll have to see some ID. And sign here in my register."

The taller of the two was the leader. "He ain't got no ID, but here's mine. We got some silver to sell."

Jerry coolly said, "Okay, just lay it out here on the counter."

The men eagerly emptied silver flatware, a tea set, and a velvet case of silverware from the pillow cases.

Jerry carefully scanned the considerable pile. "Looks like a complete set."

"It is," the shorter man blurted out.

The taller one wheeled around. "Shush, I'll do the talking." He then calmed himself and turned back to Jerry. "How much can we get for it?"

Jerry sighed. "Well, it's old and needs polishing. The silverware case is in pretty bad shape. The entire set is only worth a little more than its weight in silver. I'll give you...seventy-five dollars for the lot."

"Seventy-five bucks! Is that all? Man, I need at least two hundred."

"No. Seventy-five is my top dollar."

"Man! I gotta have more. Can't ya help me out? I mean, look at all this silver."

"No."

He kept whining, "But...come on, man, please just...150."

"No. Seventy-five, that's it." Jerry sounded irritated. "By the way, do you mind telling me where you got all this silver?"

"Uh, well, uh...My grandmother left it to me...in her will. She died last week."

Jerry looked up. "What was her name?"

"Uh, Mrs....Johnson."

"Which one, Rose, Irene, or Pearl?"

"Uh, Rose."

"Hmm." Jerry rubbed his chin. "Got a little problem. Actually, I got two problems. First off, Rose died nine years ago. She only had one grandchild, and *her* name is Clarice. Second, on the back of this tea platter," Jerry turned it over, "it says, 'To Joanne, the love of my life, yours truly, Darrel.'"

There was an awkward silence for four seconds as the two men stood frozen.

"Tell you what I'll do for you boys. I'll ask the Benson police to sort all this out."

"What!"

Jerry held the phone to his ear as he dialed the number. "Just leave all that stolen silver there on the counter."

The short man grabbed the silverware case and the taller one ripped out the register page before they bolted out the front door.

Wendall was stunned. "Oh my gosh, Jerry! They ripped out part of your book. Do you remember that guy's name?"

"Sure do. See, I wrote it down on this piece of scrap paper from his driver's license while they were unloading the silver."

"How did you know it was stolen?"

"If granny leaves you her fine silverware, you're gonna carefully wrap it in packing paper and put it in a box so it won't get scratched up. Those clowns were still carrying it around in the pillowcases from the house they robbed. Besides, the morons should have read the inscriptions so they could at least tell a believable lie."

"You never know, Jerry. Maybe they can't read."

"Hello, Benson police..."

Jerry never trusted bargaining, even though he owned a pawnshop. Maybe that's why he was so successful.

"Bill, what do you have there?"

Bill was a regular customer. His weekend hobby was picking through garage sales then selling the "treasures" he discovered to Jerry for a profit of course. Bill also didn't have a sentimental bone in his body. Everything he inherited was brought straight to Jerry.

"I got a gold watch, an antique. It was my granddad's."

"Are you wanting to pawn it or sell it?"

"Sell. Can I get three hundred dollars for it?"

"Depends on how much gold is in it. Set it there on the scale."

Jerry adjusted his reading glasses. "Looks like five and a half ounces. So half of that is two and a quarter ounces times eighty dollars an ounce is uh…" Jerry scratched out the numbers with a short pencil on a pad of paper. "Comes to 180 bucks."

"Can't you give me more than that?"

"No."

Bill protested, "But why did you cut the weight in half?"

"It's not solid gold, just the casing. All the guts in it are iron. And the casing is only 18 karat, not 24."

"But this is an antique, and it still runs. Keeps good time."

Jerry flipped the watch over in his hand. "Yeah, so it does. But nobody's gonna buy a watch with 'To Benjamin Needleman for thirty years of devoted service' inscribed on the back."

"So you would just bust it up into pieces, for the gold?"

"Yep, with my sledgehammer out back."

"Look, I'll make a deal with you."

"No. No deals. Period!"

"But you haven't heard my offer yet."

"Doesn't matter. Don't trust anyone. No deals."

"But, Jerry, I'm good for it."

"No, you're not. That washing machine you sold me last month. You said it worked fine. You didn't mention that it sounded like a jet engine."

"But…"

"No deals. No exceptions. Now, do you want 180 bucks for it or not?"

"Okay."

Jerry could not be intimidated by bullying.

Raymond was homeless, around thirty years old, and able-bodied by all appearances. But he lived off the charity of others. Usually, he slept in Benson Springs Park when the weather was good, and he wandered into the Salvation Army when it was bad. Raymond was a frequent visitor at Jerry's. He would hike two miles to the city dump and bring in other people's trash.

"Hey, Jerry. Got somethin' really good this time." Raymond held up a bent bicycle rim.

"It's junk, Raymond. Can't buy it or let you pawn it."

"It's not junk. This here came from a racer bike from the Tour of France."

"It's Tour de France, and I don't care where it came from. Unless it's made of silver or gold, it's not worth a damn thing."

"You know, it could be silver. It's silver colored."

"Silver doesn't rust." Jerry pointed to where the spokes entered the rim.

"What do you expect me to do?"

"I expect you to take it back to the dump and throw it as far as you can."

"You're just being mean to me because I'm homeless."

Jerry shook his head. "No, I'm being mean to you because you're wasting my time."

"You don't care about anybody but yourself."

"Raymond, you are *absolutely right*. And if you cared anything about *yourself*, you would go straight to the Salvation Army. They can clean you up and help you get a steady job and a place to live."

"I'm gonna report you to the Better Business Bureau. You're just rippin' people off."

"Knock yourself out." Jerry turned and proudly pointed to a framed certificate that read, "Haley's Gold, Silver, and Pawn Shop. Member: Benson BBB since 1954."

"I'm gonna call the police on you!"

"Wanna use my phone? They can pick you up for vagrancy. Give you a cot and three-square meals."

"To hell with you, Jerry!" Raymond stomped out the door.

Jerry started laughing. "Raymond, wait! You left your Tour of France junk."

Wendall asked Jerry where he learned to say no with such ease and without any feelings of remorse or pity for his customers.

"I learned in the School of Hard Knocks. You get cheated enough times, and you learn to look out for yourself."

"So you've been cheated a lot in the shop?"

Jerry laughed. "No, of course not! Otherwise, I'd be out of business. I started gettin' cheated in the first grade. Other kids would borrow my pencils and never give 'em back. Or they'd ask for a dime so they could get an extra chocolate milk at lunch and then never pay me back. But the straw that finally broke my little eight-year-old back was when my friend Billy borrowed my bike. A week later, his family moved, and they took my bike with them."

"Your parents couldn't get it back?"

"Nobody knew where they went. I remember cryin' to my mom. And you know what? She flashed a happy smile and said, 'This is a lesson you will never forget. You've got to be more selfish about your things.'"

"Did that help?"

"No. But she was right. I never forgot. And after that, I became the most selfish little kid you ever saw. I said no to everybody, every time."

Wendall's squeamish expression made Jerry grin.

"What's the matter? Don't feel comfortable telling people no? Worried about upsetting 'em? Or they won't like you? Or they'll give you grief?"

Wendall looked down and sighed. "Guess so."

"Well, you just haven't been burned enough times…yet. Tell me. Besides me, who's the most selfish person you know?"

What an easy question. "Damon, my little bother, uh, I mean, brother."

Jerry chuckled. "I'll bet you a hundred bucks he doesn't have any trouble tellin' people no."

"You're right. It's his favorite word."

"It's because he's selfish. He cares more about himself than he does about anybody else. That's the key to saying no."

"But sometimes I'm not really sure whether to say yes or whether to say no. How do you decide?"

"That's simple. If you can't say yes in *three seconds*, then the answer is *always* no. Want to know why? Because during those three seconds, you're hemming and hawing around, worrying about hurting their feelings and trying to come up with some excuse."

Wendall admitted, "You're right. I don't like to make other people feel bad."

Jerry looked straight at Wendall. "*Better them than me.* Do you know how bad it feels to lose a thousand dollars on a counterfeit Colt revolver because you didn't listen to your gut and insist on a professional appraisal before you bought it?"

"No. But I know what it's like to be trapped in a filthy trailer house with a sexual psychopath."

"*What!*"

Wendall laughed and told Jerry the story of Mona Lisa and her term paper. "When Danny asked me to help her, I knew *in my gut* that I should say no."

"Right, listen to your gut. And if you find yourself stammering around, then don't hesitate any further. Say no."

Wendall frowned. "But when I say no, they always ask me, 'Why not?' or 'Why can't you?' They demand some kind of explanation. What do I tell them?"

"Tell 'em *the truth*. 'Because you don't want to. Because you don't have the time. Because you don't have the money. Because you don't think it's a good idea. Because you don't trust them. Because you don't think it's legal. Because you don't…whatever.' Just fill in the blank."

"Okay."

"Okay? Is that all I get for teaching you the most important lesson of your life?"

Wendall had to smile at Jerry's feigned upset. "You're right. I really do appreciate it."

"Just remember one other thing. Practice makes perfect. Practice being selfish and saying no in front of a mirror until it becomes second nature."

Wendall told Jerry about Thurman's training method of saying no. Jerry let out jovial laugh followed by a long sigh. "Yep, sounds just like my old man. He definitely 'trained' me and my brother. Our dad would scowl at us and say, 'What the hell do you need that for? Do you think I'm stupid? You know better than to ask me that! Don't ever ask me that again!'"

Wendall was shocked. "Oh my gosh! What kind of training is that?"

Jerry was still smiling. "The kind that taught us, 'Don't ever ask for anything.' One time, I'll never forget. My brother wanted to go on a double date on Saturday night. I tried to tell him that Dad wouldn't let us use the car. But Roger argued, 'If he says no, then we're no worse off. What have we got to lose?'" Jerry shook his head. "Famous last words. Our dad was working in the garage when Roger asked him. He looked up, pointed his finger at us, and said, 'The *last* time you borrowed the car, you were supposed to put gas in it. And ya didn't.' He snapped his fingers. 'Ten bucks from the both of you, and you *still* don't get to use the car!'"

"Ouch."

"Exactly. But he taught us well. Roger and I have enough *selfish self-respect* to put ourselves first. You'll never catch us being afraid to say no."

Over the years, Wendall reaffirmed that Jerry was absolutely right. *The ability to say no is the most important skill in life.* If you cannot say no, then you cannot control your life, which means someone else will. Your money, property, time, and even your freedom can easily be taken from you. Mable Clarkson learned this sad truth after Thurman's death. Like a scrap of paper in the wind, she was helpless. However, mastery of saying no gives clarity, peace of mind, and ultimately happiness. Why? Because to be happy, you must get what you want, which requires you to say no to all the things you don't want. Remember what Mrs. Brown taught her grandchildren: Happiness begins with the self-respect to say no.

But saying no is not easy. The pressure to "be nice" and "help others" and "get along" is overwhelming in our society. We even say "sorry" when we "have to say no." Our natural instinct to be defiant when we were "terrible" two-year-olds has long since been crushed.

As adults, we must *relearn our "childish" self-centered ability* by doing the following:

1.  Caring more about what *we* want, or don't want, than what *anyone else* wants.
2.  Ignoring or rejecting all three *B*s no matter how dramatic they may be.
3.  Telling the blunt truth. "Because I don't..."
4.  Questioning or ridiculing, if necessary, their request or demand.

There are also a few caveats to keep in mind. Remember that saying no includes *refusing to accept* bad behavior. "No! You don't talk to me that way!" "No! You don't treat me that way!" "No! Children, you will obey me." Also, it is certainly wonderful to help other people, *as long as* you don't go too far. If you begin feeling resentment or regret for your benevolence, then you are giving and sacrificing *too much*, and it is time to say no. Finally, many of us make the mistake of *not* being selfish enough, or honest enough, to say no to our loved ones, friends, coworkers, or employers. As a result, "little resentments" form inside us. These unspoken, seemingly insignificant irritations can unconsciously accumulate day after day, month after month, and year after year until we've finally "had enough" and the marriage, friendship, or job are destroyed. Therefore, *don't let the little resentments build up*. Speak up immediately when you feel that twinge of unfairness, anger, or disgust. Because if you cannot say no *in* a relationship, then you will eventually have to say no *to* the relationship.

Despite our best selfish efforts to say no, we can sometimes be exhausted by a loved one or a master of the three *B*s. Therefore, *if all else fails,* tell them the following:

*   "Dr. Wendall said no."
*   "He doesn't want me doing that."
*   "He told me absolutely no."
*   "Forget it. I'm not even going to think about it."

This honest excuse can cover *everything* in your life. Because if you do not want to do something, Dr. Wendall doesn't want you to do it either. Why? Because it's *bad* for your mental and physical health. Stay healthy. Say no.

# 8

# Prune Your Tree

You have to prune the sucker branches if you
want the tree to produce better fruit.
—Jack Williams

Jack Williams was a neighbor. His day job was managing a local lumberyard. But his passion was his garden. Jack loved to brag about his garden and with good reason. It grew as if it were possessed. His green bean plants were waist high, and his corn towered to over eight feet tall. Jack's tomatoes grew so big and heavy, his wife, Regina, would spread newspapers under the sagging tomatoes to keep them off the ground. Wendall would not have been surprised to step outside some morning to see a skyscraper bean stalk curling its way through the clouds from Jack's backyard. Jack gladly shared his bounty with the Nichols and his other neighbors. It gave him the opportunity to show off his green thumb.

But how was Jack's backyard an oasis of vegetables while the Nichols's yard was a hard clay slab of dying grass and weeds? Jack never watered his garden, not even at night. He didn't use any fertilizer either. Wendall noticed that the only thing Jack did water and fertilize were his prized young apple trees. His six trees lined the very back of his yard. Jack had dug a circular ten-inch-tall moat around each one. Then he flooded them every other day. The trees had been producing apples for about three years, and they were just coming into their own.

The secret to Jack's magical garden was finally revealed when his daughter, Sally, accidentally washed a dishcloth down the kitchen sink, and it plugged the sewer line somewhere outside the house. When Wendall came home from school, a backhoe was digging up Jack's septic tank. Septic tank? In the city limits of Benson? Who knew that Jack's house was the original farm house in the area? Over the years, it had been updated with siding, new windows, and an attached two-car garage. Therefore, it blended in with the later homes built around it as Benson grew out to the countryside. But the old septic tank remained, and its lateral lines conveniently extended underneath Jack's garden. All his family's pee and poop were silently, and continuously, watering and fertilizing all their tasty vegetables. Yum! To his credit, Jack never claimed to be a better gardener than any of his neighbors. But he didn't mind letting them think that he was.

That's not to say that Jack wasn't a skilled gardener. His apple trees didn't receive any benefit from his sewage system, yet they were thriving. That fall, Jack pruned them. Wendall was surprised by the large pile of limbs in the corner of Jack's yard. Damon saw the branches and was determined to get some of the clippings. His army men desperately needed "tree cover" from the enemy. Damon enlisted Wendall to requisition the military supplies.

Jack waved. "Good morning, Wendall. I just picked another five-gallon bucket of tomatoes."

Wendall walked over. "Wow, Jack! Those are incredible."

"Here, take some. We can't eat 'em all, and Regina's already canned thirty quarts."

He handed Wendall the bucket of ripe tomatoes.

"Thanks, Jack. Your tomatoes are the best I've ever tasted."

Wendall nodded toward the five-foot-tall pile of apple tree branches. "What are you planning to do with all those limbs?"

"I'm gonna turn the smaller ones into mulch and the larger branches into firewood. Why? Did you want some?"

"Damon was wanting some branches to use in his war games."

Jack smiled. "Sure, take what you need. This is the first year I've cut 'em back, so there's plenty."

"Thanks. I have to admit. I don't know much about apple trees. But, uh, why did you prune them back so much?"

"You have to prune the sucker branches if you want the tree to produce better fruit."

"Really?"

Jack nodded. "Oh yeah. When you prune, the water and nutrients go to fewer branches so you get larger apples."

"That makes sense."

"Well, there's another thing too. If a tree gets too many branches, it can die."

Wendall nodded, but his frown signaled that he didn't understand.

Jack explained, "If you have a drought in the summer, the tree won't get enough moisture to feed all the limbs and leaves. Of course, I can always give my trees plenty of water. But the winter is the real threat. If an ice storm hits, all the little branches get coated with ice. Then the weight bears down on the main branches. That's how ice can split a tree in half and kill it."

Wendall thought about the last ice storm in Benson three years before. Many of the elm and maples throughout town were shattered. Wendall reminded Jack of that storm.

"Yes, I remember. Luckily, my trees weren't big enough to need pruning at that time. People don't think about pruning their shade trees. They're no different from fruit trees. The main branches can get stressed to their breaking point from too much ice."

Wendall thanked Jack again for the tomatoes and started walking back to the house. The vision of a sagging ice-ladened tree suddenly splitting in half stuck in his mind. He remembered his parents and grandparents using various phrases to describe "overload." Someone had "too many irons in the fire" or "bit off more than he could chew" or had "too much on his plate." "Supporting too many branches" could easily take its place among these expressions. Wendall thought of his mom and all the unnecessary "branches" she was struggling to hold up, which included many of the things she did for Damon and him. As he stepped through the back door, Wendall felt a twinge of guilt. There were a lot of chores that he could, and should, be doing to help his mom. Washing the dishes, doing laundry, folding clothes, and helping Damon to clean his room were just a few. Wendall could easily "graft" some of his mom's branches to his own tree.

Wendall rinsed off the tomatoes in the sink and opened the refrigerator. It was completely full of Jack Williams's cucumbers, green beans, and more tomatoes. Wendall didn't want to let the new arrivals spoil, and he certainly didn't want to throw them out. Then it occurred to him. If you have too much, do what Jack does. Give them away. Don at Don's Motorcycle Shop loved tomatoes, and Wendall wanted to drop by the shop anyway to talk to his assistant, Phil, about a scooter.

Don Murphy was a motorcycle authority. As far as Wendall could tell, no one knew more about motorcycles than Don. He specialized in Indian brand motorcycles, the "best cycles ever built" from 1901 to 1953. Wendall always wondered: if they were the best ever built, why did they go out of business? But you didn't dare ask Don an insulting question about Indian motorcycles. They were rare and popular, which made them expensive. He was even known to pay big bucks for rusted and broken frames, motors, wheels, gauges, and gas tanks that had been pulled out of pastures and old barns. Don could restore any motorcycle. His waiting list from all over the country was over a year long, which is why he hired Phillip, a young "kid" of twenty-eight who was a worthy apprentice of the master.

Wendall walked in the front door, past all the rows of new motorcycle accessories, to the counter next to three rebuilt Harley's for sale.

"Hi, Francine. Are Don and Phil in?"

"Yeah, Don's in the back. What's in the bag?"

"Oh, I brought some garden tomatoes. I got them from my neighbor and we just can't eat 'em all. They're really good."

Wendall handed Francine a bright red tomato the size of a softball.

"Wow. Those are a lot better than anything in the store. Don loves tomatoes. He eats them like fruit. Please, go on back."

Wendall walked into the shop strewn with a hundred motorcycle parts. Don was rebuilding a 1937 Harley "knucklehead" engine.

Wendall had hung around his shop enough to recognize its distinct shape.

"Hi, Don."

Don paused only long enough to glance up. "Hi yourself. What's in the bag?"

"Brought some tomatoes from my neighbor's garden."

"Ya stole 'em?"

Wendall laughed. "No, no. He gave 'em to me. But we've got too many. Thought you might like some."

"Sure." Don peered inside the bag. "Just one of those would make a whole meal. Thanks. Thanks a lot." He went straight back to work.

"You're welcome."

Don looked up again. "Anything I can do for you?"

"Actually, I wanted to check with Phillip about a Honda scooter he was rebuilding."

Don shook his head. "Sorry, he quit."

"Really? I thought he was a good mechanic."

Don nodded in disappointment. "Yeah, he is. But he just wasn't dependable anymore."

"What happened?"

Don ratcheted off the last bolt to the head of the engine and lifted it off to reveal a head gasket older than Wendall's father. "His girlfriend's bloodsucking friends happened. He let 'em take advantage of him."

"I never met any of his friends."

"He doesn't have any." Don's voice was full of disgust. "He's got a sleazy girlfriend and all *her* dope-head friends."

"Did they take all his money?"

"More than that. They took all his time. He was in here late at night repairing all their cycles."

"Let me guess. For free."

"Oh, they paid him all right, with deadlines and complaints, when he didn't work fast enough."

Don paused and then grimaced. "You know, I didn't mind him using my shop after hours. But he was so damn tired after working all night, he'd lay his head down on the work bench and fall asleep during the day."

Wendall thought about his mom working for free on all those cheerleader hand warmers when she should have been sleeping.

Don set down his wrench and chuckled. "And there's more. Get this. Phillip's girlfriend made him take her two kids to school every day, because they didn't want to ride the school bus."

"Why couldn't she take them?"

"Because she couldn't get her fat butt out of bed before noon!"

"What?"

"No joke. Phillip started coming in here late every morning. I told him, 'What you do on your own time is your business. But showing up late *and* falling asleep at work isn't gonna cut it.' So he tried to stand up to her."

"What did he tell her?"

Don smiled. "He tattled on me. Told her that it was *me* demanding that he stop taking her kids to school." Don started laughing and coughing at the same time. "So she called me up, here at the shop, and started bitchin' at me to mind my own business."

Wendall started to laugh. "Oh boy."

"I had so much fun. I'm not exactly sure when she hung up. I didn't let her get a word in sideways."

They both laughed as Wendall imagined Don disassembling her over the phone.

"What happened then?"

"Phillip quit. Said he was going back to Michigan where his family lives."

"That's too bad."

"Well, it *will be* too bad if he doesn't learn to cut those suckers off."

The word "suckers" reminded Wendall of Jack pruning the "sucker" branches off his apple trees.

Wendall now knew two pathologically polite people, his mom and Phillip, who were being weighed down by suckers.

"Wendall, I'm sorry about the Honda. But I'll keep my eyes open for another scooter. If I find one, I'll let you know."

"Thanks, Don. I'll see you later."

"Oh, and thanks again for the tomatoes."

After Wendall left the shop, he wasn't concerned about the scooter anymore. He was determined that his mom would not suffer a fate similar to Phillip's. Back at home when Wendall opened the front door, the air was filled with the smell of chocolate chip cookies and Damon's whining.

"Mom! Can't I have just one?"

"You've already had three."

"But I need one for Ranger Rick and the squad."

Wendall quickly walked to the kitchen, picked up a freshly baked cookie, shoved it toward Damon, and said, "Beat it. *Now!*"

Damon looked at Wendall with fear, grabbed the cookie, then turned and ran.

The kitchen mess was familiar. Wendall knew exactly what was going on. It was Saturday afternoon, and his mom "had to" bake 150 chocolate chip cookies for the children's Sunday school. Susan's routine was a grueling four-hour marathon of measuring, mixing, baking, and packaging over twelve dozen cookies. Wendall didn't even ask how much all the ingredients cost. This weekly "donation" had been going on for over a year.

Wendall looked at his mother's haggard face as she struggled with a spoon to mix in the chocolate chips with the dough, a task for which you can't use a mixer.

"Mom, let me do that." Wendall took the large spoon from her hand. "Do you enjoy making all these cookies every week?"

She sighed. "No, I don't. But I have to." Tears started to well up in her eyes.

Wendall shook his head and thought, *Enough is enough.* Everything he had learned about self-respect, happiness, saying no, and pruning was beginning to coalesce inside him. Time to stand up, say no, and prune some branches.

"No, Mom. You don't 'have to do' anything …well, except pay taxes and die. At least that's what Grandpa Nichols always says. This is the *last* batch you will *ever* make for the Sunday school. We're cutting it off right now."

"What?"

"We're going to prune your tree and chainsaw the branch that produces cookies."

She started crying. "But…how, how am I going to do that? They're expecting me to…"

"Simple. Cut 'em off, *now*. Call Deloris and say fifty cookies is all you have for tomorrow and no more after that. They can go buy cookies.

"But they're counting on me."

"No, they're *using* you. It's got to end. The world is not going to dry up and blow away if they don't have free cookies tomorrow. And why are *you* doing all the baking? Does no one else own a working oven?"

She wiped her tears. "You're right. They don't even say thank you anymore."

"Another thing. I thought you finished all those hand warmers for the junior high cheerleaders. Why is your sewing machine covered with more cutouts?

"Those are for all the high school cheerleaders. Sharon insisted they had to have some too, after seeing the junior high girls with them."

"Call Sharon and give her the unfinished warmers. She can pay someone to finish them."

Susan sighed. "I get a headache every time I look at those. I just wish I had the strength to tell Deloris and Sharon all that."

"Oh, you have the strength. You just need to unleash it."

Wendall described the three *B*s to his mother as they placed spoonfuls of cookie dough on the baking sheet for the last time. Like any parent, she immediately recognized the *B*s. Wendall explained how to say no effectively, "Mom, when you face the three *B*s, above all else, *be selfish, be bluntly truthful,* and *never say sorry.*"

Wendall offered to make the pruning phone calls to Deloris and Sharon, but his mom insisted that she do it. Although Wendall was proud of her, he wasn't completely confident in her ability. Therefore, he found four index cards and wrote "beg," "bargain," "bully" and "don't say sorry" with a black felt marker. He would eavesdrop on the calls and silently point out any *B* she might encounter. Now they were ready.

"Hello, Deloris. This is Susan."

"Oh. Hi, Susan."

"I'm not going to make the Sunday school cookies anymore. I've got fifty for tomorrow, and then that's it."

"Oh my! Is anything wrong?"

"Yes. I don't have the time and energy anymore."

"Is there any way you can get us the 150 for tomorrow, just this once?"

Wendall held up the "beg" sign.

"No. You can buy some cookies at the Big Girl Bakery. They're open until nine." (Advice given.)

"If money is a problem. Perhaps I can get some church funds for you. I know flour and sugar cost."

Wendall held up the "bargain" sign.

"No. It's not the money."

"Well, the children are going to be so disappointed. You're really leaving everyone in a bind at this late hour. They all look forward to those cookies."

Wendall finally got to wave the "bully" sign. (Guilt induction.)

"They won't be disappointed if you get to Big Girls on time. Tomorrow, I'll bring the fifty I've got."

"But…"

Wendall made a fist, raised his thumb like a hitchhiker, lifted his chin, and then raked his thumb across the front of his throat. His mom understood the sign language.

"I've got to go now, Deloris. See you tomorrow." *Click.*

Susan looked relieved. She actually smiled.

"That wasn't nearly as hard as I thought it would be. For the first time in a long time, I don't feel like I'm riding down a hill in a car with no brakes."

Wendall reminded her, "Sharon is next."

The phone call to Sharon was short and sour. Sharon went straight to bully.

"All the girls are going to be so upset. You know they've been waiting patiently for two weeks already!" (Guilt induction.)

"Sharon, do you want the patterns or not?"

"Well...I guess we'll just have to take what we can get." (Guilt induction.)

Sharon's final failed comment was a stab at Susan's sewing ability, "Well at least we can now have mittens personalized by a *professional* embroiderer." (Insult.)

"That's right, Sharon. I hadn't thought of that! I am so glad I decided to turn them over to you. Goodbye."

Wendall burst out laughing as his mom hung up the phone. "Good try, Sharon, and good riddance!"

During the course of our lives, we tend to grow and "branch out" much like a tree. As we become more responsible and competent, we tend to take on more and more responsibilities and thereby add branches, large and small. The main branches are the people and obligations most important to us. The progressively smaller branches are, of course, the lesser important responsibilities to friends and organizations. Over time, we can take on too many branches. Anyone can be "sapped" with marriage, children, jobs, aging parents, other relatives, church, civic organizations, needy friends, mortgages, car payments, and other unending bills to pay. It's not that any of these people, responsibilities, or commitments are inherently "good" or "bad." The point is this: *everyone must be wary of becoming overloaded.* Just like Jack's apple trees, too many branches give small, inferior fruit and place the entire tree at risk for collapse. The same thing can, and does, happen to people.

Take time to step back and look at your tree. If you don't have the time, energy, and money for the people and activities you *really want* in life, then you must do some serious and aggressive pruning. This is not easy. You will have to say no to good people and worthwhile activities, and pruning requires you to be *selfish, bluntly truthful, and unapologetic.* But the health and well-being of your tree of life depend on it.

# 9

# Great Expectations

> No child ever wakes up on Christmas morning and
> says, "Ugh, I don't want to get up. Today is going to
> be a horrible day." No! They *expect* to have a great day.
> We should all be just as excited about *every* day.
> —Marvin Stewart, a.k.a. Marvelous Marvin

The most positive person Wendall ever met was Marvin Stewart, a.k.a. Marvelous Marvin. No, he wasn't a motivational speaker, a minister, or a professional wrestler. He sold Ford cars and trucks. He sold *a lot* of Ford cars and trucks. His celebrity status in Benson was as big as his frame, six-foot-three and 250 pounds with a smile and handshake to match. Marvin's appearance and exuberance were that of an offensive lineman who had just led his running back into the end zone for the winning touchdown. He knew everyone in town, and everyone certainly knew him.

Marvelous Marvin's son, Sean, lived in the shadow of his celebrity father. Sean didn't develop his dad's extroverted, overpowering personality, but he did inherit Marvin's physique, which made him an excellent defensive lineman on the Plainsman football team. However, Sean's eligibility was in jeopardy. Although he was otherwise a B student, Sean struggled with geometry. It just didn't make sense to him with all those lines and planes and points. But the bottom line and the plain truth and the point was Sean would have to sit out the second half of the football season if he couldn't raise his geometry grade from a "high F." Sean sought help from the geometry teacher, Mr. "Bowtie" Bodie, who was gracious enough to tutor Sean over the noon hour. Poor Sean had to pack a sack lunch, miss the most important social hour of the day, and suffer the humiliation of everyone knowing his dilemma. But it all came crashing down when Coach Gordon provoked a shouting match with the otherwise demur and diminutive Mr. Bodie. Allegedly, Coach became furious because Bowtie wouldn't assign Sean a little extra homework, for extra credit, to get his grade up to a D. An appeal to the superintendent, a former football player himself, was shockingly and sadly rejected. Frustrated and desperate, Coach Gordon asked Wendall to tutor Sean. Coach Gordon told Wendall that he would be doing him "a personal favor as well as saving the team and uh, the entire community." Even though Wendall didn't play football, he could become an "honorary member of the team." Since he could also stand on the sideline during the games, near the cheerleaders, Wendall agreed to do his part.

Wendall met Sean at the Stewart home, a two-story colonial mansion with four marble columns in the front and an Olympic-size pool in the back. The lawn reminded Wendall of the putting greens at the Masters golf tournament on TV. The Stewarts didn't have one front door. They had two. Both were massive eight-foot-tall, side-by-side, carved wood slabs on heavy brass hinges. Marble floors and a crystal chandelier adorned the entry way. Their living room glittered like the trophy room at school. Trophies, plaques, and framed photos of Marvin accepting awards lined the shelves and walls. On the wall above their big screen TV hung a dozen shield-shaped "Salesman of the Year" plaques. Wendall commented on all the awards.

Sean nodded. "Yeah, my dad's a great salesman. He could sell sand to nomads in the Sahara Desert."

Wendall shook his head in awe. "How does he do it?"

"I think it's his attitude. He just *expects* to sell a lot of Fords, and well…he knows everything about the cars and trucks he sells."

"So it's his positive attitude."

Sean laughed. "You don't know the half of it."

Wendall smiled with curiosity. "What?"

"The first thing he yells before he's even out of bed is, 'This is the greatest day of my life!'"

"Really?"

"Oh yeah. It's like my alarm clock. If the day ever comes that I don't hear my dad yell that from the other side of the house, then I'll know he died in his sleep."

Wendall chuckled. "That's hilarious."

"Oh, there's more. He has motivational slogans everywhere around the house: in his closet, on his bathroom mirror, even inside the shower."

"What do they say?"

"Lots of things. 'Sell a Car, Save a Life,' 'You Get, What You Expect,' 'Attitude is Everything,' 'You Can't Fail Unless You Quit, So Never Quit,' and my personal favorite, 'They Came, They Saw, They Bought a Ford.'"

Wendall laughed. "That's from Julius Caesar..."

"I know, I know." Sean smiled sheepishly. "I came, I saw, I conquered. It sounds crazy, but it works. By the time my dad leaves the house every morning, he's unstoppable."

Wendall pointed to some of the framed color photos. "Who are all those other people in the pictures?"

"Those are regional and national sales managers. He goes to sales meetings where they give out awards. I went to one in Dallas last year." Sean rolled his eyes.

"What happened?"

"Let's just say they make our Friday afternoon pep rallies look like prayer vigils."

"Oh yeah?"

"Talk about loud! And all the chanting." Sean raised his right hand like a witness being sworn in at a trial. "Honestly, I thought, these people must be drunk. But they couldn't have been, it was nine in the morning."

"Is that all they do, have a rally and hand out awards?"

Sean shook his head. "No, they have training sessions. You know, go over the new models and latest features along with the

114

rebates and financing. But my dad keeps a picture of every award ceremony. Heck, he keeps a hand-shaking picture of every person who buys a car or truck from him."

Wendall was genuinely surprised. "That must be a lot of pictures."

Sean pointed down a hallway. "The walls of his study are covered with them. He says they remind him of all the people he's helped."

"But what about all the times when people don't buy a car or truck?"

"You know, I asked him about that once. Doesn't faze him at all. He told me that he's still done the customer a 'huge favor' by teaching them about safe vehicles and how to survive crashes. He can't wait to talk to the next person."

"What's the best way to survive a crash?"

Without hesitation, Sean shot back, "The three $S$'s: wear seat belts, stay sober, and slow down. My dad really stresses the three $S$'s, even here at home. And on the Fords, my dad talks up the wide seat belts, padded dash, safety glass, disc brakes, cabin strength, and uh… oh yeah, the large brake lights. Almost forgot that one."

Sean conjured a mockingly stern expression on his face and wagged his index finger. "Other brands just don't care about your family's safety like Ford does."

They both laughed.

Wendall joked, "Sounds like you're well on your way to selling Fords yourself."

Sean smiled but shook his head. "No, I'm too shy."

Wendall thought out loud, "Your dad psyches himself up every morning and then constantly reminds himself of his previous successes throughout the day."

Sean nodded. "Yeah, he's like a steam-roller barreling down a steep hill. He can be contagious too. If I'm moping around the house, he is all over me to find out what's pulling my attitude down. Asking how he can help."

Wendall could picture it. "Like this geometry?"

"Yeah, he asked me, 'Who's the best student in your geometry class?'"

"And you said *my* name?"

"Well…"

Wendall protested, "But Jenny Parker is the best student in the class."

Sean cringed. "Yeah, but my girlfriend doesn't like her. No way I could ask her for help. After that, Dad called Coach Gordon, and the deal was done."

"So uh…there really was no way for me to say no."

Sean took a big breath. "Right. My dad would have called your dad, then your mom, then your grandma, then your other grandma. You get the picture."

"Well, we might as well get started."

Wendall quickly realized that Sean was a bright student. He just couldn't visualize the concepts of lines, planes, and points in his mind. Wendall told him to imagine he was in outer space and that a line was a red laser beam of light that went on forever in both directions and a point was a single dot of red light and a plane was a sheet of paper-thin light with no borders that stretched out flat in all directions. Now, Sean could easily "see" and manipulate them in his mind. By the time Marvin came bursting through the front doors with a loud, "Wow, today was a great day!" Sean was zipping through the geometry word problems. His dad was extremely grateful for Wendall's help, especially when he saw how quickly Sean had mastered the subject. They were in the living room finishing up what was likely to be their first, and only, tutoring session.

"Wendall, I can't tell you how much I appreciate you helping Sean. In a couple of years, you'll need a Ford to drive, and I'll make you an unbelievable deal."

"Thank you, Mr. Stewart…"

"Oh please! Call me Marvin."

"Yes, sir, I mean, Marvin. I really appreciate that. Sean just needed a different way of looking at geometry."

Marvin nodded. "How you look at things makes all the difference. I'm proof of that."

Wendall couldn't resist asking, "How so?"

"Well, you might not believe this, but there was a time when I thought I was the worst car salesman in the world."

Wendall was stunned. "Really? Why would you think that?"

"Probably because I *was* the worst car salesman in the world." Sean snickered.

"But I turned it around. Started looking at the world differently."

Sean smiled and leaned back in his recliner. He had heard this story before.

"I couldn't sell a car or truck to save my soul, much less feed my family. My manager must have felt sorry for me because one day he gave me a ringer."

Wendall tilted his head. "A ringer?"

"Oh, I'm sorry. A ringer is a sure thing. A sure sale. You'd have to trip the customer, knock him down, fall on top of him, and break his hip to lose the sale."

"Got it."

Marvin continued, "This customer had bought a new F150 pickup two weeks before in Ponca City, Oklahoma. He got sideswiped by a drunk driver on Interstate 35 and ran off the road and rolled his truck, totaled it. But he walked away with just a couple of bumps and bruises. He finally got his insurance money, and he came in to buy the exact same truck, same options, same red color. He kept going on and on about how that truck saved his life. The salesman who sold him the first F150 had told him, 'This truck is loaded with new safety features.'"

Marvin glanced at the plaques on his wall before looking back at Wendall. "I had never thought of car and truck sales that way. I always thought I was just…selling transportation. But the truth is, I was keeping people alive. Saving them *and* their families from harm."

Wendall nodded. "That could definitely change your perspective."

Marvin began pacing while gesturing. "It changed everything! My motivation and my confidence went way up. Now my customers weren't just potential buyers to 'win over,' they were my friends for me to protect out there on the road. Yes, sir, I saw the world in a different way and my attitude changed completely."

"So attitude is everything." Wendall shamelessly borrowed one of Marvin's quotes.

"Right!" Marvin pointed his finger at Wendall. "That's *exactly* right."

Meanwhile, Sean was observing the rah-rah session with amusement and working hard to suppress a laugh.

Marvin was on a roll. "Every morning I wake up and say, 'This is the greatest day of my life!' And you know why? *Because there's no reason it shouldn't be!* I am smarter, more experienced, and more successful than on any other previous day of my life."

Wendall stopped smiling. Marvelous Marvin had a point. Suddenly, his positive affirmations and slogans didn't seem so over the top anymore.

Wendall murmured, "I hadn't thought of it that way."

Marvin raised his hand toward the ceiling like a praying evangelical. "There we are again! See the world in a different way, and it can change your life."

Marvin sat down and said thoughtfully, "You know, when Sean and Lydia [Sean's sister] were little, I noticed something. No child ever wakes up on Christmas morning and says, 'Ugh, I don't want to get up. Today is going to be a horrible day.' No! They *expect* to have a great day. In fact, they are so excited the night before, they can hardly go to sleep. We all should be just as excited about *every* day."

Wendall tried to imagine every morning feeling like Christmas Day. "Yeah, that would be great."

"Oh, believe me, it is great." Marvin stood up and looked out the patio doors at two men working on the pool house. "But there's a little more to success than just *deciding* to have your greatest day."

He motioned for Wendall. "I want to show you something." Wendall followed him outside to the patio. Meanwhile, Sean had already quietly slipped out of the room to finish all his overdue geometry homework.

Marvin pointed to two workers standing on ladders leaned against the pool house. "See those men cleaning out the gutters."

"Yes."

"They are an analogy of *all* success and failure in life."

"No kidding."

Marvelous Marvin smiled. "No kidding."

As he motioned toward the workers, they stopped working. "Oh, it's okay, guys. You're doing fine."

Marvin continued, "First, those workers both have a purpose: to clean all the leaves out of the gutters. *My* purpose is to save people's lives by selling them Fords. *Everybody* needs an important purpose in life."

He turned to Wendall. "Do you know your purpose in life?"

"Uh, no. Not yet."

"Not to worry." He slapped Wendall on the back. "I didn't realize mine until I was married and had kids. Thank goodness for that ringer from Ponca City."

Marvin nodded thoughtfully. "Just like those two men, everyone is standing on a ladder, an imaginary ladder. Our purpose in life is the reason we are climbing the ladder. Our goal is at the top and our past is at the bottom."

"So you never look down?"

Marvin broke off his stare at the two workers. "No, no. You've got to keep your eyes on *both ends* of your ladder. At the *top* is your big goal that *inspires* you. At the *bottom* is your past that makes you *grateful* for how far you've climbed."

Wendall bit his lip gently. "But a lot of people don't have big goals because ...they don't want to fail."

"You're right. Most people worry about failure. I call it s*hort ladder syndrome.*"

"Short ladder?"

Marvin nodded confidently. "Short ladder syndrome. They don't have a strong purpose, so they're too afraid to climb. They might slip on the next rung. So they stand there, uninspired and bored, on their short ladder. You see, *the right purpose has a way of bulldozing even the most stubborn fear of failure.*"

"Is short ladder syndrome a real disease?"

Marvin smiled. "No, not a disease. But it's real all right. It's been around forever. I just call it that. It's my description for being afraid to set higher goals, build a longer ladder, and be happy."

They walked from the patio back into the living room.

Wendall had to ask, "But what about people who *do* have goals and work hard and are successful, but they're never happy? They act as if no amount of success is ever good enough."

Marvin rubbed his chin. "Yes, I've seen that. Those people are doing *two* things wrong. First, they're *not looking at the bottom of their ladder* to remember how far they've come and to feel grateful for the success they've achieved. Second, they're *comparing themselves to someone* who's even more successful but isn't having to work as hard."

Marvin smiled. "Imagine struggling for years to pull yourself up your ladder one rung at a time. Then you glance over, and the guy next to you is riding one of those hydraulic extension ladders they carry on fire engines. He just smiles and waves good-bye as he flies by you."

Wendall laughed. "Does that really happen?"

"Oh sure. It happened to me. Billy Bartley sells Fords in Wichita. In the previous ten years, he had never sold more than thirty vehicles in any given *month*. Two years ago, I sold more Fords than any year in my career. But guess what? I wasn't the national salesman of the year. I wasn't our regional salesman of the year. I wasn't even the top salesman in the Oklahoma-Kansas district. Billy Bartley, out of nowhere, dethroned the champ. Of course, everyone, including myself, wanted to know how he sold so many cars and trucks. Billy spun an elaborate yarn about how to make people *like* you, because people won't buy a Ford from you if they don't *like* you. But some of the other salesmen in Wichita knew the truth, and they told me what happened.

"How did Billy do it?"

"Two of the older salesmen at his dealership retired after thirty or forty years. They both turned over their *entire* customer bases to Billy. Basically, they gave him a hydraulic extension ladder."

"That's too bad."

Marvin walked over to his wall of plaques. "Well, don't feel too sorry for me. The next year I was back on top."

"What happened to Billy Bartley?"

"He got lazy. He started taking for granted all the customers he had inherited. He didn't give them the attention they deserved. Those customers didn't *like* that. And just as Billy had lectured us, 'People won't buy a Ford from you if they don't *like* you.'" Marvin grinned. "You know, he was absolutely right about that."

"Did his sales drop?"

"Like a Chevy skidding off a cliff. Yes, sir, Billy cut the hydraulic hoses that powered his extension ladder. It was a quick ride back down to the bottom."

During the next week in geometry class, Mr. Bodie assumed full credit for Sean's amazing turn around. Sean and Wendall agreed that it wouldn't hurt to let Bowtie believe it. Besides, it was fun watching him strut and cock his head like a little banty rooster. Coach Gordon kept his promises. Wendall even got to ride the team bus to the away games. Sean made all-conference and nearly made a B in geometry despite his terrible start. Wendall was privileged to be a regular guest at the Stewart's mansion. Sean's family believed that Wendall gave them much more than he received. But Wendall would insist that it was the other way around.

Ten years later, Wendall would have another lesson in "expectations." As a young medical student, he discovered a biochemical explanation for Marvelous Marvin's great attitude.

Wendall couldn't understand why some of his friends and classmates took drugs. In high school and college, whenever Wendall refused to "party," he was accused of being "chicken" and chided that "you only live once." His accusers were absolutely right. Using drugs scared the hell out of Wendall. And everyone *does live only once*. However, Wendall wanted his one trip around the block to take as long as possible.

Wendall often wondered what drugs did to people's brains. He reasoned that if a chemical (drugs) could alter a person's behavior and sensations, then some natural brain chemicals must control our normal behavior and sensations. In medical school, Wendall learned that these "brain chemicals" exist, and they have names: endorphins and neurotransmitters. But what controls the levels of these mysterious, naturally occurring chemicals in our brains? And how could people boost their levels without taking drugs?

Wendall presented these important questions to a few of his medical school classmates. Their answers weren't particularly convincing:

"Music is the way." Carol seemed certain. "Why do you think people sing when they're happy? It's really God's gift to our souls."

Harry disagreed. "Exercise, you know, pumpin' iron. It works for me." Wendall was pretty sure that Harry's weekly testosterone shots were doing most of the work instead.

It was a no-brainer for Sally. "Oh, just have sex. It'll get your levels up. You should try it sometime."

Wendall finally discovered the truth in human behavior class. The professor presented a research study of a new class of anti-depressants that would later revolutionize the treatment of depression. Sixty-four study participants with confirmed major depression were enrolled. Many of them were unemployed and some were homeless. It was a "double blind" study meaning that neither the patients nor the physicians knew who was taking the study drug and who was taking the placebo sugar pill. Every week, the study subjects were paid one hundred dollars in cash for lab work, psychological testing, and a PET scan of their brain. PET scans are positive emissions tests that show the amount of chemical activity in different parts of the brain. The brighter the color on the scan, the more the activity in that lobe of the brain.

The study was proceeding as planned until week 6 when "Bill" didn't show up for his checkup. Of course, the biggest concern during the study was the risk of suicide. After all, half the people were only taking sugar pills. Maybe Bill killed himself. It took several weeks to find Bill because he had given the researchers a false address, and his emergency contact number had been disconnected. The local police eventually spotted his car parked behind a McDonald's dumpster where he waylaid teenage employees for unsold fries and hamburgers just after closing. Bill told the police he wasn't going back to the clinic. Reluctantly, the clinic sent an assistant to interview him in his car.

"Bill, we are so glad that you're okay."

"Thanks, I'm doin' fine! Better than fine. Doin' *great!*"

"Why didn't you come in for your weekly checkup? Didn't you need the hundred dollars?"

"Oh, well, I took some of my clinic money and bought me some lottery tickets. I won $39 million! I feel great! I quit takin' that medicine."

For a few seconds, the assistant wondered if Bill was delusional or psychotic. But his overwhelmingly congruent body language, facial expressions, words, and tone of voice could not be denied.

"Oh my gosh! Really?"

"Yeah! But I need a ride. Don't have enough gas to turn in my ticket. Give ya a thousand bucks if you'll drive me to the lottery office downtown."

"Oh, uh, my boss won't let me take your money. But we really need for you to come to the clinic one last time."

"Why?"

"Since you stopped the medicine, we need to do one last lab draw, a psych test, and a PET scan before we can withdraw you from the study."

"Do I have to?"

"Yes, we really need you one last time. Otherwise, it could ruin the entire study for everyone."

Bill sighed. "Okay, if it's for science. But only if I get that ride downtown."

"With the hundred dollars they'll pay you at the clinic, you can buy gas and drive down there yourself."

Bill scratched his head. "Oh yeah. I hadn't thought about that."

At the clinic, Bill's lab results were unchanged. However, the psych testing indicated no evidence of his previous depression. The real shocker was his PET scan. It was off the scale. Parts of Bill's brain lit up bright red and orange that the doctors had never seen before. But why? What was different? Physically, nothing was different. Bill was still living in his car and eating out of the McDonald's dumpster. And when the researchers "broke open" his file, he was taking the placebo sugar pill. The *only* differences were his *expectations* of what the future would bring and his *interpretation* of how his life would change from a homeless bum into a globe-trotting playboy with cars, mansions, jewels, and women. When asked, "What is the first thing you're going to do when you get your lottery money?" Bill immediately snapped, "I'm gonna buy that McDonald's."

"You're going to become a restaurateur?"

"No! I'm gonna have it torn down so all those sons of bitches lose their jobs! They were mean to me!"

The fascinating lesson is that our *expectations* and our *interpretation of how we are doing determine our brain chemistry*, as shown by Bill's dramatic PET scan changes. Marvelous Marvin would have understood it well. Wendall could visualize a new slogan for Marvin's office, "Great Expectations, Great Brain Chemistry." Marvin Stewart enjoyed one great day after another because he controlled his brain chemistry. He *expected* each day to be the greatest day of his life, and he *interpreted* every customer interaction as a success, whether they bought a Ford or not.

Wendall imagined how Bill's PET scan would have changed if the lottery officials told him, "Well, Bill, sorry to tell you this. You had the right numbers. But those numbers were for the week *before*. Not this week. So you didn't win." No doubt, Bill would have crashed emotionally and his PET scan would have quickly lost all its brilliant, new color. The wonderful, expensive, and decadent expectations would have evaporated along with most of Bill's brain neurotransmitters. But in reality, Bill did win. And Wendall was certain that his neurotransmitter levels remained sky high until the money ran out.

# 10

# The Luckiest Man Alive

Do those three things, and you'll be "lucky" your entire life.
—Clyde Watkins

Wendall was fortunate to grow up with two fathers. No, his parents were never divorced. Wendall's second father was his first employer, a wheat farmer named Clyde Watkins. Together, Max Nichols and Clyde guided Wendall through the transition from a blissful childhood to the problem-filled adult world.

Wendall met Clyde Watkins through a classmate, Donnie McIntire. Donnie had worked for Clyde during the previous summer with a high school senior named Frank who graduated and immediately joined the army. Donnie joked that Frank went to boot camp to get away from all the cursing and profanity at Clyde's place. Donnie admitted that although Clyde habitually swore, he was never mean. He wouldn't curse or cuss at people. However, broken down equipment, bad weather, and ornery cattle were all fair game.

Born in a clapboard farmhouse near Hardtner, Kansas, in 1920, by the mid-1970s, Clyde was a middle-aged, overweight, master wheat farmer. He was molded, and to some extent scarred, by the Great Depression and the dust bowl of the 1930s. As a teen, he had seen the dust clouds rolling in from the horizon like billowing brown thunderstorms. For the rest of his life, blowing dirt was the only thing that made him nervous. Forty years of farming had been good, and bad, to Clyde. It lifted him out of poverty, kept him out of World War II, and found him a perfect-match wife. However, the Kansas summer sun and winter cold had taken a heavy toll. Clyde's knees were swollen with arthritis. His hands were calloused, weathered, and reminded Wendall of a pair of old leather gloves. His hair was still jet-black but now receding and thinning. His face had the ridges and furrows from a million smiles and laughs and just as many frowns and curse words. But his eyes were still bright and his mind was sharp. He stood only five-foot-four (with his boots on), and he probably weighed two hundred pounds. His bulging belly certainly didn't help his worn-out knees, which gave him a painful limp when he walked. To Wendall's surprise, Clyde was once a sprinter in high school when his short legs could pump like pistons. Clyde's body may have deteriorated since then, but not his spirit. He was brash, unpretentious, and direct. He believed in God and attended church on Sundays, unless there was wheat to be harvested. Clyde was guided by fairness and common sense, both of which he demanded from everyone else. His work philosophy was simple: "Take what God and the weather give you, and then work like hell."

Wendall arrived for his first day of work on a Friday, June 13. But he wasn't superstitious, not yet anyway. Wendall was a greenhorn, and he looked the part in his long sleeves, starched white shirt, new blue jeans, and leather work boots straight from their shoe box with the factory shine still gleaming. When Clyde's nephew, Mike, met Wendall, he shook his head and said, "Oh brother." Mike was twenty-six, and it was his fifteenth year helping Clyde with the wheat harvest, which made him justifiably cocky. But because his full-time job was a jet engine mechanic at Vincent Air Force Base in Benson, Mike could only help out on the weekends. Physically, Mike was the exact opposite of Clyde: six-foot-tall and a string bean at 140 pounds. His new job was to teach Wendall how to operate Clyde's 1958 Gleaner combine. It was the newer of the two combines Clyde had bought back in the 1950s, two years before Wendall was born.

Mike liked to brag. "I was only twelve when I got started in the fields. You ever driven *anything* in your life?"

Wendall rolled with the punch. "Not yet, but show me how, and I'll do it."

Mike cleared his throat. "Well, pay attention. 'Cause on Monday, I've got to go back to work at the base, and you'll be on your own."

Wendall learned his first employment lesson: Sometimes you have to work with people you don't particularly like. But you do your best to learn everything you can from them as quickly as possible. Then you don't have to rely on them to help you.

They started cutting wheat that day on the *home place*. Clyde farmed six quarter sections of land. Each was roughly 160 acres, and they were scattered over a five-mile radius. The old Gleaner combines didn't have a cab to protect the driver from the wind, dirt, sun, bugs, and wheat chaff. As Mike drove the mammoth machine to the first field, Wendall stood on the combine's platform trying hard to hold on and yet stay clear of Mike's long arms and legs. Although Mike was stern and abrupt, Wendall appreciated his running monologue describing what he was doing and why. Mike gave condescending attention to every detail.

"Listen to what I tell ya. See that paved road?" Mike nodded toward Highway 132 that bordered the west side of the field.

"Yeah."

"Watch out for bottles and other crap that people throw out of their cars into the field. Oh yeah, and dead tree branches too. If your combine eats any of that shit, it'll lock up the guts of your machine and then…" He paused and looked directly at Wendall for emphasis. "There will be hell to pay."

Trash and tree limbs were not obstacles on this day, but a ravine cutting through the field soon appeared that caught their attention. Spring rains had carved a gully three feet deep and twelve feet wide. Mike cut the wheat to its edge and stopped. Wendall climbed down the steps from the platform to check it out. When he returned, he made a big mistake. He asked Mike a question.

"Do we cut around it? It's pretty deep, about three feet."

Mike sneered. "No! That'll make a bunch of zigzags in the field. We want straight lines to cut a full swath of wheat at all times."

Wendall instinctively grimaced. "But you might get stuck in there."

"You got any mud on those fancy-dude boots?"

Wendall looked down at his barely scuffed leather boots. "Uh, no."

"Then I won't get stuck."

To understand the impending disaster, the design of the old Gleaner combine must be described. The two front tires are four-foot-tall and resemble tractor tires with thick, angled tread. Since the combine is front-wheel drive, these tires carry most the weight and provide all the propulsion. The two back tires are tiny by comparison: only eighteen inches in diameter with thin longitudinal grooves for tread. They do the steering and allow the combine to "turn on a dime."

Now, back to the crossing of the Grand Canyon: Mike raised the combine's fourteen-foot-wide header all the way up and eased the two large front tires into the ravine. The old Gleaner crawled into the gully, and then the rear end tilted down, indicating that the small back wheels were rolling in. Suddenly, the steering wheel spun, as if possessed, out of Mike's grip followed by a loud *pow* that could have passed for a shotgun blast. The rear end jolted down, and the combine lurched to a stop. Mike jammed his feet on the clutch and brake pedals.

"What the hell happened!"

Wendall jumped off and spotted one of the back tires rolling down the gully toward state Highway 132. He chased it down just in time to prevent a second disaster. Wendall looked back up the gully to see that both back tires had wedged sideways and then popped off like a pair of buttons from a fat man's vest. Meanwhile, Donnie, who had been following them on the other combine, cut a serpiginous, winding swath around the gully and its tributaries. So much for straight lines in the field.

Mike was right about one thing. There was now hell to pay. Here came Clyde driving the wheat truck across the field in a hurry. "Oh hell!" is all he could say over and over. Clyde eventually calmed his nerves, stopped swearing, and looked thoughtfully at his crippled combine. Wendall could sense that there was no question in Clyde's mind that it would be rumbling across the field the next day.

First things first: Get the right people with the knowledge and tools required. Clyde needed a "damn good welder" to weld the axles of the wheels to the frame of the combine. Clyde had cultivated many friends over the past forty years because he knew the value of treating people with fairness and respect, especially people in the farm service industry. He carried a well-worn two-by-three-inch vinyl address book in his pocket and a duplicate in the glove compartment of his pickup truck. Clyde wiped his hands off on his jeans before thumbing through his little black book to find Preston Johnson, owner of Johnson's Welding. Preston's service truck sported an electric arc welder, a gas-powered generator, and flood lights, all of which made "Bessie" an ideal ambulance for innocent farm equipment injured in wheat field accidents. Clyde and Wendall drove back to the house to call Preston (no cell phones in those days). Mike wisely opted to stay behind in case Donnie "needed any help."

After loading up the necessary shovels, a hydraulic jack, and a large sledgehammer, Clyde and Wendall returned to the crash site. The task seemed simple enough. Dig under the rear frame, jack the rear end of the combine up out of the dirt, and then have Preston weld the axles, back wheels, and frame back together. However, an unwelcome, but predictable, complication soon developed. Wendall noticed that the digging started getting easier. The dirt was getting moist, then sticky, then muddy, and finally, just brown water.

Clyde was undeterred. "Are you deep enough for the jack?"

"I think so."

"Then stick it in the water."

The jack fit under the frame, but instead of jacking the combine up out of the dirt, Wendall was burying the jack down deeper into the mud. With every up and down stroke of the three-foot-long jack handle, a pulse of brown sludge oozed out of the hole around the jack. Wendall's new leather boots were ankle deep in mud. Wendall stopped and looked at the muddy mess. Visions of the Roman army popped into his head. But why? Perhaps it was because he was standing in the mud and grasping an iron bar that looked something like a spear while Clyde was cursing like a centurion. History class told the story of Roman legions marching north toward Germania until they were stopped by the Rhine River. To the astonishment of the terrified Germans, the Romans built a mile-long bridge across the Rhine by pile driving the trunks of trees through the mud and down to the bedrock of the river. Wendall offered his suggestion to Clyde. But he didn't mention the Romans.

"What if we used a sledge hammer to drive a piling down until we hit bedrock? Maybe we could use a tree trunk or a wooden post."

"Good idea." He motioned to Mike. "Take the pickup and go to the CO-OP and buy two creosote corner posts."

Meanwhile, Wendall abandoned the mud pit to begin digging an exit ramp in front of the combine's large front tires. After an impatient hour, Clyde demanded, "Where the hell is Mike? It's gonna be dark before long." A few minutes later, Mike returned empty-handed. The CO-OP had sold out of wood fence posts and the farm supply stores twenty miles away in Benson would be closing in ten minutes. To make matters worse, Preston Johnson pulled up in old Bessie, and he charged $75 an hour. Wendall scanned the horizon for anything made of wood. The only trees were in the front yards of farmhouses far in the distance.

*Wait a minute. There were some nearby fence posts. But they were already in the ground, with fence attached to them, on the neighbor's property. Surely, old man Cauldwell wouldn't mind if Clyde "borrowed" one or two, temporarily, in his time of great need.*

Cauldwell's posts were a standard six and a half feet long, and Wendall needed every inch to hit bedrock. Under the glare of the floodlights from Preston's generator, the "old tin bucket" was raised from the mud. Preston could finally work his welding magic. He had obviously done this before.

"Yeah, this is a design problem on these Gleaners. Years ago, some kid, probably fresh out of college with a slide rule, drew this up. I'll wager he never set foot in a wheat field before. Most times, these kiddie wheels pop off when you're backin' up in heavy mud. They catch a rut, flip sideways, pop off, and end up *under* the frame. I never had one in a gully like this before."

Preston used a torch to heat the bent frame until it was white hot, and then pounded it back "straight enough" with a sledgehammer. Steam billowed off the metal when Wendall poured the last of their drinking water from the ice bucket to cool it off. Welding the axles was the easy part. The combine was now in one piece, but it was still stuck in the ravine. It was midnight before Mike and Wendall finished digging the long exit ramp that Wendall had started earlier. Thus, ended Wendall's first day of his first job, Friday, June 13, 1975.

Over the next two weeks, Wendall and Donnie cut wheat every day from morning to midnight. They even ate lunch in the field during harvest. Mary would set up a card table and two folding chairs in the shade of the wheat truck and serve fried chicken, mashed potatoes, corn, rolls, and apple pie. Meanwhile, Clyde would "spell" Wendall and then Donnie by driving their respective combines once around the field, which meant they had to eat fast. The weather stayed hot, and it didn't rain. Although Wendall and Donnie both hoped it would so they could rest a day or two. Then one morning, they finally got a break. There was a heavy dew on Clyde's lawn, almost as if it had rained the night before. Without a strong breeze, it would be after lunch before the wheat would be dry enough to cut. Nothing to do but "hurry up and wait." Wendall didn't want to bring up a bad subject, but as usual, his curiosity could not be contained.

"Clyde, what if we couldn't have gotten the combine jacked up out of the mud?"

His response was pure attitude. "Well, hell, you can't just sit down and cry when things go bad. You find a way. My dad always told me, 'The dirt roads of life are full of ruts and detours. To make it to town, you work hard, get help when you need it, and do the best you can with what you've got. But whatever happens, you *never* give up on your crop.'"

Wendall later realized that this dirt road philosophy was the famous American "can do" spirit. It was a potent blend of confidence, determination, and pride.

But Clyde wasn't finished. "When you're facing a problem, you always need two things: the right tools and the right people with experience. Sometimes you already have the tools and the experience, but not always. That's when you have to find both, which is why friends, neighbors, and people you do business with are so important."

Wendall nodded. "That's why you have a little notebook."

Clyde smiled. "No, that's why I have *two* copies of my little notebook, in case I lose one. And you *always* treat people with respect and pay 'em for their honest work. People don't forget. And it damn sure makes a difference when you're askin' for a favor in the middle of the night."

That afternoon, the harvest resumed. Every year, Clyde wanted to finish cutting wheat before July 4 so he could enjoy the holiday. The July 2 weather forecast called for a cold front to move in by late afternoon with a near 100 percent chance of rain. A steady south wind blew all night into the storm system approaching from the north, which meant no morning dew on the wheat and an early start in the fields the next day. By four in the afternoon, the frantic harvest was done. As Wendall finished unloading his combine into the wheat truck, a cold, driving rain swept in.

Clyde yelled, "Wendall! Help me get this tarp on the truck."

Wendall quickly climbed down the slippery combine steps, now wet with rain, onto the side of the wheat truck bed. By the time he and Clyde jumped into the cab, they were soaked, but happy. The old truck lumbered across the freshly cut field with the last load of the year.

"Clyde we sure are lucky to finish before this storm."

"So you think Lady Luck shined down on us?" Clyde shot Wendall an unexpected, disapproving glance.

"Uh, sure." Wendall felt more than a little confused. He assumed that Clyde would be happy that they finished before the rain.

Clyde lectured him, "Well, you're wrong. We made our own luck. We started making ourselves 'lucky' back in May when we got the combines and trucks ready. Then we continued our good luck by working most of the night to weld the back tires onto the combine. Then we cut wheat every minute possible, every single day for the last three weeks. We made ourselves 'lucky' by being prepared, working hard, and taking advantage of what God gave us: dry weather."

"I hadn't thought of it that way."

Wendall understood Clyde's point, but he was still having a hard time dismissing the concept of luck: something he had believed in all his young life.

"But what about people winning the lottery or a million-dollar jackpot in Vegas? Isn't that being lucky?"

Clyde pounced all over him. "Those games are for suckers. In Vegas, everybody knows the odds are stacked against you before you even lay down your bet, same for the lotteries."

Trying to save face, Wendall added, "Of course, I'm too young to gamble."

Clyde grunted, "Well, I hope you're too *smart* to gamble."

"Oh sure."

But Wendall couldn't let it go just yet. "But, Clyde, what if I'm walking along the sidewalk and look down and find a dollar that someone dropped? Isn't that lucky?"

"No. That's your reward for paying attention. Ever heard of the superstition that you'll have good luck if you find a penny on the ground?"

"Yeah."

"That just means you're paying attention to where you're walkin', and because of that, you're not gonna step in a hole, twist your ankle, fall over, and break your neck."

"That makes sense."

"Of course it makes sense! Do you think I'd tell you some nonsense?"

Wendall chuckled. "No, definitely not."

Clyde slowly shook his head. "But there's a lot of non-sense out there. Think about all those superstitions about 'bad luck.' Breakin' a mirror or spillin' salt. Those things just mean you're clumsy or careless. And clumsy, careless people get hurt more often. Walkin' under a ladder isn't bad luck. It's just plain stupid."

Clyde continued, "What superstitious people call 'luck' doesn't just happen. 'Luck' comes from three things." Clyde held up his right hand and counted with his fingers.

"Being prepared."

"Workin' hard and…"

"Grabbing the opportunities that God gives you."

"*Do those three things, and you'll be 'lucky' your entire life.*"

When they arrived at the elevator, the usual long line of wheat trucks around the block was conveniently absent because of the rain. After dumping their load, Clyde and Wendall went inside the office. The manager greeted them at the counter.

"Howdy, Clyde."

"Charlie, meet my new hand, Wendall Nichols. And he's damn good help too."

Wendall extended his right hand. "Glad to meet you, sir."

Charlie shook his hand firmly. "Likewise."

He turned to Clyde. "How long do ya think it'll be before you're cuttin' again, Clyde?"

Clyde smiled with pride. "Oh, we're finished. Got the tarp on the last load just as the rain started."

Charlie shook his head in disbelief. "I swear. You're the luckiest man alive."

Wendall had to bite his lip to stifle a smile and suppress a laugh.

Clyde glanced at Wendall before declaring. "We made our own luck. We worked our butts off to get the crop out of the field as soon as the weather would allow."

He spoke the absolute truth.

Later, after they climbed back in the truck, Clyde shook his head. "People just don't get it."

Wendall smiled at Clyde's disappointment. "Well, most people believe in good fortune and being 'lucky.' I did before you explained it to me."

"That's why Charlie never made it as a farmer. Even though he inherited two good quarters of land. He was just too lazy to get things done when they needed to be done. Then he'd complain about all his 'bad luck' and how the 'weather wouldn't cooperate.' That's as stupid as complainin' that the sun shouldn't come up until you're ready to roll out of bed."

With the harvest finished, they drove back to the house. The now gentle rain would soften the fields for the plowing, which would commence in three to four days. It was a rare chance to finally relax.

Clyde decided to tell Wendall the story of how he met his wife, Mary. Or rather, Clyde bragged about how he "picked a peach."

Clyde married the love of his life when he was twenty. Unlike many of his high school classmates, he did *not* marry a girl from his high school in Ames, Kansas. Instead, he met an "out of town girl" at a barn dance. Dances were the 1930s equivalent of today's computer dating services. At a spring dance in 1939, Mary wore a sleek black dress that highlighted her long blond hair. Clyde said she was a "hidden angel" at Drummond High School.

"I could tell right away that she was a sincere girl. I couldn't take my eyes off her. I scribbled my name on every line of her dance card before we even started to dance."

Clyde added that he almost got into a fistfight with Mary's "damn fool" boyfriend when he tried to cut in on them. Clyde explained as a matter of fact, "He couldn't get it through his thick head that Mary and me were gonna end up gettin' hitched."

Wendall asked Clyde if he felt bad about stealing Mary away from another fella.

"Oh hell no! He deserved to lose her. What kind of an idiot takes his girl to a dance and gives her a dance card?"

Clyde and Mary were married within months. They worked hard, saved their money, and raised a daughter. Thirty-five years later, they were still happily married in the same two-bedroom farmhouse.

Clyde was determined that Wendall's love life would be as fortunate as his own. "Findin' the right woman is the most important thing in a man's life."

"You know, Clyde, I hadn't thought of it that way."

"Well, you better. 'Cause it's true."

"So…how do you know the right girl when you see her?"

"She'll be a *sincere* gal, and you won't be able to stop thinking about her. And everything you do, you'll want to do better because of her."

Wendall was surprised by this romantic streak hidden under Clyde's tough crust. But Wendall wasn't clear about something. "What do you mean by *sincere?*"

Clyde frowned. "You know. She's kind and considerate and hardworking, and *never* petty."

"Of course. It helps if she's pretty, right?"

Clyde slowly shook his head. "Believe it or not, looks don't really matter. Looks are like paint on a barn. It doesn't tell ya how strong the barn is, and the paint fades and peels off when the barn gets old."

Wendall smiled at the comparison.

Clyde nodded. "Yes, sir. You'll do well to marry a sincere, hard-workin' girl instead of some beauty queen who thinks she's a diva. Then you treat her like an angel and pray to God that she's forgiving enough to accept all your bad habits."

Wendall had been around Clyde long enough to know that the best way to get on his good side was to compliment Mary. So he brown nosed a little. "You know, Clyde, you are so *lucky* to have a wife like Mary." His grin gave him away.

Clyde immediately knew that he was being baited, but he didn't mind. "I made my own luck."

Wendall laughed.

"With my temper and foul mouth, I could have run Mary off a thousand times. But I'm no dummy. I know when I got somethin' wonderful. I work hard every day to appreciate her and everything she does. That's how an old cuss like me can keep such a beautiful woman around for thirty-five years."

Clyde shook his finger at Wendall. "You remember that. When you find a sincere gal, you compliment her every chance you get. Never swear at her. Never call her a bad name and never *ever* lay a hand on her."

Wendall nodded respectfully. "Yes, sir."

"'Cause if you do…and I find out about it, I'll kick your ass all the way to Wichita."

Wendall smiled. "Fair enough. I won't forget."

Years later, Wendall would consider Clyde's relationship philosophy to be the best advice he had ever received.

There was no doubt, Clyde and Mary's marriage was rock solid. But how? And why? Time to pay attention and keep asking questions. It took no more than a week for Wendall to discover the secrets of their union. They both practiced three persistent habits.

*First*, they expressed and demonstrated *sincere appreciation* to each other for *everyday* tasks.

"I sure like the way you fix these eggs, and this bacon is always just right."

"I appreciate you working so hard."

"You always keep the house so clean."

"Thank you, sweetheart. You didn't have to do that."

"This fried chicken is better than Kentucky Fried."

"Wendall, be sure and take your boots off so we don't track in dirt."

*Second*, they both *bragged* on each other, *a lot*. They bragged to Wendall and Donnie, to family, to neighbors, and to people in Drummond: at the elevator, the gas station, the grocery store, and everywhere in between. And since people in small towns like to gossip, *everybody* knew Clyde and Mary appreciated and loved each other.

"Mary is a peach. They don't make 'em like her anymore."

"Clyde is so thoughtful. He's always asking me if he can help me with anything."

"The café's fried chicken is really good, but I'll take Mary's over theirs any day."

"It's a wonder some fella taller and better lookin' hadn't snapped her up before me."

"I just hope our daughter, Paula, finds a man as wonderful as her father at college."

*Third*, and best of all, Clyde and Mary both *knew how to argue*. Although it was rare, they disagreed better than any couple Wendall had ever known. One argument in particular stood out. It was in March. Wendall had already worked for Clyde and Mary the summer before. Their cattle had been grazing on the "wheat pasture" since December. In Kansas, winter wheat is planted in September or October. If it rains enough, by December, cattle can graze on the dark green fields through the winter months. Even snow and ice won't kill the wheat. But sometime in the middle of March, the wheat heads that yield the grain begin to form in the stems near the base of the plant. It begins "booting." If the cattle eat the wheat at this point, there won't have any grain to harvest. The exact day that wheat begins booting varies from year to year by up to two weeks, depending on the specific variety of the wheat and the weather that spring. The trick is to leave the fattening cattle on the wheat pasture as long as possible without damaging the crop.

Clyde, Mary, and Wendall were kneeling in the middle of 160 acres of ankle-high green wheat pasture on March 10. They are looking for the first evidence of booting. Wendall really had no idea what he was doing. Mary confidently called him over, "Wendall, this is what we're talking about. See that little bit of a bump in that stem? That's what becomes the head of wheat."

Clyde craned his neck and shook his head. "No. That's not it. That's just a node on the stem."

Mary looked up. "No, that's the head. We have to take the calves off the field right away."

"No. We're not doing that. It's not bootin' just yet."

Mary presented two more stems as evidence. "These two have heads as well." She carefully peeled back the overlapping layers of the stems like parting the husks on tiny ears of corn. Wendall could clearly see the miniature heads of wheat.

Clyde still wasn't convinced. "That's just the pulp of the stem. Besides these calves can gain two pounds a day out here, and that's a lot of money."

"But they're eating our crop, and that's a lot *more* money."

"No, I think you're wrong. We can leave 'em on at least another week."

Mary wouldn't back down. "No. I'm right about this. With the warm winter we've had this year, these calves should come off now."

Wendall could tell that Clyde *really* didn't want to give in, and Wendall didn't dare jump in and take sides. But he did know one thing. It was supposed to rain the *next* weekend. He had helped Clyde and Mary move cattle and repair fences on most weekends during the winter, and Wendall learned to pay attention to the weekend forecasts. He honestly didn't care who was right or wrong. He just didn't want to herd cattle in the rain.

"You know, Clyde, I just remembered something. They're calling for rain to move in next Friday and Saturday. This field could be a mess next weekend."

Clyde seemed surprised that Wendall brought up a relevant point that Clyde himself should have considered: the weather. Clyde nodded and smiled. "You know, I think you're both right. We'll move 'em off today."

Turning to Wendall, he added, making certain that Mary overheard, "And let that be a lesson to ya. Always marry a woman smarter than you."

They all laughed as they walked back to the truck. Then Wendall realized something. As passionate as both Clyde and Mary were about being right and as passionate as they were about attacking the other's argument, neither of them attacked the other *person*. There was no swearing, no name-calling, and no accusations. Wendall *never* heard either of them say,

- "You're an idiot."
- "Don't be a jackass."
- "You're just being stupid."
- "Stop your bitchin' at me."
- "Are you blind? Can't you see that?"
- "Quit bein' so stubborn."
- "You just don't want to admit you're wrong, again!"

There was *never* any caustic, divisive, and demeaning language or attitude. Clyde and Mary always *made their bond more important than any argument.*

Wendall concluded without a doubt in his mind, that Clyde Watkins was the luckiest man alive. Although Clyde would never accept that title, he was completely responsible for it because he made his own luck. He also found and appreciated the two most important things in a man's life: the right woman and the right profession. Despite his rough edges, he knew exactly how to treat his beloved wife. Their marriage was cemented by three simple habits: complement each other, brag on each other, and argue with respect. And despite his profanity and temper, Clyde knew exactly how to solve life's inevitable problems. Find the right tools and the right people, and then "never give up on your crop."

Wendall worked for Clyde and Mary the next summer as well. He came to realize that he was only one in a long line of young boys whom they had trained to become men. Their life lessons became deeply ingrained into Wendall's personality and *just in time* for the extreme challenges of the next chapter of his life.

# 11

# The Mule-Headed Formula

If you're *determined* to do something, you'll make it
happen: despite every obstacle. But if you only *wish for it*,
you'll just make excuses: despite every opportunity.
—Max Nichols

Life was good. School was out for the summer of 1977. A beautiful June morning was dawning, and Wendall was daydreaming of
becoming a legal driver in September, buying a car, and then dating a
teenage Farrah Faucet look-alike. Little did he know that his pleasant
fantasy would soon be shattered by a single house fly buzzing around
fifteen miles away.

It was a typical farm sale in the Kansas summer: windless, cloud-
less, and sweltering. The men in the crowd wiped their brows under
their cowboy hats and baseball caps. The women fanned themselves
with their auction fliers. The auctioneer was rattling away like a
machine gun. It had been a long day selling all the old tools, vehicles,
and worn-out farm implements, one by one. The final items were the
farmhouse and the farm itself: a three-bedroom, red-brick house on
160 acres of clay dirt fields and cocklebur-filled pastures.

"Ninety-two, ninety-two, ninety-two even, ninety-two thousand, ninety-two, ninety-two. Who'll give me ninety-two?"

One of the auctioneer's spotters threw up his arm and called
out, "Yeah!"

"Now ninety-two five, ninety-two five, ninety-two and a half, ninety-two and a half. Who'll give me ninety-two and a half?"

Somewhere in the middle of the crowd was Wendall's great uncle, Cecil Banks. He was the older brother of Grandmother Dent. Cecil rarely went to auctions. In fact, this was his first in over thirty years. If there ever was a modern-day Scrooge, it was Cecil. The only difference: Cecil married Mrs. Scrooge. They decided early in their marriage that they couldn't afford children; therefore, nieces and nephews were their only occasional family. Together they scrimped and saved and gradually paid off the home place and even bought a second farm closer to town. When the city of Benson expanded, developers paid Cecil a handsome price for his second farm. As a child of the Great Depression, he never trusted banks, stocks, or bonds. He only knew farming, which is why he was now sitting in the hot sun. He had no intention of buying anything. He just wanted to "eyeball the market." And although he would never admit it, Cecil wanted to feel respected as a successful farmer who could buy another farm if he wanted to. But this old rundown farm was too much work at his age. The ten-year-old farmhouse featured an eighty-year-old septic tank in the backyard. It was a remnant of the original wood frame house built in 1897. The septic tank had caved in two months before and left a round swimming pool of raw sewage. Even so, Cecil had made some early, meaningless bids. He was about to leave for the comfort of his air-conditioned pickup truck when a pesky fly, probably from the septic tank, landed on his nose. Without thinking, he brushed it away with his right hand…the same hand holding his auction tag number 85.

"Yeah!" went up the cry from the nearby spotter.

The auctioneer instantly responded, "Now ninety-three, ninety-three. Who'll give me ninety-three? Now ninety-three thousand."

Oops. Cecil wasn't certain if the auctioneer thought he had just bid. He looked around nervously. Did he have the bid? If he did, surely someone else would pick up the bid, and then he'd be off the hook. But no.

"*Sold*! For $92,500 to number 85: the gentleman in the white hat."

The auctioneer pointed his gavel straight at Cecil.

Stunned and unable to speak, Cecil looked around dumbfounded.

The auctioneer finished with, "That concludes our auction. Thanks folks, for comin' out. See ya next time."

Strangers with sly smiles brought Cecil out of his fog when they began patting him on the back.

A spotter approached him. "Congratulations, partner. Got a lot of work ahead of ya. You did see the disclaimer on our auction bulletin?

"Uh, no. What disclaimer?"

"The well went dry last summer."

Cecil drifted back into in a state of shock. "There's no water on the place? What about the water in the septic tank?"

"Oh, that's all rain water. Toilets in the house don't work." The spotter motioned to a row of blue plastic outhouses. "That's why we got all those port-a-potties. Before he died, old man Derrick told me the well was only thirty-four-foot deep. I got a nephew that can dig ya one all the way down to the aquifer for only three thousand dollars. Here's his card."

The rest of the afternoon was a blur for old Cecil. He was too embarrassed to say he didn't place that bid. Besides, who would believe him after he had placed all those early bids? Cecil needed some youthful and enthusiastic help. That's when he thought of the young, energetic Nichols family.

Max Nichols jumped at Cecil's offer to finance the rundown Derrick farm. Grandma and Grandpa Nichols had lived on a farm for a few years when he was a kid. They rented a run-down dairy and, with the help of their seven children, made it a success. After three years, the landowner refused to renew their lease, took the dairy away from them, and reaped the rewards of their labor. But now, Max could buy his own farm, and with Wendall's recently acquired farming experience, the timing seemed perfect. Susan Nichols reluctantly agreed but insisted that Cecil first "fix the plumbing" and replace the septic tank. She refused to set foot in a house without running water. For financial security, Wendall's dad would keep his full-time job with Monroe Calculator Company and farm on the side. Or rather, he would have Wendall farm for him. In other words, Wendall's dream life of a car and a pretty girlfriend was about to be plowed under.

Two weeks later, Wendall and his dad began inspecting the old wooden barn and the overgrown pastures covered with ragweed and wild sunflowers standing six feet tall.

Max squinted and grimaced. "Wendall, there's a tractor, a three-bottom plow, and an eight-foot-wide disc out here somewhere."

"How can you tell?"

"Cecil told me. They didn't sell at the auction. Of course, that was before all these weeds grew up."

"Why didn't they sell?"

"Uh, well, they probably needed a little work. But they belong to us now, and we'll use 'em to farm this place once we find 'em."

Wendall noticed a dilapidated windmill, the farm's original water source. The galvanized metal derrick was intact although the fan had been blown off the top, likely from one of the violent thunderstorms that routinely sweep over the Kansas plains every spring.

"Hey, Dad. I'll climb up the windmill, and maybe I can see something."

From thirty feet above the ground, a tractor muffler peeked through the weeds about twenty feet from where Max was standing.

They then embarked on a short archeological expedition into a jungle of bee-infested wild sunflowers. Wendall groaned at the site of the ruins they discovered: a faded-yellow tractor buried to its axles in the dirt. The old Minneapolis Moline tractor, M&M for short, had a bird's nest in the driver's seat and a small cedar tree growing up through the hitch. The half-graves of the plow and disc were alongside.

Wendall shook his head. "No wonder they didn't sell. They're not even worth digging out for scrap."

"No, no. They're still good. We can get them up and running."

His dad studied the tractor tires closely. "I can't tell if they're flat. The tractor's buried so deep."

Wendall felt deflated. "Dad. I'm sorry, but…this looks impossible. I wish we had one of Clyde's John Deere tractors."

Max shot back, "*Nothing's* impossible. If you're *determined* to do something, you'll make it happen: despite every obstacle. But if you only *wish for it*, you'll just make excuses: despite every opportunity."

Max sat down on the right front tractor tire. "You just have to use the mule-headed formula."

"What's the mule-headed formula?"

"Your great-grandfather Nichols taught it to me. It's the best way to get things done. First, you've got to know *exactly* what you want. See it in your mind as clear as day."

Max patted the side of the tractor engine. "You know, there was once a day when this tractor was brand-new, state of the art, and it pulled that plow and that disc, on *this land*, season after season. Visualize *that*."

Wendall was not encouraged. "That day was long before I was born."

"You're right. But you can *imagine* it. And if you can *clearly* imagine something, you can get it."

Wendall had seen some "old" tractors with the classic 1930s bulbous headlights at Clyde's place. Clyde only used them in his pastures to move portable cattle feeders. He hadn't used them in the fields for decades.

Mr. Nichols continued, "Then you've got to want it, really *bad*. That's where the mule-headed part comes in. Be stubborn and accept *nothing less* than what you want."

Wendall squinted at the tractor's rotting spark plug wires. "But how do you get motivated to want something when it looks hopeless."

Max smiled. "That's easy. Consider the consequences. On the good side, imagine truckload after truckload of our wheat going to the elevator year after year until we pay off the entire note and own this place free and clear."

Wendall remembered the summer before when Clyde was standing on the side of his wheat truck as Wendall augured the first load of red wheat from the combine onto the old truck's wooden bed. Clyde was so happy. "Hot damn! Sounds like buck shot hittin' that bed!"

Max then became more solemn. "Now consider the consequences of failure: no crop, no money, and no mercy from the bank. Imagine being escorted off the farm by a sheriff's deputy and living in a beat-up, two-bedroom trailer loaned to us by my uncle, Jacob. Believe me. I know what that feels like."

The prospect of losing everything flashed in Wendall's mind. It was a horrible and sickening image that included sharing a room with Damon and seeing his mom crying. Suddenly, failure was not an option.

"Always remember: the greater the consequences, good and bad, the stronger your motivation. And the more mule-headed you'll become to get it done."

Max continued, "Once you have your vision and the motivation, then plan it out. Write down all the mile markers."

"Mile markers?"

"The steps along the way. For instance, the first mile marker is digging the tractor out of the dirt. Then, getting the engine running, and so forth. If you get discouraged, instead of mile markers, you write down yard markers.

Wendall smiled. "Yard markers? Really?"

"Oh yeah. Really small steps to get you moving and off square one. *One* shovelful of dirt is your first yard marker."

"It's gonna take a lot of shovelfuls."

His dad nodded. "But it's not an infinite number. Each one gets you a little closer to the end. The point is, break the job down into small, manageable steps and write them down."

"Why write them down when we already know what needs to be done? Why not just get started?"

Max sighed. "Because it will save you time and frustration in the end. You can avoid 'unexpected' problems and backtracking. And writing down your roadmap does one other important thing."

"What's that?"

"It keeps you *motivated* to do the work. Instead of feeling overwhelmed, you can *enjoy your progress*, one little step at a time, like walking to the candy store."

Wendall was still cringing at the challenge of resuscitating the dead tractor. "But what if you've never done anything like this before?"

"Then you either figure it out on your own or get advice from someone who *has* done it before. That's the advantage an expert has when tackling a project. They've done it so many times, they already know every step and all the tools, materials, and people they need. And they can anticipate problems and setbacks. But I guarantee ya, they still write things down."

Over the next one hour, father and son imagined, jotted down, scratched out, notated, and otherwise amended a detailed description of all the steps required. Darkness and mosquitoes ended the day, but Wendall now had a step-by-step plan.

The following morning Max drove to Kansas City for a ten-day training seminar for his job with Monroe. After two hours of digging out the front tires, Wendall went inside the house to take a break. The "short break" soon stretched to lunchtime. He would "get back out there" right after the noon news on TV, but then *Gilligan's Island* came on, so another thirty minutes was lost, and Wendall still couldn't get out the door.

He thought, *What is holding me back? Am I afraid of failing and proving that it was all a big waste of time? Afraid of looking stupid? Afraid of being ridiculed or laughed at by our neighbors? Afraid of trying things that don't work and feeling like a failure? Too proud to ask for help? Afraid of being turned down if I do ask for help?*

Wendall reviewed the written, detailed steps and thought about what his dad had said, "If you're determined to do something, you'll make it happen: despite every obstacle. But if you only wish for it, you'll just make excuses: despite every opportunity." Then Wendall realized that he hadn't *really* wanted anything his entire life. Oh, he *wished for* a car and a pretty girlfriend. But did he "make it happen"? Did he scrimp and save every cent so he could buy a car? Did he ever ask Clyde for a raise? Had he even started calling any girls? No. No.

And finally, no, he hadn't. As Wendall sat in the living room with his chin resting on his fist imitating the statue The Thinker, he heard a familiar commotion in the kitchen.

"But, Mom! I gotta have one more! It's super important."

"I said no. Now go on."

Damon stomped his foot. "You don't care about me!"

"You know that's not true. You've already had two cookies. Now go outside and play. I've got work to do."

"Okay, okay!"

Wendall smiled. Perhaps Mom had finally learned how to stand up to Damon's three *B*s. Then about a minute later…

"Damon! You get down from there!"

Damon was so desperate to reach a plate of freshly baked chocolate chip cookies sitting on the top shelf, he was standing tiptoed on two telephone books on a kitchen chair and awkwardly swinging a plastic hockey stick at the plate. Wendall burst out laughing. The little maniac was going to break his neck. But then it dawned on Wendall: Damon was demonstrating *exactly* what he needed, unrelenting determination, a "mule-headed" stubbornness that smashed through every seemingly immovable obstacle. Damon made no excuses. He wasn't proud. He didn't worry, or even care, what anyone thought of his efforts. He wasn't afraid of being turned down, laughed at, scolded, or even punished. He wasn't afraid to try *anything* to get what he wanted. He was fearlessly stubborn.

Mom capitulated, "Oh, okay! Here!" She handed him a cookie. "But that's the last one until after supper."

Sweet success, which in the end sweeps away *all* previous failures and disappointments.

Dad was right, and Damon had just proven it. Damon was mule-headed. He was determined to get another cookie no matter what. He didn't *wish* for it. He made it happen.

Back to digging one yard-marking shovelful at a time. Wendall kept repeating his dad's consequences and the rewards of success and the punishments of failure. After three hours, the tractor was "dug out" and now stood in a two-foot-deep pit. To his surprise and relief, the tires weren't flat.

Next step, the engine. Wendall unscrewed the oil drain plug, and nothing came out. He stuck his finger up into the drain hole and immediately wished he hadn't. His finger was coated with a black sticky tar. He removed six screws and pried the oil pan off the bottom of the engine. The inside of the rectangular pan was coated with a thick slab of black oily fudge. Opening the top of the engine wasn't going to be as easy. The bolts that held the "head" of the engine were rusted solid. Now Wendall needed advice from an expert. He gave Slick 'n' Greasy a call. To Wendall's surprise, Slick offered to drive out the next day.

Slick brought his own secret concoction for removing rusted bolts. He called it Nut Buster. Because of its acidic smell, Wendall was certain it would never have been approved by the Environmental Protection Agency. Slick approached the old tractor like a surgeon treating a trauma patient with multiple injuries. He "sterilized" the six head bolts with Nut Buster then carefully "broke them loose" with a socket wrench to remove the top of the engine. Just as he thought. "The pistons are rusted inside the cylinders." Slick dowsed the inside of the engine with Nut Buster.

"We'll let it sit for twenty minutes while I check the transmission."

The transmission had liquid in it, and thankfully, it wasn't rainwater. Slick thought that the fluid probably just needed to be changed. At least the transmission didn't leak. Slick then crawled under the engine to inspect the crankshaft.

"It looks and feels okay but everything's coated with dried up oil. Tell ya what. I'll leave a gallon of Nut Buster. Find a one-inch-wide paintbrush to paint the inside of the engine with it and clean all that old oil off. I'll come back out here tomorrow, after five, and we'll try to bust those pistons loose."

"Thanks so much, Slick."

It was now scavenger hunt time. Wendall intently scanned the inside of the old barn. Unfortunately, there wasn't a single paintbrush on the farm. How was he going to clean the engine? Suddenly, Wendall gasped. Ice-cold water was freezing the nape of his neck and running down his back.

"Great shot, Ranger Rick! Your freeze gun got the enemy in the neck!"

Wendall wheeled around just in time to be "shot" in the chest by Damon's Super Soaker water rifle, which as full of ice water.

"Damon, you little jerk!"

Wendall jammed his palm against the end of the barrel. "Can't you see I'm looking for something." *Wait a minute.* He looked down at the plastic water gun. "Damon. I need your squirt gun."

"No!" Damon took off running for the house. "Momma!"

After convincing his mother that Nut Buster was not going to destroy Damon's "favorite gun," Wendall found it very effective at dissolving the gummy, grime coating from the underneath side of the engine. Using a piece of broken mirror, he reflected sunlight up inside to reveal a silvery clean but still frozen-in-place engine. True to his word, Slick came out the next evening.

Slick crawled under the engine and shined a flashlight inside. "You did a real good job cleanin' that engine."

Wendall smiled with pride. Any compliment from Slick was something to remember.

Slick 'n' Greasy grasped the trigger of Damon's water gun with his right hand. "I gotta get me one of these."

Without thinking, Wendall blurted out, "You can have that one. It's the least I can do for all your help."

Slick smiled. "Do you know the best thing about these old engines? They have a crank. We'll use it to free up these pistons inside the cylinders. There's only four of 'em, but since this is a tractor, they're big."

The "crank" was standard equipment on all cars, trucks, tractors, and any other internal combustion engine before reliable electric starters were invented. Cranks are a solid metal bar with a notch on one end and a handle on the other. By sliding the notched end through a hole in the front of the engine, the driver could "crank" the engine over and start it. Wendall had never cranked an engine before. He remembered seeing it done on Ford Model T cars in old movies, and it looked simple enough. He carefully slid the notched end into the hole until it hit metal; then he turned it a few degrees and felt the notch catch. Slick felt it to be sure it was "in right."

"All right, Wendall, let's try to turn it over."

"Wait! What if it starts?"

Slick laughed. "It can't. Got no battery, no alternator, no gas. Hell, we don't even have any spark plug wires. How's it gonna fire?"

For a brief second, Wendall felt like a complete idiot. "Oh yeah. I'm just not thinking."

"No. You *are* thinking. And you're thinkin' right. Never crank an engine without making sure it won't run over ya when it starts."

Together, they pushed down on the handle, straining hard. Suddenly, the crank swung down half a turn. A *pop, pop, pop, pop* came from the top of the engine.

"Yeah, baby!" Slick gave a thumbs-up. "Broke her loose. Let me pour a little oil into the cylinders. Then you can turn it over nice and slow."

Wendall felt a surge of accomplishment and satisfaction. The cranking became progressively easier with the oil lubricating the pistons, rings, and cylinders. He could feel a definite stuttering resistance with each full turn as the four pistons came to the top of the engine in rapid succession.

Slick smiled. "I like the sound of those pops. The rings and cylinders are nice and tight. The old engine is in good shape."

They bolted the oil pan and the head back on the engine, but they didn't put any oil in it yet.

"Wendall, you'll need new gaskets for the engine head and the oil pain before adding any oil. I'll see if I can find some in Benson."

"Thanks a lot, Slick."

"Now for the spark plugs." Slick checked the four plugs on the right side of the engine block. "Don't recognize the brand. Wonder if they've ever been changed? Probably not."

"Really?"

Slick nodded. "Bet so. And they're rusted in solid. Gotta be careful. Don't wanna twist any of 'em off. We better Nut Buster 'em."

Slick used Damon's water gun to spray all four. "Man, I really like this thing."

Slick slid a socket wrench over the first spark plug before reaching for a hammer. "Wendall, this is the *only* time you should *ever* hit a wrench with a hammer. Tap it gently to vibrate the plug and get the Nut Buster down into the threads. You gotta be patient. Tap for a little while, then pull on the wrench. Just keep spraying and tapping till it breaks loose. But *never* put a cheater pipe on the wrench. You'll twist off the top of the spark plug every time." (Note: A "cheater" pipe is any length of pipe that can be slid over the end of a wrench to provide more leverage to turn the wrench.)

"Thanks, Slick."

"I'll be back day after tomorrow to check on your progress."

"What? Day after tomorrow? You mean, it's gonna take that long?"

"Yeah. Like I said, you gotta be patient. Just remember, it's a hell of a lot easier than drilling out busted plugs and then retapping new threads into the engine block."

Wendall kept spraying and tapping, alternating between the four plugs, until the mosquitoes, fatigue, and fading sunlight finally stopped him. Early the next morning, his staccato *tap, tap, tap, tap, tap, tap* of steel on steel sounded like a robotic woodpecker. Instead of yard markers, he began thinking that each tap was an inch marker. Slick was right. It was midmorning before Wendall got one of the plugs to budge. He let out a victory yell.

"All right! Yes! I got one!"

Wendall examined the old rusted spark plug. This small but winning confirmation of eventual, inevitable success felt good. By late afternoon, the fourth and final plug gave way. Wendall carefully screwed the new spark plugs in by hand before tightening them with a wrench. The next day, Slick brought out the gaskets for the engine.

"So you didn't twist any of 'em off?"

Wendall grinned. "No. I was careful."

"Good! Most guys can't help themselves, and they end up using a cheater bar. You did good."

Wendall was starting to enjoy the addictive feelings of pride and accomplishment with each small success.

With a new battery and battery cables, shiny spark plugs, soft rubber water hoses, ten quarts of 40-weight engine oil, a gallon of thick transmission fluid, a full tank of gas, and two gallons of fresh antifreeze in the radiator, the old M&M reminded Wendall of the Frankenstein monster. It was a hodgepodge of old and new parts, which, with the help of some electricity, could be brought to life. But without an ignition key to start it, he would have to use the crank. It sounded inherently dangerous. What if the tractor started and the crank stayed in the engine slot? It would twirl like a propeller at the same speed as the engine. Wendall decided to talk to someone with "crank experience." Therefore, he called a neighbor, Gerald Ratliff, who was glad to teach a skill he hadn't used in half a century.

Gerald began with "The trick is to give a quick half-a-turn and then immediately pull the handle out about an inch to slide it out of the engine slot. Otherwise, it could break your arm."

"What if the engine starts and the crank is still in the slot?"

"Then you don't wanna be holdin' on to it. So you gotta be quick and shut the gas off to the engine to kill it. It should be…here it is. See that little toggle switch on this gas line?"

Wendall craned his neck. "Oh yeah."

"The only other way to shut off the engine is to pull all the spark plug wires off."

The first three tries by Gerald were unsuccessful. "No worries. Gotta let the fuel pump prime the cylinders with some gas. Then it should start."

On his fourth try, the engine popped, then stuttered as black smoked puffed from the muffler before the engine gradually built up a rhythm and finally began to purr. The black exhaust quickly became invisible.

Wendall was jubilant. "Hot damn!" an expression borrowed from Clyde.

Above the engine noise, Gerald shouted, "It sounds good…and no smoke. This tractor might be old, but I know for a fact that the engine doesn't have that many hours on it."

It was like bringing something, or someone, back from the dead. Wendall decided to name the old tractor "Frankie," short for

Frankenstein. After idling the engine for a few minutes, he drove it out of its pasture grave up to the barn and then flipped the gas line toggle. The engine died a few seconds later. Now it was Wendall's turn to try the crank. His first two attempts were fruitless. Then Gerald pointed out that he hadn't flipped the gas toggle switch back on. Wendall smiled with relieved embarrassment, then started the old engine with the next try.

Wendall fist pumped. "Yes!"

After killing the engine for a second time, they walked back to the pasture to "look over" the plow and the disc.

Gerald groaned. "What a shame. These two have sat in the weeds and dirt for at least twenty years. I can remember John Derrick using this plow and disc year after year."

Wendall took a deep breath. "Yeah."

Gerald rubbed his chin. "But it can be done. All the tires are shot, but the frames are intact. Definitely a pain in the butt. But it's still doable."

As Gerald was leaving, Wendall extended a firm handshake. "Thanks for everything, Gerald."

Like the tractor, the plow and disc would have to be refurbished where they sat buried in the pasture weeds. Back to one shovelful at a time, only this time, it was easier. Wendall's previous success with the tractor inspired confidence and enthusiasm. It took two days to dig them out, replace all the tires, and pack the axles with new grease. Frankie easily pulled the plow and then the disc out of their respective trenches. Wendall would have to wait until after harvest to try them out in the fields.

On June 28, 1977, Wendall watched a custom harvest crew with three massive John Deere combines make short work of the farm's one hundred acres of dry, waist-high, golden wheat. He was eager to test the disc. The next morning, he got an early start before the sun had even peeked above the horizon.

Although the disc was old, it wasn't worn-out. The individual discs were all sharp, and the heavy steel frame resulted in "a good deep cut" into the field. But its swath was only eight-foot-wide, guaranteeing six full days would be needed to disc the farm. Fortunately, only one of those days was humbling. That was the day their neighbor, Roscoe Hamilton, disced his field just south of the Nichols farm. Roscoe smiled and waved from the cab of his towering four-wheel-drive tractor as he rumbled past Wendall and dusted him with a twenty-eight-foot-wide disc. Roscoe's bright-orange Versatile tractor had dual wheels on the front and the back axles, and each tire was twice the size of the rear wheels of the old M&M. Roscoe enjoyed power steering, a plush cushioned seat, and air-conditioning with a stereo and a small refrigerator inside his cab. By comparison, the old M&M had a few comfort features of its own: a wide bare-metal seat that was molded to the shape of the average farmer's butt, "natural" air-conditioning if the wind was blowing, and an extra-large steering wheel, which provided the leverage needed for the driver to have any hope of turning the front wheels.

The rest of Wendall's days of discing in the summer heat were pure enjoyment. Clyde drove out to visit and was giddy at the sight of the old equipment "choppin' the hell out of the stubble." Almost as satisfying was a fairly frequent event that cost Wendall twenty minutes each time it happened. The neighboring farmers would stop their pickups on the side of the dirt road and wave him down to ask about the old M&M. Like Gerald, they had grown up seeing the yellow tractor work the Derrick farm as teenagers. After five days, Wendall reckoned that he had met every old-timer in the county.

Max Nichols taught Wendall the "mule-headed formula" for success. It consists of only four, preferably written, equally important steps.

1. *Visualize exactly* what you want. See it in your mind with as much detail as possible.
2. *Consider the consequences.* Feel the successful results that will inspire you and the devastating failure that will terrorize you. Decide with stubborn determination that you must succeed; no excuses.
3. *Break it down.* Write down mile markers, yard markers, and inch markers and include all the tools, talent (people or

skills), materials, and money needed. Of course, your plan will need to be flexible because unforeseen problems will arise.

4. *Work without shame or hesitation.* Imitate Damon reaching with a hockey stick for another cookie. Failure is not an option. You must be willing to beg, borrow, buy, ask, learn, hire, and consult everyone and everything you need to get what you want.

The *truly amazing fact* is that most people will help you *if* you ask them, *and* they see your determination and enthusiasm. Why? Because people want to be part of something successful. Helping someone fulfill a dream or achieve a worthy goal, even just a little, is good for the soul. Also always keep a simple truth in mind: *Nothing is impossible with unwavering determination and the generous help of other people.*

However, you will encounter roadblocks, setbacks, procrastination, and doubt. Count on it. How do you keep motivated, energized, and unafraid of failure?

*First,* you burn the very real consequences of satisfying success and devastating failure into your mind. Remind yourself of them as often as needed.

*Second,* you *enjoy the inch and yard markers along the way—not just the final result.*

Wendall will forever remember the joy and satisfaction of hearing the tractor engine *pop, pop, pop* when he and Slick broke it loose or when each spark plug finally gave way or when the old M&M started for the first time or the smiles of the old farmers when they stopped him in the field. You must *enjoy the journey* because the little successes along the way are the majority of your life.

That summer on the farm, Wendall grew two inches taller, gained fifteen pounds of muscle, and matured into a young man with confidence. He would need every inch of height, every pound of muscle, and every ounce of self-confidence for the challenges awaiting him. High school in small-town Kansas was to start in mid-August.

# 12

# Pure Evil

He really enjoys hurting little kids. He laughs when
they scream and cry. He's just pure evil.

—Freddie Lindman

Like many of its rival in rural Kansas, Clearwell's school struggled to maintain Kansas's minimum daily attendance requirement. It faced "consolidation" with surrounding small-town schools if its average daily attendance for grades nine through twelve was less than fifty-five. Since the local Mennonites withdrew their children after the eighth grade, each of the high school grades had only ten to fifteen students. During flu season, the principal was known to taxi sick students to school just long enough to be counted as "present" for one morning class. Unfortunately, the consolidation threat meant that Clearwell would tolerate *any* high school student, regardless of their bad behavior, as Wendall would soon learn.

On the first day of school, Wendall was disappointed that he was the only high school student on his school bus. All the kids were elementary age except for a couple of junior high girls. His daily commute was eight miles of bumpy dirt roads on worn-out shocks. On arrival, Wendall noted something odd. Although Clearwell's football stadium was state of the art with artificial turf, a massive score board, and VIP box seating, the school building itself was a relic. The single-story cinder block structure featured cracked and peeling white stucco and large plate glass windows. Without any air-conditioning, the windows were hinged open in August, September, and May to allow the breeze and dozens of sparrows to share the classrooms with the students. During the winter months, everyone wore their coats and gloves in class because the old wall furnaces had been disconnected years before after two of them caught fire. Fortunately, Wendall's Grandpa Nichols was a captain in the Benson fire department. In December, he made one call to the fire marshal. By the next week, brand-new gas heaters, each of them half the size of a Volkswagen, were installed high in a corner of every classroom. As a result, an order for new football helmets featuring an updated "Hawk" logo was delayed until the next year.

Back to the first day of school, Wendall was eager to start making friends. In the gymnasium, students milled around before classes, waiting for the first bell to ring. Raised wooden bleachers ran along both sides of the basketball court, and a five-step stairway on each end led up to the stands. A three-foot-high pipe railing ran the length of the stands to keep spectators from falling four feet onto the court. The west side was roped off. Apparently, the custodians didn't desire to clean both bleachers every day. But Wendall noticed something peculiar about the east side. Only a handful of guys in letter jackets and a few cackling girls were sitting in the stands. But why?

"Hi, I'm Freddie. You must be new."

"Oh. Hi. Uh, yeah. I'm Wendall. Just moved here this summer. My mom and dad bought a farm north of town.

"You play football?"

"No, just baseball. I pitch and play first base."

"We don't have a baseball team. Just football and basketball. But mostly football. Why don't you play football? You could play cornerback."

"I grew up in Benson, and I wasn't big enough or fast enough to make the team."

"Well, we play eight-man football. We were 2 and 8 last year. But the Thompson twins are freshmen this year, and they'll anchor our offensive and defensive lines. We might go undefeated."

"That's great. Uh, Freddie, why are there only a few students sitting in the stands?"

Freddie nodded toward the bleachers. "See that asshole sitting at the top of the stairs."

Wendall squinted at the lanky frame, the stringy-brown, shoulder-length hair, and the sneering smile. "The Ted Nugent look-alike?"

Freddie laughed. "Yeah, but that jerk is no rock star. He's the school bully."

"Really."

Freddie smirked. "He's the 'king of the bleachers.' If you want to sit up there, you have to give him a dollar."

Wendall shook his head. "That's ridiculous. What does the principal think of his little business enterprise?"

"Oh, he knows all about it. But he's too afraid to say anything."

"The principal is afraid of a student?"

"Mr. Green's afraid of Rance's parents. They've threatened to sue him if he 'harasses' their 'innocent boy' and 'destroys his self-esteem.'"

"Rance? His name is Rance? As in rancid?" Wendall had to chuckle.

"His real name is Randy. But he insists everyone call him Rance ever since he came back from reform school in the third grade."

Wendall studied him sitting in the stands as he would a wild steer that needed to be corralled. "Too bad someone didn't fix his wagon back then, before he was over six feet tall."

Freddie nodded. "Yeah, you're right."

Wendall smiled. "Yes, sir, Randy—what a dandy."

Freddie didn't appreciate Wendall's attempt at humor. "He'll kill ya if you call him that."

Wendall motioned toward the stands. "So all those people up there gave him a dollar?"

"Nope. None of 'em did. Those guys are all the jocks and over there are the popular girls. He doesn't bother them."

"Why not?"

Freddie smiled. "'Cause the football team would gang up and put his head in the locker room toilet."

"Why don't they do it anyway?"

159

"Good question," replied Freddie. "Probably because they don't care about us weaklings down here on the court."

"Who are those three guys sitting next to the jerk?"

"They're his 'lieutenants': Raymond, Jason, and Rodney. They're all juniors."

"Oh...right." Wendall nodded. "They're called toadies. They're so afraid of the bully, they tagalong kissing his butt so he won't bully them." Wendall wondered out loud, "What if some new kid, who didn't know any better, dared to pass without paying the dollar toll?"

Freddie shook his head. "Rance would shove you back down the stairs."

"Sounds like a real nice guy."

Freddie didn't miss the sarcasm in Wendall's voice. "Yeah, he's been a troublemaker all his life."

"How long have you known him?"

Wendall could see the pain in Freddie's face even before he spoke.

"Since he beat me up the first week of first grade. When I was in the third grade, he broke my arm just for fun. My parents were going to sue his parents for the doctors' visits until Mr. Hill paid up."

"Who's Mr. Hill?"

"Rance's dad. Then, two weeks later, we found my mom's cat. Rance had cut Fluffy's head off. But we couldn't prove it was him. After that, he left me alone, and I haven't had anything to do with him since."

Over the course of the next week, Freddie told Wendall of the sadistic and cruel trail of pain, suffering, and destruction left by Dandy Randy. In kindergarten, he pulled the girls' hair, flicked the boys' ears, stuck his fingers in other kids' brownies and cupcakes, snapped all their pencils in two, and marked up their clothes and faces with Magic Markers. His teachers tried to discipline him. But sitting Rance in a corner or at the front of the class only made him feel special and privileged. Of course, his parents blamed the teachers for his bad behavior.

Rance never attempted any of his schoolwork. Old Mrs. Koehn was brave enough to make him repeat the first grade, twice, because he couldn't, or rather, refused to learn to read. Her best intentions unknowingly sentenced children yet unborn to terror and misery. Because Rance's parents had already "redshirted" him for one year before kindergarten, he was now three full years older than his classmates. It was the perfect arrangement for a bully. He was bigger, stronger, and meaner than the "babies" around him. No other teacher dared to flunk him. One year of Rance and his parents was all that any faint-hearted elementary teacher could take. They just kept pushing him into the next grade. Their frustration was compounded by Rance's parents who refused to allow anyone to spank him. Rance's favorite taunt to the teachers and principal became, "You can't touch me or I'll tell my daddy."

Rance's first brush with the law was at age ten. He thought it would be cool to set fire to a train. So he did. The Clearwell volunteer fire department saved the locomotive but not three boxcars. Rance carelessly left the metal gas can at the scene of the crime. The sheriff fingerprinted every high school and junior high boy in the school but no matches. Then he heard about some first grader "laughing his ass off" about the train fire. A year in "reform school," for gladiator training, only made Rance more dangerous. By the time he was twelve, he had broken six arms (including Freddie's), three ankles, dozens of fingers, and one skull. Recess was no longer Rance's favorite "torture time" after the teachers began following him around the playground. Therefore, he rescheduled his "fun class" to begin immediately after school. Rance took great delight throughout the day deciding who he was going to "hunt," meaning, run them down and inflict enough pain to make them scream "I'm a pussy" at least three times. Rarely did any of the children report his reign of terror to their parents since Rance promised to burn their houses down if they did. They all knew about his train fire. Freddie could count at least ten families who had pulled all their children out of the Clearwell school and began homeschooling because of Rance.

Freddie shook his head. "I've never understood it. He really enjoys hurting little kids. He laughs when they scream and cry. He's just pure evil."

Rance was illiterate, but he wasn't stupid. He steered away from kids who had older, bigger, and stronger siblings. He backed off from kids whose parents showed up with a gun at his parents' doorstep. He also didn't mess with Mennonite children. Their parents were organized, met every Sunday at church, and they had the voting clout to have the school board expel him. But on occasion, Rance would make a mistake. Freddie told Wendall about a new fourth grader, Johnny Millony, a foster child of the Hendricks family. They were farmers in their late fifties who now had an empty nest after their youngest son joined the marines. Rance was a sixteen-year-old seventh grader who decided that little "Baloney Millony" needed to be "initiated." Freddie wasn't certain of exactly what Rance did to Johnny because Johnny never came back to school. Unfortunately for Rance, marine basic training in South Carolina ended two weeks later. Little Johnny's much bigger "brother," Marine Private First-Class Hendricks, made a personal visit to his alma mater in full dress uniform. He had a book for his friend, Randy Hill. Hendricks casually dropped by the principal's office but insisted on delivering the large, hardcover World Atlas personally. The blushing young secretary nearly tripped in her high heels leading him to Rance's English class. The marine had no problem recognizing Rance sitting in the back row, a foot taller than his much younger classmates. Dandy Randy was, in military terms, a "lit-up target" with his feet on the desk in front of him. Hendricks ignored the puzzled look on Miss Stetler's face and marched straight down the aisle to the back. With one grand slam swing of the book, he flattened Rance's nose, blackened both eyes, and knocked him out cold. Rance fell to the floor like a sack of potatoes. Hendricks calmly laid the blood-splattered atlas on Rance's desk, stepped over his unconscious body, strolled out the rear door of the classroom, and exited the building. The marine never said a word. An ambulance finally arrived from Benson to cart Rance off to Sisters of Mercy Medical Center.

Meanwhile, back at the school, the county sheriff just smiled and shook his head as the janitor mopped up the dried blood on the floor. The sheriff and Rance were well acquainted. "Did anyone see anything?"

Wide-eyed silence filled the air.

"No? I didn't think so."

The sheriff pointed at Patricia Slader. "Young lady, you didn't see anything, did ya?"

Patty quickly shook her head no.

"Miss Stetler, is it entirely possible that this lazy student fell asleep and then fell forward landing flat on his face, knocking himself out?"

"Uh, well…"

"Isn't it true that he falls asleep a lot in this class?"

A visibly nervous Miss Stetler stuttered, "Yes. Yes, he does." (A true statement.)

"Well…there you have it! Just an unfortunate accident. Maybe that boy can catch up on his sleep in the hospital."

No further investigation was made. No charges were filed.

Rance was in the hospital for five days. Three weeks later when he came back to school, Rance still had a slight yellow-green eye shadow, remnants of his black eyes. But with Rance, it was never over. One year later to the day, fifty of farmer Hendricks's best Holstein milk cows were found dead. Their water tank had been poisoned.

Jump forward five years to present day, and Rance was enjoying his senior year of high school at twenty-one years of age. He was at the top of the pecking order. Since Wendall was so new, his place in the primitive hierarchy had yet to be established. But he was under scrutiny. Not enough was known about him. Did he have older siblings? Any family in the military? Who was his father? Did they have a lot of money or own any guns? Wendall obviously wasn't a Mennonite since he was in high school. And he didn't play football. But he did live on a farm, and he was well tanned, which meant he worked outside. Also, puberty was trying to wake Wendall up, but he stood only five feet, eight inches, and weighed a skinny 130 pounds. Wendall knew he would have to enter the ring eventually. He was determined to be ready. But first, he needed two things: permission and a corner man.

The permission needed to come from his dad. Wendall found him tinkering with an alternator in the machine shed.

"Dad, I need to ask you something."

Max Nichols looked up from the workbench. "What is it?"

"I got a problem at school. A bully. He's been terrorizing the school for years."

"Who is he?"

"Rance Hill or Randy Hill. His dad works for the county."

"Hill? Don't know any Hills in Benson."

"His parents have lived in Clearwell for years."

"What's he doing?"

"Besides beating up younger, smaller kids, he sits at the top of the bleacher stairs demanding a dollar if you want to sit in the stands before the first bell."

"Sounds to me like everybody needs to throw him out on his head."

"Well, Dad, that's the problem. Everybody is too afraid of him. Nobody is willing to even think about standing up to him."

"Well, someone needs to kick his ass."

Wendall wasn't surprised by this response. He knew that his dad wasn't a violent man. But Max was the oldest of seven children. Growing up, he took it upon himself to stand up and protect his younger siblings. It was a point of pride that he had instilled in Wendall. Wendall knew that Damon could irritate him to no end, but he would *never* allow anyone to bully Damon.

Wendall replied, "Yeah, he does need his butt kicked, and I'm thinking that I'm gonna have to be the one to do it."

"Has he bothered you?"

"Not yet. But if I have to fight, I wanna make sure it's okay with you."

"Sure it's okay. Just make certain you get in the first punch. And don't stop until he's on the ground."

Wendall didn't mention that Rance was five years older, nearly a foot taller, and fifty pounds heavier than him. He kept reminding himself of the old saying, "The bigger they are, the harder they fall."

One advantage to living on a farm is that you meet other farmers, and Wendall had met most of the locals while discing with the old M&M tractor. Back in the 1970s, many of them were veterans of the Korean War or World War II. Most of them had been in combat, and they knew how to fight hand to hand. The Nichols's neighbor on the next mile, Gerald Ratliff, immediately came to mind. He fought in Guam in the Pacific against the Japanese. Wendall knew Gerald was going to be working some calves that weekend, castrating and dehorning them. Gerald had been waiting for colder weather so the flies wouldn't bother the calves afterward. Wendall called and invited himself over to help, "for the experience." After four hours, they finally finished the last of the thirty calves.

"Thanks for helping me, Wendall. Are you sure I can't give ya twenty bucks for your time?"

"Oh no, but thanks anyway. I still owe you for helping me learn to crank start my old M&M. But I could use some advice."

Gerald smiled as he took off his work gloves. "Sure. I don't know how much good it'll do ya. But I can tell ya what I know."

"Well, there's this bully at my school…"

"Bully? Don't ya mean, coward?"

"Yeah, he's that too."

Gerald nodded with disgust. "All bullies are cowards. They have to push others around to convince themselves that they're more than just an ass wipe. Who is he?"

"Rance Hill."

"Hill? Hmm…" Gerald rubbed his chin for a second. "Isn't he that little bastard that set fire to that train?"

Wendall smiled. "Yeah, that's him. Only, he's not so little anymore. More like six-foot-three and 180 pounds."

Gerald shook his head. "Size doesn't matter. The Japanese taught us that. Ike [General Dwight D. Eisenhower] always said, 'It's not the size of the dog in the fight, it's the fight in the dog that matters.'"

Wendall added, "He also has three 'lieutenants' that hang around him."

Gerald let out a belly laugh. "Lieutenants? Shit! Those are pissant toadies. They're the biggest cowards of all! Those yellow bellies are so afraid of the bully they grovel at his feet so he won't pick on them."

"What will they do in a fight?"

Gerald chuckled. "They'll turn into tit-less cheerleaders."

Wendall laughed at the thought of the three in cheerleader costumes complete with makeup and ribbons in their hair.

Gerald looked puzzled. "Why hasn't everybody set him straight?"

"Because they're afraid of him."

"In my high school [in the small town of Clayton forty years before], he wouldn't have lasted half a day. We would have run him out on a rail."

Wait a minute. "We? Who's we?"

"All of us, the guys and the gals. If anybody tried to pick on somebody else, we would jump in and say, 'Why don't you pick on somebody your own size?' It let 'em know. We didn't put up with that kind of nonsense."

Wendall was instantly envious of Gerald's school and student body. "I wish my school had some backbone. I'm thinking that I'm gonna have to take the point on this."

Gerald adjusted his cowboy hat. "Well, if you're gonna be in a fight, do what my sergeant taught us. Fight with your head first. Plan it. *You* pick the battlefield and the time. Always attack from the higher ground with the sun at your back and the enemy up against a river, the ocean or the edge of a cliff, as if anybody is stupid enough to camp next to a cliff."

Wendall laughed. "All good advice when you're fighting outside, but we'll be inside the school."

"Sure. In that case, hit first and hit hard. And remember, the weakest points on a man are his eyes, his balls, his throat, and his knees, in that order. Don't waste time hitting anywhere else."

"So fight dirty?"

"Oh hell yes!" Gerald frowned. "You think we followed the queen's rules of boxing in the jungle? *No!* We put the enemy on the ground as fast as possible."

The following Monday morning, Wendall noticed something new in the gym, the sound of a bouncing ball. Rance had a tennis ball and was bouncing it at his feet as he sat on his usual throne at the top of the east bleacher stairway. Wendall's glaring stare did not go unnoticed. As he turned his back to say hello to Freddie, the tennis ball whizzed past his left ear and bounced off the west bleachers.

"Oh! Almost! Good throw, Rance." His toady chorus sang his praises.

"Hey, Nichols, you sonovabitch, fetch my tennis ball."

Without turning around, Wendall held his hand out for the ball from an eighth grader who had retrieved it.

Rance was now standing. "Nichols! Don't make me come down there, you pussy."

Wendall stuffed the ball in his coat pocket and calmly walked into the principal's office to deposit it in the lost and found box as the first bell rang. Thus, the gauntlet had been thrown down.

Later that day, Wendall formulated his battle plan. It would have to be inside the school to keep both of them alive. The obvious battlefield was the gym. The best time would be before the first bell. Rance would already have the high ground at the top of the stairs. Wendall would have to somehow get past him and up into the bleachers where the fighting would commence. There was one other important aspect to consider, psychological warfare. Wendall had witnessed it during Damon's war games.

"Ranger Rick, is from Kansas! His rebel yell terrifies the enemy as he charges them. Come on, men! *Aaaaaaaaaaaaah*!"

"Damon! Stop that screaming!"

"*Aaaaaaaaaaaaaah*! The enemy line breaks. Ranger Rick shoots 'til he's out of bullets. Use the bayonet! *Aaaaaaaaaaaaaah*!"

"Damon! Quit yelling!"

"Mom! I'm not yelling! It's Ranger Rick. He's psyching out the enemy."

Wendall thought, maybe, just maybe, a sudden rebel yell would freeze Rance long enough to knock him down.

Tuesday was going to be the day. It was cold, cloudy, and windy. Wendall wore his heavy coat for padding. And he chose his leather work gloves instead of insulated gloves. He just felt stronger wearing the same gloves that he used to build fence. The gloves also reminded him of being on the farm: a place where he feared no one. Plus, the heavy cowhide would protect his hands if he missed Rance's eyes and hit his teeth.

Wendall glanced at his watch as he stepped off the school bus: 8:27. He had only three minutes until the first bell. Maybe there was still time. He quickly walked the one hundred feet from the entrance, past the office and the library, to the gym. He was on high alert. Rance was in position. Wendall immediately headed for the stairs. As expected, Rance stood up and challenged him, "Where the hell do you think you're going?"

The entire student body suddenly fell silent. They were now coliseum spectators with all eyes glued on the feared gladiator and the doomed little Christian. Wendall didn't usually swear, but it makes a runt sound tougher and unafraid. "Well, Randy, I'm gonna sit my lazy, frozen butt down on that bleacher up there and let it thaw the hell out."

Rance held out the palm of his hand. "Give me five dollars!"

The sudden price increase brought a chorus of "oohs" and "oh yeahs" from the three toadies.

Wendall intentionally raised his voice. "I had no idea you were so *poor*! Out here beggin' for money? What kind of gun have you got?"

Rance looked surprised. "What?"

Wendall picked up the pace to keep him off balance. "Gun, you know, for shootin'. Shit! If you're so desperate for food, come out to our place. We got lots of rabbits and squirrels. I'll give ya some shells, but I gotta know what kinda gun ya got." Wendall shook his finger at Rance. "But...don't go out there by yourself. We got signs up. My dad will drop you with a headshot if he finds you trespassin'."

The first bell cut him off.

Wendall grimaced with disgust. "Damn! I didn't even get to sit my ass down."

He turned and started heading down the stairs. "I'll get back to you, Randy. Bring your gun tomorrow, and I'll show you mine."

Fifteen minutes later, Mr. Green interrupted Wendall's first hour history class.

"Wendall Nichols!"

Wendall jumped to attention like a private in the army. "Yes, sir."

"Did you bring a gun to school?"

"Not today."

"Have you ever brought a gun to school?"

"Not yet."

Mr. Green shook his head in disbelief. "You...you can't *ever* bring a gun to school."

Wendall played as dumb as possible. "Oh, okay. Good to know. I'm kinda new here. I carry one at home at all times. Never know when you might need to shoot somebody, uh, I mean, somethin'."

The next day, it rained. As usual, the buses ran late due to the muddy roads. Wendall's bus pulled up to the school twenty minutes after the first bell. As he walked by the empty gym on the way to class, he noticed a confetti of white poster board littering the gym floor and stairs. Some pieces had black Magic Marker lettering on them. History class was abuzz about "the beggar sign." Someone, Wendall was guessing the jocks of the football team, had used a full sheet of twenty-four-inch-by-thirty-six-inch poster board and a black marker. They wrote, "Randy, here's $5 so you can buy some food" and taped a five-dollar bill just below. The practical jokers then propped it up on Rance's seat at the top of the stairs earlier that morning. Rance went ballistic and shredded the poster with the money still attached. He threatened to "beat the living shit out of whoever did it." Of course, it couldn't have been Wendall. He was still on the bus at the time. But Wendall knew that once the rain stopped, it would be D-Day for him and Rance.

Thursday morning was bright and sunny. On the way to school, Wendall sat in the front seat, with the first graders. He wanted to be the first person off the bus. They asked him why he was wearing work gloves and such a heavy coat on a sunny day.

"'Cause I got some serious work to do."

Wendall thought of how he might get the high ground in the bleachers. Rance would try to shove him back down the stairs as soon as he reached the top. How would he get past him? Wendall remem-

TIM JONES, M.D.

bered what his dad had said about getting in the first punch. Why not get in the first shove?

Meanwhile, in the gym, Rance had loudly announced for all to hear that he was going to "beat little Nichols to a pulp." Did anyone stand up for Wendall? *No.* Did Mr. Green, only twenty feet away in his office with his door wide open, come out? *No.* They were all too afraid. Better to let "little Nichols" absorb Satan's wrath than to become a victim themselves.

The bus screeched to a stop. Wendall jumped out and jogged through the entrance and down the hallway toward the gym. He could hear the sheep bleating, "He's coming. He's coming." They were all expecting a slaughter. Wendall was determined to surprise them. Without breaking stride, he went straight for the stairs, smiling and waving a five-dollar bill. Rance stood up.

"Randy! Did you bring your gun? I brought ya five dollars for some food."

"Nichols, you son of a bitch!"

Wendall bounded up the stairway and lunged forward into Rance and shoved him hard into the toadies. A quick turn to the right, and Wendall was three steps up the bleachers. Now he had the high ground with God's glorious morning sun at his back, shining through the gym's plate glass windows into Rance's eyes. Rance was also in a "poor strategic position," backed up against the bleacher's pipe railing with a four-foot drop off to the gym court below. Wendall screamed Damon's rebel yell at the top of his lungs and threw himself at Rance. They both cascaded over the railing and onto the basketball court.

"*Fight! Fight! Fight!*" was the chant from the gutless crowd. Just as Gerald had predicted, the toadies became nothing but "titless cheerleaders." Wendall got in the first, the second, and the third punches. He blackened Rance's right eye and bloodied his lower lip. Rance never even got his hands up. Mr. Green came running. His pot belly bounced with every short stride.

"Break it up! Break it up! What's going on here?"

Earlier that morning, Wendall had thought a lot about what his dad and Gerald had told him. Bullying did not exist in their schools because *the students* didn't stand for it. They stood up for each other. "Pick on someone your own size" was their motto. It was another way of saying, "If you want to pick on someone, try picking on me first." But their generation had principals and school boards with backbone. Bullies had their butts tanned with a paddle beginning in the first grade, and expulsions were the rule, not the exception. Lawsuits against schools guilty of maintaining order weren't even considered in those days.

Wendall put the blame for Rance's bullying squarely on the inept Mr. Green. Wendall was "past the point of caring" about anything. He fully expected to be expelled; therefore, he unloaded on Green.

"You're nothing but a damn *coward!*"

Wendall pointed at Rance who was still on his back and now crab crawling away. "Why do you allow this *jackass* to terrorize us? What is wrong with *you?*"

"Now, Mr. Nichols. You need to calm down."

Mr. Green was interrupted by the first bell.

Wendall shook his fist at him. "You knew all this shit was going on, and *you let it happen!*"

He must have hit a nerve with Mr. Green. Green knew that Rance was a hateful, sadistic bully. And Green knew that he could have prevented this fight. But he wasn't man enough to admit it. "Both of you are expelled for three days. Go to the office and call your parents. Everyone else, get to class."

When Wendall returned the next week, no one said a word to him until lunch. In the cafeteria, grade school boys, whom he didn't even know, walked by and patted him on the back as he sat alone.

"Hey, man, good to see ya." It was their way of saying "thank you."

Rance never came back to Clearwell. If he had, round 2 would have immediately started. Rance's bluff had been called. His parents transferred him to Butler High School twenty miles away. Butler only accepted him because they were also on the verge of being closed by the state of Kansas due to low-average daily attendance. Wendall anticipated some classic Rance retaliation, similar to the murders of

171

Freddie's family cat and farmer Hendricks's cows. Rance was planning something to be certain. But his evil plan was overheard at the Pizza Hut in Benson by Miss Davis, a teacher who knew Wendall from Benson Junior High. She and her fiancé were sitting in a booth next to Rance and his toadies. They overheard his detailed plan to "wipe out little Wendall Nichols." Miss Davis didn't know Rance, but she did know Wendall. Waving a plastic fork in Rance's face, she screamed, "If you touch one hair on his head, half the town of Benson is comin' after you, and I'll be leading the way!"

No doubt, her threat was reinforced by her six-foot-six, three-hundred-pound fiancé towering behind her. When Davis later described the incident to Wendall, her voice was a mix of rage and fear. "He's evil! You watch out for him. He's the devil incarnate!" (in the flesh).

Wendall couldn't agree more.

Ten years later in 1987, Wendall bumped into Freddie in Tulsa when Wendall was a resident physician. Freddie told him that Rance was in the Oklahoma State Penitentiary in McAlister. Wendall wasn't surprised. There was only one other place better suited for Rance, and Wendall was certain that Dandy Randy would eventually arrive there. After all, no one lives forever.

Randy "Rance" Hill was a sadistic psychopath: a person with no conscience, no morals, and no empathy for any living thing, man or animal. Psychopaths are real life monsters who feed on the suffering of others to fill themselves with a sense of pleasure, power, and superiority. They react violently to any opposition, and they plot even more violent revenge when successfully challenged. Psychopaths are dangerous, and inevitably, they wind up dead or in jail but not before leaving a legacy of misery.

Wendall had three choices when he faced the "devil in the flesh." Two choices were advisable, and one was stupid. Unfortunately, *Wendall made the stupid choice*. He fought Rance. Wendall was very lucky that he didn't severely injure or kill Rance, and luckier still that he wasn't injured or killed. Wendall could have ended that day in jail or the hospital or the morgue. Furthermore, Wendall was fortunate that Rance's retaliation plans were overheard and squashed by a friend. Although his fight with Rance seemed necessary at that time, it could have been completely avoided. Wendall had two other, better options. First, he could have completely avoided the sadistic psychopath. Wendall thought of all the parents who had removed their children from Clearwell school because of Rance. Is the avoidance choice cowardly or smart? Or both? It's a matter of opinion. But complete avoidance can be effective, and it is certainly safer than fighting the psychopath alone. The second, and arguably the best choice, was Miss Davis's approach: gather an army. *Just her threat of raising an army* from the town of Benson was enough to shut him down. Rance was also intimidated by the Mennonites because of their collective power. But raising a student army would have taken considerable time and effort. The Clearwell students were terrified of Rance, and they didn't have Mr. Green's support because he was terrified of Rance's parents. And even a united student body might not have been enough to drive Rance out. But additional muscle from parents, extended family and friends, alumni, the school board, sheriff, attorneys, and "half the town of Benson" could have been drafted into active service. And it all would have been worth it. The abuse and suffering would end. Students who had been exiled could return. Best of all, Clearwell students would learn to stand up for themselves and their fellow students. Yes, in the future, Wendall wouldn't be baited into a one-on-one fight. Instead, he would gather an army by inspiring, and if necessary, by shaming everyone until the psychopath was driven out of town or into a jail cell. Of course, Wendall would *love* today's cell phone videos and social media that can document a psychopath's evil deeds and then broadcast them for all the world to see. No doubt, army recruitment is actually easier today.

But old habits are hard to break. Wendall didn't fully learn this chapter's lesson until later as you will discover.

# 13

# Don't Peck on Me

Shame them. They don't have the right to bully anyone,
and they disgrace themselves when they do.
—Ruby Nichols, a.k.a. Grandma

Farm animals can teach you a lot about people, if you pay attention. Baby chicks, for example, can be so fuzzy, so cute, and...so vicious. Max Nichols bought a dozen from Johnson's Feed and Hardware in Benson. A patched up, sway-back-roof chicken house became their new home. But the Nichols family quickly noticed a problem with their little fuzz balls. Four of the chicks were pecking on one little speckled one. What was going on in their pin-sized brains? The abuse became so bad that the little victim's back was bleeding. The attackers were easy to identify by their blood-stained beaks. Wendall's Grandma Nichols knew just what to do.

"Put some Vaseline all over his bloody back. It'll keep the flies and the other birds off him."

She was right. It worked like a charm. Now when the little peckers bothered him, they got a beakful of nasty petroleum jelly. After three months, the little speckled chick didn't turn into a beautiful swan. He became a badass rooster. And his tormenters turned out to be hens. Well, you can guess how that worked out.

At Clearwell High, Wendall observed students who mimicked his little chicks in the chicken house. One of the speckled students was Clifford Smithson.

"Hey, Smithson! Have you taken a dump in your pants yet today?"

"Of course he did! Can't you smell it?"

"Who ya bringin' to the prom, Smithy boy, your show lamb?"

Clifford was the youngest of five children and the last Smithson at Clearwell High. Unlike his older, outgoing, and athletic sisters, he was tall, slim, and introverted. However, Clifford was no ninety-pound weakling. His hands were calloused, and the lean muscles in his long tanned forearms rippled when he opened or closed his fists. His family was devout, and he was destined to be a wheat farmer like his father and grandfathers before him. Of course, Smithson had been a regular target for Rance. But even with Rance gone, his schoolhouse nightmare wasn't over. A group of pecking students was still around to bloody Smithson's back.

Food and drinks were "accidently" spilled on Clifford nearly every day at lunch. He sat by himself, and he ate quickly to limit his exposure. Smithson was also a favorite subject for the disgusting graffiti artists in the boys' restroom.

"Smithson is a faggot."

"Smithy for class clown."

"Smithson sucks dick."

Mr. Green's threats to find and punish the culprits were toothless. New and original profanity and pornography defaced the walls and stalls as soon as the janitors scrubbed off the old.

The other harassed and battered speckled student was Nancy Adams. Nancy lived with her grandmother. Wendall wasn't certain what happened to her parents. Like Clifford, Nancy stayed to herself. She was petite and pretty with blue eyes, shoulder-length blond hair, and a timid pearly-white smile. She never bothered anybody, and she was always polite. And she did her best to ignore the put-downs, catcalls, and insults. In the days before caller ID, her grandmother had complained repeatedly to the school and to the police about the late-night, obscene phone calls to the house.

"This number was on the bathroom wall. I'm looking for a good time."

"Is Nancy, 'the sex addict,' home?"

"Is the little blonde available tonight? I pay good money."

The local sheriff was powerless and therefore uninterested. The phone company couldn't put a trace on her grandmother's phone without a court order. They suggested Nancy's grandmother change to an unlisted number and unplug her phone after 7:00 p.m., which she did.

For his part, Mr. Green made it a point to speak to every class and warn "whoever is doing this" to stop.

Wendall thought, *Or what?*

To their credit, Clifford and Nancy diligently followed their Christian upbringing and the old saying, "Sticks and stones may break my bones, but words will never hurt me." This philosophy kept old man Smithson blissfully ignorant of his son's suffering. Sticks and stones also kept Clifford and Nancy out of the principal's office and in class. But as much as they tried to ignore all the insults, the humiliation was painfully clear on their faces. No doubt about it, "sticks and stones" is just a Pollyanna nursery rhyme. *Words can and do hurt people*, especially decent young people trying to find acceptance in this world. Words can cause despair, anxiety, depression, and even suicide.

The four pecking students at Clearwell were birds of a feather. They weren't farm kids, and none of them had ever held a job. Therefore, they couldn't imagine working fourteen-hour days combining wheat in the heat of summer or moving hay to feed cattle in the dead of winter. But they didn't need to earn money. Their bell-bottom blue jeans, ostrich skin cowboy boots, and new pickups were all courtesy of Mommy and Daddy. The spoiled brats labored at watching TV, grooming themselves, hot-rodding around town, and securing their status within their little group.

Wendall noticed three very predictable pecking behaviors. First, the bullies rarely harassed, or even approached, a speckled student, unless they ganged up with at least one of their comrades. Second, the bullies required constant reassurance from their pecking group that they were tougher, smarter, cooler, and in general, superior, to everyone else. Third, the bullies obsessively monitored their own status within their little gang, because occasionally, there just weren't enough speckled students available to peck and harass. Pecking cliques would then become cannibalistic. They would shun, then bully, one of their own, which only reinforced the insecurity within their group.

All the bullying at school was starting to irritate Wendall. But he couldn't afford another expulsion and three more days of zeros on his class assignments and tests. Besides, Wendall had learned from the rickety chicken coop that kicking the tar out of the four little peckers didn't protect the little speckled chick after he left the barn. He would have to find a Vaseline-type solution. He needed some experienced advice. Granny Nichols knew chickens; maybe she knew people as well.

Ruby Nichols had experienced a lifetime of struggles and problem-solving in her fifty-five years. She grew up during the Great Depression of the 1930s, and like Clyde, she shared a no-nonsense approach to people. She listened silently as Wendall described the pecking students and their bullying. Her usually cheerful demeanor darkened. "Why don't you *chew them out* the next time they pull any of that nonsense?"

Her scolding response caught Wendall flat-footed. "Uh, well, they haven't bothered me. I mean…I wanna help, but it's really none of my business."

"What do you mean it's none of your business?"

Wendall stammered, "Uh…"

"It's your school, isn't it? Well, isn't it?"

"Oh yeah, absolutely."

"And it bothers you too. Doesn't it?"

"Uh, yeah, that's why I'm asking you about it."

"Good! It should bother you a lot. They're your classmates. This Clifford and…the girl …her name was?"

Wendall quickly recovered. "Nancy. Yes, they're my classmates, and like I said, they're good people."

"Then their problems are *your* problems. You've got to look out for your friends. Help the people around you."

Like a gentle hammer tap on his head, Wendall immediately understood what was so special about her generation. They looked out for other people, not just their family, but also their neighbors and even strangers. Unlike Wendall's spoiled "Me Generation" and its "don't get involved" philosophy, which bordered on cowardice.

Wendall suddenly felt ashamed. "You're right, Grandma. What's the best way to handle these jerks, short of kicking their butts?"

Grandma Nichols chuckled. "That's sometimes the best place to start. But I know what you mean."

She was aware of Wendall's previous scrape with the Clearwell school administration.

"Shame them. They don't have the right to bully anyone, and they disgrace themselves when they do."

Ruby smiled and added, "My daddy put it another way. 'They're just showin' their own asses.'"

Her colorful analogy made Wendall laugh. He imagined the pecking students proudly bending over and pulling their pants down around their knees.

"Don't let them get away with it. You go after them. And get your friends to join you and put 'em in their place."

"Yes, ma'am."

His grandmother's advice was exactly what he had previously heard from his dad and Gerald: confront and shame the bullies with, "What's wrong with you? Leave him alone. Pick on somebody your own size."

But one thing puzzled Wendall. "Grandma, why do bullies pick on people?"

"Because it makes them feel superior. But they're not. Their shit stinks just the same as everybody else's."

Wendall had to laugh again. His grandma had a knack for humbling pretentious, high-and-mighty characters.

Ruby explained, "Bullies look for kids who don't want to get in trouble, which means they won't fight back. It's little wonder why some kids drop out of school. So you've got to stand up for them. Teach 'em to stand up for themselves."

The rest of the day, his grandmother's advice kept playing in Wendall's mind. "Teach 'em to stand up for themselves." But how? He remembered Mrs. Brown. Her PaPa had instilled self-respect by telling her, at *every opportunity*, that she was important and deserving of respect from everyone. But Wendall would be working with two teenagers who were practically strangers. He couldn't be their grandfather, but he could be their friend. Somehow, he had to teach Clifford and Nancy to respect themselves "no matter what other people may say or do."

Slick 'n' Greasy had the same philosophy about self-respect but with a sharper edge.

"Don't give a damn what other people think!"

Wendall could hear Slick's voice in his mind. It made him smile. Slick was *the last* person who could *ever* be bullied. Why? Because he didn't care, *at all,* what other people called him or said about him or thought of him. Slick knew exactly who he was, and he didn't accept any degradation, a.k.a. "shit," from anyone. Wendall decided to consult the *master of indifference* for his advice on bullying. He hitched a ride to Benson with his mom on her trip to the grocery store, and she dropped him off at Slick's garage.

"Slick, I don't wanna slow you down…"

"No chance of that." He continued removing a water pump from a Ford pickup.

"Thanks. I just wanted to know. What's the best way to handle a group of bullies?"

Slick looked up. "Are some dumb-asses givin' ya trouble?"

"No. Not me. Some kids in my high school are being bullied, and I'm wondering how I can help them."

Slick turned around with a socket wrench in his hand. "Bullies are like *three-year-old liars*. Everything that comes out of their mouths is *baby shit*. You dress 'em down. Remind 'em of how stupid and worthless their opinions are. Make sure they know you don't give a damn what they think."

Wendall smiled and nodded. "Yes, sir. Three-year-old liars you say?"

Slick laughed. "And that's bein' generous."

Wendall felt inspired the following Monday morning. Clifford Smithson and Nancy Adams didn't know it yet, but they had a new best friend. The pecking students didn't know it yet, but they had a new worst enemy.

The bell rang signaling the end of the first hour of classes. The students poured into the perpendicular east and north hallways. Shortly thereafter, the pecking began. Wendall weaved his way toward the noise in the north hallway.

"Baa, baa. Hey, Smithson! It's your girlfriend."

"How's your momma? I hear she has a big mouth."

The bullies paused when they saw Wendall approaching.

Wendall instinctively made a fist with his right hand. "Why don't you pick on somebody who will fight back?" The bustling hallways came to a sudden, silent stop. "You wanna mess with someone? Then mess with me!" Wendall's invitation to a fight could be heard loud and clear all the way to the principal's office.

Jason glanced nervously at Wendall's fist. "We're just havin' a little fun, uh, no big deal."

Rodney hurried a forced whisper, "Green's comin'. Mr. Green's comin'."

Mr. Green came jostling through the crowded hall in his familiar panic. "What's going on here? Let me through. Let me through."

On arrival, Green was panting hard. "Nichols, I would've thought you learned your lesson."

Wendall shot right back. "I would've thought you learned *your* lesson and cleaned up this bullying. It needs to end." He motioned down the hallway. "These people don't want to hear this bullshit. And what about Clifford?"

Raymond interrupted with his innocent, little girl imitation, "Mr. Green, we were just joshin' and then *he* came over and tried to pick a fight."

Steve quickly added, "Yeah, he took a swing at me. Good thing I ducked."

That was more than enough for Mr. Green. "Nichols! To the office. You're expelled for the rest of the day."

"For what?"

Mr. Green nodded toward the bullies. "For trying to start another fight."

"Oh! So you believe these liars. Why don't you ask any of these other people?" Wendall motioned to the crowd of bystanders.

The bell cut him off. Students started scurrying to their second hour classes.

As Wendall followed Mr. Green to the office, he could hear the bullies whispering and laughing softly. No one answered the phone at home. Wendall's dad was at work in Benson and his mom was likely outside in the garden or hanging clothes on the clothesline. Wendall thought, *No problem, I can walk.*

Meanwhile, Clifford was in English class when he saw Wendall walking down Main Street toward his parents' farm eight miles away. Clifford leaned forward in his desk and began groaning while holding his stomach. "Mrs. Cell. I don't feel good. I think I need to throw up."

"You should go to the office if you're sick, Clifford."

Clifford gagged. "Thank you, Mrs. Cell."

Smithson hurried out of the room and then out the east side door of the school to his pickup. One minute later, Wendall was climbing into his passenger seat.

"Thanks, Clifford, for picking me up. How'd you get out of class?"

Smithson smiled. It was the first time Wendall had ever seen him smile. "Please. Call me Cliff. I faked bein' sick."

"Good for you! And for me."

Over the next fifteen minutes, Cliff explained that he wasn't afraid of the bullies or Mr. Green or of getting in trouble at school. But he was afraid of getting in trouble at home. His father was against all forms of violence. "Turn the other cheek" and "God will judge them for their deeds" were his mottos.

Wendall had a different opinion. "Why not judge 'em now? Don't wait for God. Punish them and have everyone at school help us do it like one big supportive family."

Since Cliff came from a large family, he was beginning to like the idea. "You know, I hauled hay this summer with Darrel Martin and Billy Rotan. They're like brothers to me."

"That's good. You know what? We need someone loud and mouthy, especially a girl. Nothin' irritates a jackass like being dressed down by a brassy girl."

Cliff blurted out, "Jennifer Higgins."

"Jennifer Higgins. Afraid I don't know her."

Cliff pulled to a stop in front of Wendall's house. "She's a senior. She's famous for screaming at Green two years ago when the toilets in the girls' bathroom wouldn't flush for about a month. She almost got kicked out like you. Well…except you actually *did* get kicked out."

"Can't wait to call her. Talk to you tomorrow."

Of course, Wendall's mom wasn't happy about him being expelled, again, even though it was only for one day. Max Nichols didn't mind after Wendall told him that his grandma had given him advice. Max knew Wendall was fighting the good fight.

Wendall learned that experience can be a cruel, but effective, instructor. He spent the rest of the day analyzing the mistakes he had made that morning. *First,* he had attempted to take on the bullies all by himself. *Second,* he underestimated them. They lied and played the role of victims. He should have remembered what Slick said. "They're three-year-old liars." *Third,* and worst of all, Wendall had placed far too much faith in that coward, Mr. Green, who obviously *cared more about his peace and quiet than he did about Cliff's humiliation and harassment.*

But you can't change the past. You can only learn from it. Right now, it was time to gather a family together. Wendall called Jennifer Higgins.

"Hello, Jennifer. My name is Wendall Nichols. I go to Clearwell and—"

She cut him off. "I know who you are. You're the guy who punched out Rance and got him kicked out. Glad someone finally did."

"Oh, uh…thanks. That's why I'm calling you."

"He's coming back?"

"No. Uh, not that I've heard. I'm calling about his toadies: Jason, Rodney, Raymond, and Steve."

She replied with sympathy, "Yeah, I heard you got kicked out today. I don't know why Clifford doesn't just kick their butts. He could do it. I once saw him wrestle down a five-hundred-pound steer."

"Well, his dad won't let him."

"So what do you need from me?"

Wendall immediately liked her frankness. "I'm forming a group. Call it a 'family' of students to stand up against these little peckers."

Jennifer started laughing. "Did you say little peckers?"

"Yeah. You know, like little chickens pecking on each other."

Jennifer was still laughing. "I just thought of uh…something else."

"Yeah. I know. They're just a bunch of bullies."

Jennifer regained her composure. "Well, count me in. I don't mind making Green do his job, again."

After calling Cliff, the first "family" meeting was scheduled for the next morning before school.

Wendall considered the tape recorder to be the greatest invention of the twentieth century. Tape recorders don't lie. They are the perfect *audio* witness. His recorder saved him from Mona Lisa. No wonder Wendall always became upset whenever Damon damaged one of his recorders. Fortunately, Wendall had recently purchased a new pocket-size recorder. He could only dream of today's smart phones with video capability.

The next day was a perfect spring morning with a clear sky, bright sun, and a pleasantly cool breeze. Wendall stepped off the bus, but instead of following the crowd through the main entrance, he turned to the right and followed the sidewalk along the front of the building. Clearwell school was a single-story building shaped like an *L* with two hallways, the north and the east, with outside doors at the ends of both halls. The gymnasium, office, elementary classrooms, and library were attached to the west side of the north hallway. The building's exterior was made of cinder block plastered with cracked and peeling white stucco. The flat roof explained the water leaks onto the black concrete hallways when it rained.

Wendall met the others just outside the east hallway door. After Cliff introduced Darrel and Billy, Wendall presented his plan of action.

"Cliff, set yourself up in front of the four jerks right after first hour in the north hallway. I'll be at my locker around the corner in the east hall and out of sight. Talk back to them in a loud voice and tell them to stop using foul language. Remind them that there are young ladies present, and oh yeah, tell them to leave Nancy alone too. Get them to say something about Nancy."

Cliff was puzzled. "You want me to provoke them?"

"Yeah, by not backing down. And scold them." Wendall repeated it for emphasis, "Scold them. They won't expect it, and then they'll pour on the abuse. Meanwhile," Wendall held up his tape recorder, "I'll get it all on tape."

Jennifer laughed. "Yes!"

Darrel and Billy smiled.

Wendall continued, "After they make some comments about Nancy. Then you guys," he motioned to Darrel, Billy, and Jennifer, "jump in and start shaming them too. But...*make no threats or use any profanity*. Remember, you'll be on tape. Just imagine that your mothers are standing right next to you."

Cliff asked, "What if Mr. Green shows up?"

"That's exactly what we want! Shame *him* for not putting an end to this *repeated* abuse. Remember, 'repeated abuse.'"

Everyone nodded as the first bell rang.

Wendall was in a world of his own during first hour history class that morning. He kept visualizing the north hallway scene that he would hear, but not see. Finally, the bell rang. It was show time.

"Hey, stupid! Yeah, you, Smithson!" Wendall recognized Raymond's voice. "We found out why you're such an idiot. Your retarded father married an imbecile!"

Then, "Where's your, buddy? Nichols. Too scared to face us?"

Cliff shot back with volume, "Wendall Nichols is not afraid of you."

Steve mocked him. "Oh my! String bean is getting some attitude. Careful, Smithy boy, or we'll have you expelled just like Nichols."

Rodney added his high-pitched threat, "Yeah! We'll all tell Green you took a swing at us."

Jason chimed in, "A phantom swing." They all laughed.

Cliff's voice stiffened. "You guys lied to Mr. Green. You're not being good Christians."

"Hell yes we lied to dumb-ass Green! So wadda ya gonna do about it?" Jason retorted.

"Maybe we should just kick the shit out of your Christian ass," added Raymond.

Cliff followed his orders. "Stop using foul language in front of all these young ladies."

Jason sneered. "Well, *sir*, you are sadly mistaken. These are *not* young ladies." He swept his extended arm toward the hallway. "They're all little sluts."

Cliff was now shouting, "They are *not*! And, you better stop harassing Nancy too. She's a nice girl."

Rodney immediately started chanting, "Smithy's got a girl-friend, Smithy's got a girlfriend."

Raymond was sarcastically indignant. "What! You don't appreciate our restroom artwork?"

A chorus of "good one," "oh yeahs," and high fives followed.

Their revelry was shattered by a booming, "Who called me a little *slut?*"

Like an exploding grenade, Jennifer's blast silenced both hall-ways and made Wendall jump. *That* should get Green's attention.

Immediately, Darrel and Billy jumped in together, "Why don't you..." and "Stop bullying my friend..." overlapping each other and Jennifer's barrage of, "I'm sick of your..."

This verbal firestorm triggered a human siren blaring from Green's office. "Nichols! Nichols! I warned you! Nichols! Nichols! I warned you!"

Wendall looked at the faces of the students near his hallway locker with a practiced expression of surprise and innocence. Then he released a smile and purposely dropped his pencil on the floor. Green burst from his office and stood at the intersection of the north and east hallways desperately searching the crowd, in vain, for Wendall who was bent down picking up his pencil. Mr. Green then pushed his way into the north hall.

"Nichols! Nichols! Where's Nichols?"

Wendall stood up with his pencil, raised it high above his head, and softly replied, "Hello. I'm here."

But Mr. Green never heard Wendall. The shouting from the north hall only intensified. Jennifer, Cliff, Darrell, and Billy easily drowned out the ambushed bullies. When Green finally arrived, the only clear statement that Wendall heard from the morass was Jennifer's loud and hateful, "The filth coming out of their mouths is like a toilet that won't flush."

It was an obvious reference to her previous scrape with Green. Wendall had started working his way toward the mayhem, but he now had to duck back around the corner to the east hall to let out a belly laugh.

A bewildered Mr. Green finally regained his composure, raised both arms, and yelled, "Quiet! Everybody just calm down!"

Both sides fell silent. Then the bell rang. The rest of the students froze. Should they go to class or stay still? No doubt, they wanted to see what would happen next. However, they were to be disappointed.

"Well, maybe you boys should knock off the jokes and the kidding around. Now, uh, everyone go on to class."

Call it a draw. But the bullies had been put on notice. A new family of four had arrived, and everyone would soon learn it included a fifth member, Wendall. The pecking died down to whispers, mutterings, and dirty looks. But the "family" was careful to stay vigilant just in case the bullies had any stomach for a rematch.

Wendall wanted to expand the family to include *all* the students. But he ran into a brick wall. Because Green refused to punish the pecking quartet, the student bystanders "didn't want to get involved" or "get in trouble." Besides, "you guys put them in their place already." The other students also knew something that Wendall did not. Raymond's and Jason's fathers were on the five-member school board; therefore, the abusive cowards believed that they were untouchable. And so far, they were right.

Wendall understood that people are social animals who crave the acceptance and security of a group. Our natural instinct to bond together explains the formation of cliques, "little pecking" groups, gangs, clubs, posses, fraternities, civic organizations, political parties, religions, and even nations. Each group develops a purpose with beliefs and ethics that bind their members together and distinguish them from the outside world. Wendall's "family" had a purpose: to eliminate bullying at Clearwell based on the firm belief that all students deserve respect. He just needed to *publicize it* to recruit new members. But how? Hmm? If this was going to be a campaign, why not use campaign stickers? The local Republican and Democratic parties used Morton Printing in Benson for their campaign materials. Morton could print two-color, four-inch diameter, peel-off stickers in one-hundred count rolls for ten dollars. What a deal!

The *family* met to decide the campaign sticker layout. They picked black lettering on a bright yellow background because it would stand out from a distance. But what about the campaign slogan? After much open discussion with suggestions ranging from, "Jason, Raymond, Steve, and Rodney SUCK!" to "Don't be a Little Pecker" and "Love Everyone," they agreed on the following:

- *Don't Be a Pecking Bird Brain.*
- *Respect Everyone.*

Jennifer insisted that they add a cute "little chick" logo from Morton's catalogue between the two lines. Wendall ordered five hundred stickers. Their neon-yellow background and cryptic black-letter message were irresistible. The stickers immediately became the talk of the school. "What's a pecking bird brain?" was the question of the week.

"It's a mean, little chicken-person who pecks on nice people like yourself. You know, a bully."

The most common response from the student body was, "Why didn't you say, 'Don't be a f—bird brain' instead?"

Free stickers began adorning notebooks, backpacks, shirts, and lockers. As expected, none of the bullies wanted any of the new fashion. When Mr. Green noticed all the bright yellow stickers, his only confused comments were, "But the school colors are red and black, not yellow and black. And our mascot is the Prairie Hawk."

Bullying was finally shut down. Comments of "stop pecking at me" and "show some respect" echoed the halls as students stood up for themselves and for others. But Wendall was not completely satisfied. He had not forgotten, nor forgiven, the little peckers. He knew there was often a blurry line between revenge and justice. The bullies and Mr. Green had not yet paid for their sins. And unlike Cliff, Wendall did *not* want to leave all the punishment to God. He had saved the tape recording of the "family encounter" in the north hall, and he decided to use it on a Monday night.

Clearwell school board meetings in the fall and winter were sparsely attended by the public. Why? Because they were always held on Monday nights during *Monday Night Football* with Howard Cosell. Wendall revealed his plan to his parents, and his dad proudly agreed to forgo the football game and drive Wendall to the meeting.

When they arrived at the school, Wendall was shocked to see that the parking lot was nearly full. What's going on? Was this a *special* school board meeting? Had word leaked out about the tape? Wendall later learned that the meeting was packed because of Cliff's mom. She was the biggest gossip in town. When Cliff told her that it was "really important" to be at the monthly board meeting, the suspense was too much for her. And we all know how suspense generates gossip.

Mr. Green and the entire board were surprised, and slightly alarmed, at the "great turnout." One of the board members commented, "We're not even discussing the budget or a bond issue tonight." The mundane meeting plodded along. Finally, near the end, the required question of "any new business" was asked, although typically, none was ever expected. Most of the crowd was half-asleep when Wendall shouted out, "Just one item of new business, ladies and gentlemen."

He stood up, raised his pocket recorder high in the air, pressed the play button, and broadcasted profane mortification.

Gasps and open-mouthed looks filled the room after every obscenity. As soon as Wendall clicked the stop button and declared, "That's it," bedlam erupted.

Green was shouting and pointing at Wendall's recorder. "That's illegal! That's illegal! You can't do that!"

Cliff's dad was yelling, "Those sinners," while pointing at Mr. Green.

Everyone was clamoring to know just what the heck was going on in the hallways of the school.

Meanwhile, Mr. Green was panting and waving his arms. "This should have been brought to my attention. I had no idea. Someone should have told me!"

Max Nichols was laughing to the verge of tears.

The president of the board was pounding his gavel but to no avail.

The Mennonites all sat stone-faced, looking back and forth at each other with a silent telepathy, which scared the board members more than anything else. School board elections were less than two months away, and the Mennonites usually voted as a block.

When order was finally restored, the president of the board, Raymond's father, wanted to talk to "the Smithson boy." Cliff slowly stood up.

"Who were the other boys on the tape?"

Cliff politely replied, "The boys using all the foul language were Steve, your son, Jason," nodding to one of the board members, "Rodney, and your son, Raymond, sir."

Raymond's dad was so shocked the gavel dropped out of his hand as the room once again erupted.

After everyone stopped shouting for the second time, Mr. Green was asked to explain himself. In his expected, cowardly, and dishonest manner, he denied any knowledge of any bullying by anyone. Wendall noticed Green's secretary was sitting up front taking the minutes of the meeting. Her painted eyebrows raised each time he swore ignorance.

Wendall stood up and suggested the board ask the school secretary if *she* had ever heard any of this harassment. After all, her desk was less than six feet from the office door that was always propped open to the two hallways in the high school. The poor girl appeared very nervous. When asked directly, she hesitated, then stammered, "Before that day...that was on the recorder, I heard that language every day, almost every hour, between classes."

Wendall thought, *Finally. Someone admitted the truth.*

Clearwell could not have been more cleansed that evening if the town had been baptized in the River Jordan. Green was shunned (fired). Raymond and Jason entered a private Christian school in Benson, the equivalent of a nunnery for boys, and "Pecking Bird Brain" stickers remained a fashion accessory into the next school year.

The following summer, Wendall had plenty of time to think about bullying while driving a tractor. He reached an upsetting conclusion. Bullying doesn't just happen. It is *allowed* to happen by the bystanders (classmates) and authority figures (teachers, principals, and school boards).

But why do they allow it?

Because their *fear* of getting involved is *greater than* their *respect* for the dignity and peace of mind of the victim.

But why are they afraid?

Teachers, principals, and school boards are afraid of the bully's parents, potential lawsuits, and "bad" statistics when they must report disciplinary actions to the state. Victims and spectator students are afraid of the school's dreaded "zero tolerance" policy toward all violence. Under "zero tolerance," *everyone* gets punished, the bully and the victim, if they dare to fight back. Even more damaging, any students who stand up for the victims (i.e., Wendall types) are punished as well.

"Zero Tolerance" doesn't mean zero bullying. It means zero justice. Don't try to sort out guilt or innocence. Just punish everyone involved. Zero tolerance guarantees that the victims will remain conveniently silent. It's equivalent to prosecuting a mugger *and* the little old lady victim because she hit him with her cane. It's no wonder that students "don't get involved" and don't report bullying abuse.

The end result is predictable. Everyone (students, teachers, principals, and school boards) *all* turn an uncomfortable blind eye to the criminal abuse. And yes, *bullying is often one of several crimes:*

*Assault: intentionally threatening to hurt someone:*
- "I'm going to [kick your ass, teach you a lesson, beat the shit out of you, etc.]."
- Daring someone to fight.
- Throwing something at someone, even if you miss.
- Waving a fist or taking a swing at someone, even if you miss.
- Threatening someone with a weapon, a.k.a. aggravated assault or assault with a deadly weapon.

*Battery: physically harming someone on purpose and not by accident:*
- Slapping, shoving, pulling, punching, kicking, or tripping someone.
- Stabbing, clubbing, or shooting someone.
- Throwing an object at someone and striking them.

*Harassment: intentionally tormenting or terrorizing someone.*
- Calling, texting, emailing, or writing notes or messages that threaten or deride someone.
- Vandalizing or threatening to vandalize someone's property: car, house, locker, backpack, etc.
- Injuring, killing, or threatening to injure or kill someone's pet or livestock.

*Defamation:*
- Writing or posting untrue statements (libel) or saying something untrue (slander) *as if it were fact.*
- Simply stating a crazy, untrue *opinion* about someone is not a crime.

- But if it's put out there *as a fact*, then it's a lie meant to damage someone.

Years later, Wendall realized that as bad as it was, and as much as they suffered, Clifford and Nancy had it easy by today's standards. In the twenty-first century, pecking students use texting, e-mail, Facebook, Twitter, and Instagram to commit *harassment* and *defamation*. (Note: Battery and assault are "in person" crimes.) Bullies can be cowards in so many more mediums with modern technology. But technology is a double-edged sword that can be used to document and expose bullying crimes. For instance, what could a present-day Cliff Smithson do against a pack of pecking students? Plenty:

*First, keep a record* of the bullies' abuses. Never delete any texts, tweets, e-mails, or other cyberbullying *and* record all in-person attacks (cell phone video is best). Better yet, have other people record the bullying on their phones. Hard evidence always helps when exposing three-year-old liars to reluctant, cowardly authorities like Mr. Green.

*Second, recruit a family*, the bigger, the better. Talk, call, text, tweet, and write to *everyone* (parents, friends, siblings, teachers, bosses, attorneys, and the media if necessary) about the shameful bullies. Scream and yell, jump up and down, and ask directly for help. Exposing bullying is *not* childish "tattling" or a sign of weakness. It is standing up for yourself against abuse.

*Third, shame the bullies* (Grandma Nichols's advice) while treating them like three-year-old liars (Slick's advice). Shaming could be the first step, but as Wendall learned, it's best to recruit a family first.

- "What's *wrong* with you?"
- "You're just showin' your own ass."
- "Why don't you pick on somebody your own size?"
- "Quit pecking at me/him/her."
- "Stop harassing me/him/her!"

*Fourth, get some practice.* Keep your eyes open for bullying and defend anyone being harassed. Jump in with an attitude of respect and protection and rally any silent bystanders. "Help out here! Stand up for your classmate/coworker/friend/stranger. Otherwise, you'll be next."

Finally, *be grateful* for the bullies. *What!* Yes, you read it right. Be grateful. They are the fire that changes soft clay into hard brick. Bullies can challenge you to respect yourself and everyone around you. Best of all, by defending others, their victims become your friends. Never forget Mrs. Brown's advice. "If you're not grateful for *everything*, you're never gonna be completely happy." Choose to be happy.

PS. Some *anti-bully campaign slogans from the twentieth century:*
- Satan hates God. Bullies hate *me.* (Clifford, inspired by a church service)
- Little peckers are bird brains. (Jennifer)
- Don't peck on me. (Clearwell High favorite)
- Ask me if I care what you think. (Slick)
- Don't be a three-year-old liar. (Slick)
- Self-respect gives you courage. (Mrs. Brown)
- Bullies are just showin' their own asses. (Grandma Nichols)

*Twenty-first century originals* from Wendall's teenage daughter, Wendy:
- Don't believe *everything* online, just the *nice* lies!
- Hated online by pecking idiots.
- The weak, the cowardly, the cyberbullies.
- Cyberbully: No morals, no life, no kidding.
- Lies! Lies! the price of my *celebrity.*
- Celebrity. Online it's all about *me*!

# 14

# The Con

I can't *believe* you're gonna miss out. Do you wanna
have to work hard the rest of your life?"
—Carl Nichols

"Max, I'm tellin' ya. This is the chance of a lifetime, and...I don't wanna leave ya behind."

Wendall's dad frowned and shook his head. "But, Carl, I'm already borrowed to the hilt on this farm. I don't have any extra cash to invest in a new business."

Carl Nichols was Max Nichols's first cousin. Born only six months apart, they grew up together in Benson. Like Max, Carl didn't go to college after high school. Instead, he worked odd jobs in construction and at the Johnson grain elevator. Then ten years ago, he finally found steady work with Peerless Foods, a food wholesaler for restaurants. Peerless had been a successful family-owned business in Benson for over fifty years. Carl paid attention, stayed out of trouble, and did just enough work to keep from being fired. As a delivery driver, he became friends with all the restaurant customers. Carl dreamed of being his own boss and becoming a millionaire before he was forty. He was ambitious and charismatic, but Carl lacked everything else required to build a successful business, namely, a work ethic, self-discipline, frugality, and honesty.

"I'm tellin' ya, Max. I've already got all the customers lined up."

"What customers?"

"Restaurants and drive-ins around town. You know, Dairy Freeze, Fletchers, Pack-A-Sack, Sandy's."

"But aren't those Peerless customers?"

"Well, right now they are. But not for long. See, I found out how much old man Peerless is charging them. All I have to do is undercut him a little. I mean, it's a dog-eat-dog world out there, and I plan to be the biggest and meanest dog."

Max grimaced as he thought about it. "But what if Peerless cuts his prices, and you end up in a bidding war?"

"Uh...that's exactly what I want! I can even sell below cost for a while if I have to. Old man Peerless doesn't have the stomach for business anymore. He's made his money." Carl grinned. "Besides, he's turned everything over to his kid, Roger, who's a stupid moron. Yes, sir, it'll be like takin' candy from a baby."

"Who do you have as investors already?"

Carl cleared his throat. "I haven't let anybody else have a piece of this action yet. I wanted to give you the first shot. We may not even *want* to let anybody else in on this gravy train. If we can go fifty-fifty, that would be incredible."

"How much do you need for half interest?"

"Only two hundred thousand."

Max and Wendall both gasped. Max blurted out, "Two hundred thousand dollars? That's more than twice what this farm cost me."

"But you're not thinking right. This business will make you ten times more money than your farm ever will. After five years of *this* business, you can pay cash for this farm and then buy a second one, guaranteed."

"I just don't have any free cash, and I can't borrow any more money."

"Why not sell the farm? That would free up all your cash and your time too."

Max was becoming frustrated. "But I *want* to live on a farm. Besides, I'd lose money if I sold it now. Auctioneers charge a 10 percent commission."

Carl's eyes widened. "I know! Borrow money on your tractor and equipment."

Wendall, who up to this point had been quietly and intently listening to Carl's desperate sales pitch, burst out laughing.

Carl looked around. "What? What did I say?"

Max grinned. "You haven't seen our tractor and equipment."

Wendall added, "They are so old they belong in a museum."

Undeterred, Carl continued brainstorming, "What about borrowing on next year's crop. You've got wheat growin' out there in the fields right now."

Max shook his head. "The crop is collateral for the land payment due next July."

Carl shook his head with pity. "I can't *believe* you're gonna miss out. Do you want to have to work hard the rest of your life?"

"Well...yeah. I was planning on working hard and enjoying it too."

"Absolutely! And you can...in *this business*. Then imagine in two years you're driving one those monster four-wheel-drive tractors with an air-conditioned cab and stereo. Wouldn't you enjoy farming a lot more?"

Wendall interjected, "Roscoe's Versatile tractor has a TV and a little refrigerator too."

Carl pointed at Wendall. "Right! Like I'm telling you, Max. The good life is out there. You just gotta have a little faith and go for it. The sky's the limit too. Once we take over Benson, then there's Topeka, Wichita, Kansas City, and St. Louis. Then we'll go national in five years."

Max scratched his head. "I don't know. It just sounds too good to be true."

"You're right! It *is* too good. Too good to pass up."

"Carl, I don't even have any money to help Wendall start college later this year. He's gonna have to pay for it himself."

"Who needs college? That's just a place to party, get in trouble, and go broke. Besides, you don't need a college degree to be a success."

Carl turned to Wendall. "I'm sure you could have lots of fun wasting your money in college, but trust me. In four years, instead of having a piece of paper with a gold seal on it, you could be driving a new Corvette and having parties in your own mansion."

Wendall played along. "Really?"

"Oh sure! Old man Peerless lives in a mansion. Who do you think bought that for him?"

"His wife?"

"*No*! No, *I* bought that mansion for him. I made all that money for that old fart while he laid around at home. You see, the trick in business is to be in management. Let the workers make *you* all the money."

Wendall pretended to be surprised. "You've got workers already?"

"Not yet. But I'm hiring. You got a job for this summer?"

Wendall began to feel uncomfortable. "Uh, well…I'm gonna help my dad with the farming."

Carl now completely switched his sites to Wendall. "Sure, no problem. You could work evenings or weekends, and get this: Diamond Delivery pays $2.60 an hour. How about that?"

"What's Diamond Delivery?"

Carl was taken aback. "My new company of course!"

Wendall bit his tongue to keep from grinning. "Oh, yeah…uh, right. Well, the pay sounds good. I only made $2.50 an hour when I worked for Clyde. But I've already saved enough to get a car and pay for my first year of college."

The mention of money piqued Carl's interest. "Great! How much do you have?"

"A little more than $4,000."

"Well, there you go! Instead of wasting your money on a car and college, you can buy a chunk of Diamond Delivery and be a business owner."

Wendall glanced over at his dad who gave him the slightest quivering shake of his head. "How much of the business would I own?"

"Let's see, uh…half the company is worth $200,000, so $4,000 would get you…uh…"

Wendall was more than a little concerned that Carl couldn't calculate the "chunk of business" in his head. Wendall decided to rescue him. "So the entire business is worth $400,000, and I would own $4,000 of it or 1 percent."

"Right!"

"But 1 percent doesn't sound like very much, and I—"

Carl cut him off, "But you're not thinking right. One percent of a billion dollars is uh...a lot."

"Thanks. But I think I'll hold off for now."

"But wait, wait. You're in the perfect spot. You're young and single and...no girlfriend or car payments to drain off your money."

Wendall thought, *Hold on a minute. A girlfriend and a car were* exactly *why I slaved away for the past three summers in the dusty wheat fields.*

"No thanks, Carl."

Carl regrouped. "It's only natural. You're thinking short term. But you gotta think *long* term, into the future, about five to six years. You can invest in a business, today, that's just exploding with opportunity and become a millionaire before you're twenty-five. I mean, this is a slam dunk, a homerun."

Wendall rubbed his chin. "Tell you what. Let me think about it, and in the meantime, if you need some help once you're up and running, then $2.60 an hour would be okay, but only on weekends."

Carl looked down with disappointment. "Okay. But I can tell you right now. Other people are gonna jump at this opportunity. Business friends of mine are already asking me to let 'em get in on the ground floor."

Max finally broke his silence. "Carl, have you thought about taking out a loan from a bank? Wouldn't that be a lot cheaper in the long run rather than selling a portion of the business now?"

Carl sniffed. "Of course I could. First National is begging me to borrow money from them. Heck, when I opened the Diamond Delivery checking account, the branch manager fell all over himself wanting my business. But let me tell you. Banks are not your friend. They just want their cut. I don't need any bloodsucking bankers. I wanna help my family and friends live the rich life."

For nearly five seconds, Wendall imagined being twenty-five and filthy rich. What if Carl was right? He did know the business, and Mr. Peerless was one of the wealthiest men in Benson. Wendall finally relented. "I would be glad to work for you, but I'm not sure about investing all my money."

"Sure, sure. You got four thousand. You should at least stick your toe in the water with a thousand while you still can."

Wendall looked over at his dad who shrugged his shoulders.

"Okay. I guess I can spare a thousand dollars."

Carl flashed a satisfied smile. "Best decision you ever made, so far anyway. Even better when you eventually invest *all* your money. You know what they always say. In life, you only regret the opportunities you let slip away."

Wendall felt a slight resentment at Carl's insinuation that he and his dad were too stupid or naive to go whole hog for this "obvious" millionaire-maker, once-in-a-lifetime "gift." He was relieved when Carl finally stopped talking, which wasn't until after Wendall handed him a check for the thousand dollars. As Carl's Cadillac made its way down the farm's long bumpy driveway, Wendall had a sinking feeling that he would never see his money again.

Two weeks later and to his complete surprise, Wendall got a call from Carl. The business was "up and running," and he needed Wendall to make a delivery that Saturday afternoon in Diamond Delivery's new refrigerated truck.

Although Wendall had driven large machinery on the farm, including combines and wheat trucks, he had never driven a semi-tractor trailer.

"Carl, how big is your truck?"

"Oh, it's big. Definitely big enough."

"Is it an eighteen-wheeler?"

"Uh, no. But it's a big truck."

"Maybe I should come take a look at it this morning and make sure I can, you know, drive it and get used to it."

"Sure thing, Wendall. It's impressive. Better than anything I ever drove for Peerless."

"Where is it right now?"

"At Diamond Delivery warehouse number 1. That's 2310 North Van Buren, just south of the railroad tracks."

Wendall borrowed his dad's pickup and drove to Benson. "Warehouse number 1" was formerly a small mom-and-pop grocery store that went out of business twenty years before. Wendall met Diamond Delivery's first employee, Ruth, inside the dusty wood-plank store. A two-bladed fan extending down from the original tin plate ceiling was the only air-conditioning.

"You must be Wendall. Carl said you'd be by. I'm Ruth Darby."

Wendall extended a polite handshake. "Nice to meet you, Ruth. I'm here to check out the truck."

"It's parked around back. Carl didn't want it leaking oil all over the front parking lot."

"It leaks oil?"

"Yeah. And I think it's out of gas too 'cause Carl couldn't get it started after he parked it."

Wendall glanced around the rectangular, single-room store. Ruth's "office" consisted of a wood desk with peeling black paint, a rolling office chair with a green vinyl seat, a four-drawer filing cabinet with ARMY SURPLUS stenciled on the side, a spiral ledger book, and a black rotary dial phone.

"Ruth, where are the supplies? You know, the hamburger paddies, french fries, buns, that sort of stuff."

"Oh, toward the back. We have an old freezer."

They walked in the direction of a high-pitched, grating hum that reminded Wendall of a table saw cutting wood.

"Only one of the freezers still works. I have to rotate the meat every two hours since it won't all fit."

Wendall stared in disbelief at a grimy, stand-up freezer with hinging glass doors. It was packed with cardboard boxes of frozen meat and fries. The other two freezers were incubating roaches and mold. Stacked next to them were a dozen cardboard boxes labeled "hamburger paddies," with house flies crawling all over them.

"Ruth, what about overnight? Do you rotate the boxes then?"

She chuckled. "Are you kidding me? I'm not coming up here after hours."

"Yuk! Is this even safe? Aren't there like health codes or something that, you know, regulate food storage?"

Ruth shrugged. "I'm sure there are. That's why I demanded my pay in advance, two weeks' worth, so I wouldn't have to worry."

"Well, I'll go look at the truck. Do you have the key?"

"Keys are in it. Nobody can steal it 'cause it won't start."

The "big, new" delivery truck was certainly neither. The front grill screamed 1960s. It was an old Ford one-ton pickup with a homemade refrigerated compartment built on the bed. Both front tires were bald with the fiberglass belts peeking through. The tail pipe and the surrounding undercarriage were black with soot, indicating the truck burned oil in addition to leaking it. Wendall opened the back doors of the refrigerator box and climbed inside. A frayed electrical cord snaked its way across the floor to the refrigerator's compressor motor, which was rusted solid. In the midmorning June sun, the box felt like an oven. Before the heat drove him out, Wendall found a thermometer bolted to the wall, but it was smashed. Under the truck's hood, the faint smell of gasoline signaled a leaking or cracked gas line. The circular air filter was so full of dirt, it resembled a chocolate Bundt cake. The oil dipstick was dry, and a black oil slick had formed on the pavement under the engine.

"What a piece of junk," Wendall said to himself out loud. He walked back into the building to see Ruth. "That truck needs a lot of work."

"Oh no!"

"What?"

"Uh, we've got our first delivery this afternoon to Fletcher's Drive-in. They're our first customer. Actually, they're our *only* customer."

"What time this afternoon?"

"They said they needed everything before five. Saturday evening is one of their busiest times."

Wendall looked at his watch. It was already eleven o'clock. "I'm gonna need to buy a gas line, oil, and some gas to even get the truck started. And there's no refrigeration. Putting bags of ice in the back is the only way to keep anything cold. How much money do you keep here?"

"None. Carl handles all the money."

"Do you have a checkbook?"

"No."

"You better call him and see what he wants to do."

Carl's teenage daughter, Jessica, answered their phone at home. Carl and his wife, Clare, were in Kansas City on a "sales trip" and wouldn't be back for another three days.

Ruth was confused. "But, Jessica, I thought they drove to *Wichita.*

"They did."

"But how did they get to Kansas City?"

Wendall could overhear Jessica's irritated response. "They took an airplane of course. Daddy wanted to fly first class into Kansas City and then get picked up in a limo."

"So your dad drove two hours to Wichita when it's only thirty minutes from here to Kansas City?

"Duh! Of course. Like Daddy always says, 'If you wanna *be* successful, you gotta look the part.'"

Ruth called the hotel room that Jessica had reluctantly supplied. There was no answer. Ruth was desperate to reassure Wendall, "I'm sure he'll reimburse you whatever you have to spend on the truck."

Wendall had a bad feeling that she was probably wrong. After all, she demanded to be paid two weeks in advance. He decided, "I'll call my dad."

But Max was on the tractor in the middle of a field. Wendall's mom was certainly no fan of Carl's. Her advice, "Just leave it. It'll serve him right. He knew full well he was dumping that truck on you."

"I agree, Mom, but Dad might get upset if I leave." Wendall sighed. "I've got my checkbook. I'll buy what I need, and Carl will have to pay me back."

Susan was still disgusted. "I wouldn't count on that."

Wendall spent the next hour buying a rubber gas line, an air filter, six quarts of oil, and a gallon of gas. Fortunately, he had a gas can and the necessary tools in his dad's pickup to replace the gas line and air filter. After adding six quarts of oil and the gallon of gas, the moment of truth had arrived. The motor slowly cranked over and sounded like a moaning cow giving birth. It finally spit and sputtered then roared with black smoke pouring out of the tailpipe. Wendall had trouble getting the stick shift into reverse, but he finally forced it. Next, he drove to a nearby convenience store to fill up with gas and buy all their bagged ice.

Back at the warehouse, Ruth handed Wendall a clipboard.

"Here's Fletcher's order. Since they're the only customer, everything we have is for them."

Wendall began loading the boxes of meat, fries, and buns as Ruth checked off each one. After the last box of hot dog buns was loaded, Ruth looked worried.

"What's wrong, Ruth?"

"Uh, we're missing three boxes of hamburger buns."

"How?"

Ruth shook her head. "I don't know. I wasn't here when everything was delivered. We were charged for fifteen boxes of buns, but we only have twelve."

"How many buns are in a box?"

"Twenty-four."

"So we need seventy-two more hamburger buns to fill the order."

At the grocery checkout line, the cashier jokingly ribbed Wendall about his nine bags of Bond Bread hamburger buns with eight buns to a bag. "Looks like someone volunteered to bring buns to the family reunion cookout."

Wendall wasn't in a talkative mood. "Not exactly."

Fletcher's Drive-in was on the far south end of town. Wendall had eaten there many times in the past, but not lately. Like most people in town, he had noticed a distinct change for the worse after Mr. Fletcher's son, David, took over the business two years before. French fries now cost extra when you ordered a hamburger, and the Cokes were smaller, but not any cheaper.

Wendall's drive to Fletchers was nerve-racking. He knew the ice would melt quickly in the June heat. To keep the food boxes dry, he loaded them on weathered wood pallets left over from the old grocery store. Wendall knew that he must drive slowly and smoothly enough to keep the boxes from sliding off the pallets, yet fast enough to arrive before all the ice melted.

Finally, Wendall pulled up to Fletcher's back door. A small tidal wave of water poured from the back of the truck when he opened the doors to the "refrigerated" box. Thankfully, the food boxes were still on the pallets, dry and at least cool to the touch. Mission accomplished. David Fletcher carefully checked off each box and bag as Wendall unloaded them into Fletcher's freezer. When Wendall sat the last box down with a sigh of relief, David complained, "You're missing a box of hamburger paddies."

Wendall quickly glanced at Ruth's clipboard. "Are you sure? That's everything on my list."

"Of course I'm sure. You're seventy-two hamburger paddies short. The number of paddies has to equal the number of buns."

Fletcher smiled sarcastically. "We don't sell buns as a solo item."

Wendall stood there in an embarrassed rage. That stupid Carl! He had screwed up both the bun and the hamburger paddy order.

Wendall thought, *Where am I going to find seventy-two hamburger paddies in the next two hours?*

Peerless was the only other company in town selling premade quarter-pound paddies, and Wendall was certain they would laugh him out of their building. There was only one place he could buy hamburger, the same place he bought the buns.

Safeway's butcher was gracious enough to measure out seventy-two quarter-pound portions of ground chuck and press them into paddies. He layered them with wax paper and packed them in a plain cardboard box. After reloading the truck with fresh bags of ice, Wendall was off to Fletcher's again.

"Hmm?" Fletcher inspected the newly minted paddies. "These are better quality than the first ones you dropped off. I think I want this brand from now on. Let Carl know. Okay?"

Wendall was too upset to explain. "Sure thing."

During the trip back to "warehouse number 1," Wendall worried about two things. Would the truck run out of oil before he got there? And would he ever see his thousand dollars again? Forget the fact that he had just spent over ninety-five dollars of his own money to repair the truck and buy buns, hamburger paddies, and ice. Thank goodness this day was over, or so he thought. A flashing red light and a siren would add some additional misery and expense to his day. Wendall pulled over and glanced in his rearview mirror. A clearly agitated Benson police officer was approaching the truck.

"I'll need to see your license and registration, son."

Wendall had never been pulled over before, and therefore, he didn't know the routine.

"Yes, sir." He fumbled with his wallet before handing his license over.

"Did you know that your tag is expired? And," the officer peered at the driver's side windshield, "your safety inspection is over four years old?"

Oh no! Wendall had assumed that Carl got the truck tagged and inspected when he bought it. He stammered, "Uh, no. No, sir, I didn't. This is the first day I've driven this truck to deliver food. You see, I'm working for Diamond Delivery. Carl Nichols actually owns the truck."

"But you're the one driving it. So you get the ticket."

Wendall was stunned. "I…Uh."

"You say you deliver food with this truck? What's all that water dripping out of the back?"

"Uh…the refrigerator compressor doesn't work, so I loaded it up with bags of ice to keep the meat cold."

The officer frowned. "You got a thermometer in there to monitor the temperature?"

"Yeah. It's got a thermometer mounted on the wall."

He nodded. "Good."

"But it's broken. Somebody must have accidently smashed it."

The officer looked up at Wendall then shook his head. "Not good. That's a health code violation. If you can't monitor the temperature in a refrigerated truck, then you can't be sure the food is kept at a safe temperature. I'm gonna have to write you up for that too."

A minute later, the policeman handed both tickets to Wendall. "You'll have to appear in court next Tuesday to either pay the fine or serve your time as determined by the judge. Of course, you can bring an attorney if you think that'll help."

Wendall was numb. "Uh, sure...Why not."

The officer put his sunglasses back on. "One other thing I need to mention, you can't legally drive this truck until it's tagged and inspected. But I'm gonna cut you a break. Instead of having you towed, I'll give you an escort to where you're going, as long as it's here in town."

"Yeah. It is. Thanks."

Wendall led the flashing police car the remaining two miles to where all the trouble began. Meanwhile, Jessica had called back. Carl and Clare said they wouldn't be available until the next morning. They were attending a Kansas City Royals baseball game, and then later that evening, they would be hosting a reception at the hotel, both as "business expenses."

The following Tuesday at 10:00 a.m., Wendall was writing a check to the county clerk for combined fines of $455. At that very moment, Carl and Clare were stepping off their first-class flight from Kansas City back to Wichita.

Wendall never got a dime of his money back. His total loss was nearly sixteen hundred dollars of hard-earned cash that represented a summer and a half of working in the fields. Wendall was certain that his original $1,000 paid for first-class airline tickets, box seats at Royals stadium, and a fancy reception. Carl's flippant excuse that "business can be risky" didn't sooth Wendall's anger. But *karma* quickly came around. David Fletcher was terribly disappointed with his next shipment of hamburger paddies. They weren't "the good kind" the previous delivery driver had promised. Fletcher's Drive-in promptly switched back to Peerless. First National Bank turned down Carl's application for a business loan after making an unannounced visit to warehouse number 1. Ruth hung around for the two weeks she was paid in advance, then walked out. She was the only intelligent person in this sad story. Security National Bank eventually repossessed Carl's Cadillac. Wendall's only consolation: he wasn't the biggest sucker to lose money to Carl's con job. Several local and out-of-town loan sharks took it on the chin. They quickly convinced Carl to run and hide in California.

A "con man" is a "*con*fidence man" and often an ex-*con*vict. He or she *con*vinces or "cons" you into giving him or her something valuable, usually money. For the con man, it's a game and an easy way to make a living. You are the prey, and they are the predator. The con enjoys the "take" or the "kill." He feels no remorse for stealing your money. Literally, the con laughs all the way to the bank. He even has special names for you: the "sucker" and the "mark." Whether the scheme is pitched over the phone, in person, or online, *the game is always played with three specific lies*:

*The first lie:* There is some *incredible opportunity* that you greatly desire or some *impending disaster* that you horribly dread. The incredible opportunity is limited only by your desires and *greed*. The *con* man promises to make you a millionaire in business or help you collect your foreign lottery winnings or buy something at a huge discount and then resell it for a windfall profit or find the true love of your life or pursue a glamorous, lucrative career. On the other hand, the impending disaster plays on your *fears*. Thank goodness, the benevolent *con* man will save your good credit or save your Social Security benefits or stop the IRS from taking your home or keep criminals from stealing your checking account or protect your freedoms from the radical left socialists or the radical right fascists. Both of the *con's* strategies, greed and fear, *always* require you to hand over money or your financial information so he can steal your money.

*The second lie: You must act now.* Time is crucial. Otherwise, you will miss out and the "window of opportunity" will close or you will be too late to "prevent disaster." In greed-based cons, other "smart" people will swoop in quickly when they learn about this incredible deal or some urgent deadline is quickly approaching that will "wipe out" your chance of a lifetime; therefore, you must not delay. In fear-based schemes, you must open your wallet and act immediately to prevent certain disaster. Of course, who wouldn't?

*The third lie: The con is doing you a favor* because he sincerely wants to help you. He or she is your friend and someone you can trust. The *con* pleads for you to let him help you help yourself.

Con men and women repeat these three lies over and over, again and again, to wear down all your hesitations, objections, and excuses. You, the "mark," are repeatedly reminded of the following:

(1) the great reward or the terrible danger
(2) the urgency to act now
(3) the sincere friendship of the *con* man

Even the strongest-willed person can eventually succumb to the *con*. Your defense is simple. Remember two things:

- The *three lies,* which are *always* present in a *con*.
- *If it sounds too good, or too terrible, to be true, then it's a con.*

*Never give or send the con man any money or financial information!* Say no, and if necessary, say, "Dr. Wendall Nichols said no." Then zip your lips and listen for the three *B*s, unless you're on the phone, in which case, you can immediately hang up. Fight off the begging, the bargaining, and especially the bullying by telling the *con* man that you will let some other "lucky" person take advantage of their "golden opportunity." Or you will contact the police or other appropriate authorities and let *them* help you confront the IRS, the Social Security administration, or whatever other boogeyman whom the *con* man has invented.

# 15

# Emotional Fatigue

No, you're not crazy, and you're not weak.
You just got tired and worn out.
—Wendall Nichols

Over the past eighty years, the old hay barn had endured hundreds of thunderstorms with hail, high winds, and pounding rain. Its red paint had long since faded and peeled off. The original wood shingle roof was hidden by rusting galvanized tin sheets that curled on the corners when the wind blew. Wendall noticed that the roof line sagged on both ends giving it the profile of a camel's back. He was nervous when he climbed into the barn's empty loft for the first time. Wendall wasn't afraid of heights, but he was terrified of falling ten feet through the loft floor. It was designed for loose hay in the days before balers were invented. Modern bales of hay are much denser than loose hay because the hay is compressed and bound by two strands of wire. Each bale weighs about sixty pounds. Wendall wondered, *How many bales can this old barn support?* Unfortunately, he was about to find out.

If your farm has pastures, then you must own cattle. Cattle eat the grass, gain weight, get fat, and make you money. But during the winter, grass doesn't grow in the pastures, and you have to feed hay to all those hungry cows. That summer, Gerald made Max Nichols a real bargain on a thousand bales of alfalfa hay. Gerald even offered to "put it up" in the barn for Max. On the day of delivery, Wendall was worried. A thousand bales at sixty pounds per bale was thirty tons of hay.

"Dad, I'm afraid the loft might fall in with a thousand bales."

"Nah, it's strong enough. I'm sure it's been full of hay lots of times."

"Why not stack some of the hay on the bottom floor just in case?"

"Can't do that. That's where the cows are gonna be when it snows."

Gerald's crew stacked the bales "to the rafters" and completely filled the loft. Only five bales had to be placed in the bottom floor.

Max wrote Gerald a check for the hay, shook his hand, and he and Wendall waved goodbye to the crew as their bale wagons rumbled down the driveway.

Max smiled and nodded toward the barn. "What did I tell you. See, the old barn did just fine."

Wendall saw a sparrow fly into the loft and perch on one of the bales. Of course, it wouldn't be fair to blame the subsequent disaster on that innocent little bird. But technically, he was the sparrow that broke the barn's back. A high-pitched screech scared the sparrow out. Then the *crack, crack, crack* sound of snapping floor boards quickly followed. The sides of the barn sucked in as it exhaled 995 bales onto the bottom floor with dust billowing out of every opening. Then the barn took a full breath as the walls sprung back into place. Miraculously, the roof stayed on.

Well, everything, including the old barn, has a breaking point. And Wendall was soon to learn that *everyone* has a breaking point too.

Summer turned to autumn, and autumn turned to the winter of Wendall's senior year at Clearwell. He looked outside his window to see a frozen, windy Saturday morning. The only good thing about winter was the absence of flies, wasps, and searing heat outside. The only bad thing about winter was the absence of anything to do outside, after the cows were fed. Yes, another "indoor day" of watching TV, reading comic books, doing homework, and tolerating

Damon's war games. Until…Wendall heard the phone ring, and then his mother called out to him,

"Wendall, it's for you."

As he took the phone from her, he asked, "Who is it?"

She whispered, "Jeanne. She sounds upset."

"Hello, this is Wendall."

"Hi, this is Jeanne Cochran. Lawrence is in the hospital."

"Oh my gosh. What happened?"

"He"—sobbing—"he was alone at home, and he must have fallen."

"Oh no!"

"Last night, he said he didn't feel good, and he didn't want to go to the movies with us. I should have stayed home with him."

"Is he okay?"

"He won't talk to anyone. I thought maybe he would talk to you."

"Then he's awake? Why can't he talk?"

Jeanne was crying so hard Wendall had to wait a few seconds for her response. "I'm not sure. He won't even look at us."

"I'll have my dad drive me to Sisters of Mercy."

"No, no. Charles will drive out and pick you up. You're Lawrence's oldest friend."

"Don't worry, Mrs. Cochran. I'll talk to him."

Lawrence, better known as Larry by his friends, was Wendall's first friend. Their mothers had been friends since their high school days. Wendall and Larry were born only one month apart and learned to crawl, walk, and ride bicycles together. They were as close as brothers until the Nichols family moved out to the farm. They slowly drifted apart as their lives became busy with Larry at Benson High and Wendall at Clearwell. But there was no erasing a friendship that was imprinted during their infancy. Larry's father, Charles, pulled up to the Nichols's farmhouse, and Wendall got in his car.

Wendall was surprised that Mr. Cochran didn't appear sad or afraid. He looked perturbed, even angry. The tone of his voice confirmed Wendall's perception.

"I overheard what Jeanne told you on the phone. There's more to the story than just a slip and fall. What I am about to tell you is *never* to be repeated. You understand what I'm saying?"

Wendall felt curious and threatened at the same time. "Yes, sir."

"The truth is, Lawrence overdosed on Jeanne's prescription nerve pills, and he drank half a bottle of Scotch whisky. Then he took a handful of Tylenol, which the doctors say is the worst thing he could have done."

"Tylenol is bad for you?"

Charles nodded slowly without taking his eyes off the road. "Apparently, it destroys your liver if you take too much."

"Didn't know that. Was he trying to hurt himself or did he just get drunk and, you know, disoriented?"

Wendall could see that Mr. Cochran was getting more upset. "We don't know. He won't say a word."

Wendall sat staring at the dash of the car and thinking, *He's one of my best friends, and yet I've hardly talked to him in three years. What could have happened?* Wendall knew that Mr. Cochran had always demanded perfection from Larry. Years before, during their Little League baseball days, Charles Cochran wanted his son to be a star pitcher. Larry was a good athlete, and he could throw hard for a ten-year-old. But he had no control. He was more likely to hit a batter than to strike him out. Mr. Cochran was particularly upset when Larry wasn't voted as the team's most valuable player (MVP) at the end of the season. Henry Dobson, their best pitcher, was the unanimous winner that year. Larry was now a senior in high school, but nothing had changed. The rumor in Benson was that Charles Cochran had a heated argument with Coach Simmons in August. Mr. Cochran was furious that Larry wasn't named the starting quarterback of the varsity team. Instead, Coach made Larry a wide receiver. Of course, there were academic expectations as well. Larry once told Wendall that his dad said, "There's no reason why you can't be a Rhodes scholar someday, so you better get your butt in gear."

Mr. Cochran stopped in the circle drive in front of the hospital's main entrance. "He's in room 209. There's one other thing you should know. His girlfriend, Amanda, broke up with him. That's probably what triggered all this stupidity."

"I didn't know he was dating anyone."

"She's not just anyone. She's trash."

"When did they break up?"

"Katy [Larry's sister] said last week."

Wendall opened the car door. "I'll find out what happened."

Wendall had never visited a hospital before. He was struck by the smell of disinfectant, loud overhead intercoms calling for doctors "stat," and people dressed in white uniforms pushing metal carts down the halls. He found room 209, but it had a No Visitors sign on the door. Well, Wendall wasn't a visitor. He was a best friend. He walked straight in.

"Hey, man. How are ya feelin'?"

Larry was lying on his back in the hospital bed. He rolled his head toward Wendall. "Oh hell. They called you."

Wendall chuckled. "You damn right. I'm your brother, remember?"

Larry sighed. "I don't want you to see me like this."

"Well, I don't want to see you like this either."

Larry produced a small, fleeting smile then looked away.

Wendall tried to reassure him. "You can talk to me. *Nothing* leaves this room. If anyone asks me what you said, I'll lie. Okay?

"Okay."

"What happened?"

Larry's eyes filled with tears. "I screwed up, big time. I took a bunch of my mom's nerve medicine and then drank, I don't know, half a bottle of my dad's Scotch. Then I got such a bad headache. So I took a handful of Tylenol."

"But you're gonna be okay, right?"

A tear began rolling down Larry's cheek, and he quickly wiped it away. "Maybe not. The doctor is really worried about my liver because of the Tylenol. They keep checking my blood every few hours and giving me something through this IV line."

Wendall looked up at the plastic bag of clear fluid connected to a spaghetti-sized tube running to Larry's forearm. He tried to be reassuring. "I'll talk to the doctor if you want. I'll find out what they're doing."

"Thanks, man. You always were good in chemistry. I never learned anything in that class."

"Remember this?" Wendall mimicked a terrified, high-pitched voice, "Mr. Ramsey! Mr. Ramsey! My experiment is on fire!"

They both started laughing. It was a good to see Larry laugh, even if it was for only a few seconds.

Larry shook his head. "What a dumb-ass Starkley was."

"Yeah. It's a wonder he didn't burn down the lab."

A subdued "yeah."

Wendall turned serious. "Your dad told me about Amanda. Even though I've never met her, I'm really sorry."

"Thanks. But it's not just her. There's a lot of other crap going on."

"Like what?"

Larry looked down and fell silent.

Wendall sat down. "Don't forget who you're talkin' to. I'm not gonna judge you."

Larry looked up. "I just don't want you to think I'm some crazy person for tryin' to kill myself."

Wendall shook his head. "I've known you my whole life, and you're definitely not crazy. Sounds like you just got worn out and… overloaded."

Angry tears welled up in Larry's eyes. "Yeah, I finally got tired of takin' shit from everybody. No matter what I do, it's never enough. I'm such a damn 'disappointment' all the time. So I thought, fine! To hell with everything! I'm checkin' out!"

Wendall sat silent for a few seconds, then said, "Sorry, I didn't know. I should have been there for you."

Larry regained his composure. "It's my fault. After you moved, I quit keeping in touch, and…my dad told me you were a loser."

"He called me a loser?"

Larry smiled. "Sure did. I believe his exact words were 'Stop associating with losers like that Nichols kid.'"

"He called me a kid and a loser?"

"Kinda pisses ya off, doesn't it?"

"He doesn't even know me. And today, not twenty minutes ago, he asked for my help. What a jerk!"

"Right! Now ya know how I feel."

Wendall let his disgust drift away. He was thankful that Charles Cochran wasn't his father. "I can't imagine what you've gone through. Your dad drove me over here. In the car, I got to thinking about our Little League days. I remember him screaming from the bleachers at the umpire behind home plate every time you came to bat."

Larry grimaced. "After I wasn't the MVP, he rode me for a year. But did he ever come outside and play catch with me? Hell no. Same thing with football. He wants me to be a star quarterback. But he's never even offered to catch any passes from me."

"Did he and Coach Simmons get into it last August?"

"Yeah, humiliated me in front of the entire team. And you know Coach. If anyone tries to tell him anything, he does the opposite. I'm surprised he didn't put me on defense."

"Changing the subject. What about Amanda? Any chance of getting back together?"

Larry slowly shook his head. "No. She really dumped on me. I don't ever want her back."

"What happened?"

Larry sat up on the side of his bed. "Well, Zales had this garnet ring, and she wanted it for Christmas. Garnet is her birthstone."

Wendall cut in, "How much?"

"Eighty-five bucks."

"Ouch. Where'd ya get the money?"

"Well, I couldn't ask my parents for it. They hate her. So I pawned my ten-speed."

"Really! I've never pawned anything."

"Benson Pawn down on Broadway gave me only seventy bucks."

Wendall was shocked. "That's a top-of-the-line Schwinn! Didn't that bike cost around two hundred?"

"Two-fifty actually. But the seventy was enough to get the ring, and I wasn't worried. My grandma Cochran always, always, gives me a hundred dollars for Christmas, and I planned to use that to pay the pawn and get back my bike. But…" Larry looked away.

"What went wrong?"

Larry let out a long breath. "I made a B+ in calculus, the only B on my report card. My dad said I needed to spend more time studying and less time 'running around with a hussy.'"

"You're kidding. He got upset about that? About one B+?"

Larry snorted. "Yeah. So he called his mother, and instead of a hundred bucks, I got a college calculus textbook for Christmas."

"Oh shit."

"Right. Now if I want it back, it'll cost me two hundred and twenty-five bucks."

"And your parents don't know?"

"Of course not. They don't pay any attention to me, until they find out that I've messed up in school."

"Uh…How are your grades this semester?"

"Terrible. Nine-week report cards come out next Friday, and I've got straight Fs."

"Oh no! Really?"

Larry found Wendall's alarmed reaction somewhat amusing. He decided to push that button again. "Hell, I had an English midterm paper due yesterday. I never even started it. At this rate, I won't even graduate."

"What happened?"

Larry stared out the window. "I just gave up. Why even try anymore? Nothing I do matters. Besides, I can't concentrate long enough to study anything. I'll read something, and two minutes later, I don't remember any of it."

"Are you getting enough sleep?"

"Not really. I try, but I'm up till one in the morning most nights. But you know the worst part? Every, little, f—thing irritates the hell out of me."

"Like what?"

"Stupid things like…the phone ringing or a car on the street playing loud music. And when I hear my dad or my mom's voice, I just want to rip their damned heads off. I scream at Katy for hoggin' the bathroom and talkin' on the phone all the time. I almost killed her cat for shedding on my bed. Then I punched Amanda's locker at school so hard I dented it. Can you believe it? She didn't like her ring. It didn't look as good on her finger as she thought it would. Well, excuse me, you ungrateful bitch!"

Wendall shook his head in disbelief. "I'm really sorry, man."

"Oh, and don't let me forget that pissant, Jason Begley?"

"Who's Jason Begley?"

"He's a smartass on our basketball team. Laughed in my face after he blocked one of my jump shots in practice. Made me *so mad*! I shoved him as hard as I could. He fell on his ugly face and bloodied his nose. That got me kicked off the team."

"You got kicked off the basketball team!"

"Doesn't matter. I would've been suspended anyway after my grades came out. Like Coach says, 'If you don't pass, you don't play.'"

"Your mom and dad don't know about that either?"

Larry smiled sarcastically. "Oh, they'll find out soon enough, when they're in the stands at the tricounty tournament next weekend." Larry mocked his father's deep voice. "Where's my boy Lawrence? Why isn't he out there? He's gonna be the tournament MVP!'"

Wendall was desperate to throw Larry any kind of lifeline. The last person Larry had any feelings for was Amanda. Perhaps she could help. "Do you want me to call Amanda?"

Larry's sarcasm immediately turned to hatred. "Of course not! She was the final straw! She dumped me!"

"Why?"

Back to sarcasm, "Because Harold Douglas is a 'real man' who drives a Camaro. Whoop-de-do! Oh yeah. And his parents think she's *wonderful*."

"Did you get the ring back?"

Larry's hateful stare answered Wendall's question.

They both sat silently and stared at the floor. Larry finally spoke, "I don't know why, but one minute I'm so damned angry at my parents, Amanda, and everybody else, especially myself. Then two seconds later, I feel completely overwhelmed and hopeless. I don't know whether to hit something and scream bloody murder or curl up and cry like a baby. I even thought of hitchin' a ride out of town and never looking back."

"At least that would be better than killing yourself."

Larry raised his voice. "You think so? Well I don't! My parents would hunt me down, just so they could punish me. Then *never* let me forget how 'stupid and weak' I am. So last night, I decided they could say that to my cold dead body."

"I understand."

"Do you! Do you really!" Larry's anger was flaring again. "Have you *ever* felt like just giving up, laying down, and dying?"

Wendall slowly nodded. "Yeah."

"Oh yeah! When?"

"You remember that ridiculous President's Fitness Test four years ago when you were on the junior varsity football team?"

"Yeah. It was a stupid waste of time. Cost us a week of practice."

"Well, all of us weaklings in the regular PE class had to take the same test. I don't even remember the last lap of the six-hundred-yard run. What I *do* remember is lying face down in the grass in my own vomit. I thought I was gonna die. I couldn't breathe. I was completely worn out. It took me fifteen minutes to get on my feet and only because Coach helped me. Then I missed school the rest of the day. So yeah, I understand what it feels like to give up...physically anyway. Right now, you've given up emotionally."

Larry looked at Wendall suspiciously. "Did you talk to some shrink before you came in here? Did they tell you what to say to me?"

Wendall shook his head emphatically. "No. No, of course not. I haven't talked to anybody."

Larry looked down at the IV line in his arm. "So you think I'm 'emotionally' worn out?"

"Yeah. I mean...think about it. Every little thing irritates the hell out of you. Your moods swing from being so angry you want to kill someone to being so hopeless you want to kill yourself. You can't think straight or concentrate. It's no wonder you can't decide what to do."

Larry plopped back onto his hospital bed. "Maybe my dad's right. I'm not tough enough. I'm just a weak-minded disappointment."

Wendall stood up and looked straight at his friend. "You're not weak. Just because you got pushed to your limit doesn't mean you're weak. Don't ever let anyone tell you different."

"Then how the hell did I get to this point?"

Wendall sat back down. "Simple. I think you tried too hard."

"To do what?"

"To please everybody and obey all the rules."

"What rules?"

"The rules of civilization."

Larry frowned. "Give me a break. Now you're talkin' psycho-babble."

Wendall extended his right hand like a traffic cop. "No. No, I'm being serious here. Just follow me on this. In the wild, there are no rules, no laws, and no ethics. If two animals face off against each other, they either fight it out or one of them runs away. Then it's over. Done. No more stress. But people don't live in the wild. We have to live in a 'civilized' society where we have to be polite, respectful, follow the law, do what we're told, and be 'good.' If some jerk irritates you, you can't beat 'em up. You'll get arrested or, in your case, thrown off the basketball team. And if you run away, the police or your family will track you down. So you have to grit your teeth and take it again and again until the stress is unbearable."

"No shit."

"Speaking of wild animals. Did you know that wild animals never get depressed? You never see a depressed lion or bear or coyote in the wild. But once you put 'em in a cage, then they fight and bite at you, and if you keep 'em caged long enough, isolated, by themselves, they finally give up. They won't eat or drink, and they will literally lay down and die."

"What's that got to do with me?"

"You've been in a cage for years. Except your cage doesn't have steel bars. It has invisible bars made of all the 'civilized' rules and expectations of how you are supposed to behave."

"Oh, okay. You're saying it's *my* fault. I should've broken all the rules and become an asshole or a criminal?"

"No. Not at all." Wendall was starting to feel frustrated. "*None of this* is your fault. Like I said, you just tried too hard to be a decent, 'perfect' person for everyone else. That's how you got worn out."

Wendall took a deep breath. "Think of it this way. Every time you have to make a decision or meet a deadline or bite your tongue or force yourself to do something that you don't want to do, then you burn emotional energy. It's like working out in the gym non-stop. Eventually, you run out of energy. You get fatigued, *emotionally* fatigued. It is every bit as real as *physical* fatigue. It's just harder to measure."

Larry sat up again. "You're probably right. I tried so damned hard. Then I finally quit trying and thought screw it."

"Yeah. You quit everything, even trying to stay alive."

"So you don't think I'm crazy or stupid…or a coward?"

Wendall shook his head. "No, you're not crazy, and you're not weak. You just got tired and worn out. And just because you did one stupid thing doesn't mean you're stupid. You're no coward either. You've been hanging in there for years."

Larry sat silently for a few seconds. "So what do I do now?"

Wendall smiled. "You do what Slick 'n Greasy taught me."

Larry and Wendall had known Slick since they were little kids. "What? Tell everyone to kiss my ass?"

Wendall laughed. "Yeah. Pretty much. You gotta quit trying to please *other people* and stop worrying about what *they think*."

Larry grinned. "Slick said that?"

"His exact words were 'Don't give a damn about what other people think.'"

Larry nodded solemnly. "I think I'm getting there."

"Good. 'Cause that's how you escape from the cage."

Larry smirked. "The one with invisible bars?"

"Yes. But…uh, you'll need help from other people."

Larry sighed. "Just what I don't wanna do, ask anyone for help."

"There's no other way. Throw your pride out the window. Take all the help you can get and don't be embarrassed to ask for it. First, who can make your dad and mom lay off?

"Grandma Cochran."

"Good. When she comes up here, you tell her *everything*. Then you ask her for help. Let her run interference for you."

"What's that mean?"

"Block for you. You know, like on the football field. She can order your parents to stop all the ridiculous expectations. Meanwhile, I'll be blocking downfield by helping you get back on track with your classes. But you're gonna have to ask your teachers for some leeway. You'll need more time and some extra credit work to turn your grades around."

Larry sighed. "All right."

"You can do it. You'll be surprised. Most people will gladly help you if you ask them."

"Okay."

"Oh one other thing. You've got to write a letter to that player you shoved."

"Begley?"

"Yeah, and to Coach Simmons and the entire basketball team. Sincerely apologize for lettin' 'em down, no excuses either. I know you had a good reason for what you did. But just straight up say you're sorry."

"Why should I do that?"

"So you can put it behind you. Besides, they're your friends, and they can help you. Also, you need Coach Simmons on your side to play baseball this spring."

Larry paused for a few seconds. "Okay, I'll do it."

Wendall started walking toward the door. "I'm gonna go talk to your parents."

Larry stood up. "Wait, wait! What are you gonna tell 'em?"

Wendall stopped. "That you've discovered the problem and agreed to talk to your Grandma Cochran."

Wendall kept his word and repeated that one-line message to Mr. Cochran. Meanwhile, Susan Nichols arrived at the hospital with Damon to pick up Wendall. As they were leaving, an ambulance was backing up to the ER entrance. Little did Wendall know that another victim of emotional fatigue, Elmer Hensman, had just arrived at Sisters of Mercy. But unlike Larry, Elmer was overwhelmed in a matter of days instead of years.

Elmer and Mary Hensman were married for fifty-four years, reared two sons and three daughters, and never spent a day apart that entire time. But eight days ago, Mary suffered a massive stroke and died suddenly at home in Elmer's arms. The funeral was beautiful, full of tears, and attended by dozens of family and friends. Then everyone went home, including Elmer. He sat down on his couch, lost and catatonic with grief, and he didn't get up. Two days later, his oldest daughter called to check on him. She immediately came over when he didn't answer the phone, and then she broke in when he didn't answer the door. Dehydrated, unresponsive, and near death, he was now being unloaded at the emergency room as Wendall was leaving. Despite the wonders of modern medicine, Elmer's mind and body could not be revived. He joined Mary later that day.

Fortunately, Larry's struggle had a happier ending. He recovered from his emotional fatigue and pulled out of depression. He got his grades up, played baseball that spring, and graduated. But it wasn't an easy road. He had to learn to say no to his parents and fend off their three Bs, particularly their bullying guilt induction. Charles and Jeanne Cochran attempted to shame Larry for "humiliating" them with his suicide attempt and "ruining" his grades the last semester of his high school career. Larry was finally cured when he realized that his first obligation in this life is to *himself* and not to his parents or *anyone* else.

Society has called it by many names: "mental breakdown," "burned out," "stressed out," "down in the dumps," "depressed," and "feeling blue." But in the medical field, emotional fatigue is called major depression. However, when most people think of the word "depression," they think of sadness and grief. But major depression is so much more. It is a devastating, incapacitating mixture of hopelessness, anger, and dread, and it is a *normal response* to overwhelming *or* persistent psychological stress. We can be emotionally overwhelmed by a single devastating event, such as the loss of a spouse, a child, or a cherished friend or relative. But more often, dozens of smaller stressors pile up overtime and eventually wear us down. When we suffer from major depression, *there is nothing wrong with our brain or personality or character.* The changes in our concentration, emotions, and decision making are due to *expected* changes in our brain chemistry caused by emotional and psychological stress. It is simply how humans are wired.

But make no mistake about it, normal reaction or not, major depression is as serious as a heart attack. *Suicide is the most dangerous, potential consequence of emotional fatigue.* If stressed enough, anyone will begin to think of giving up and ending their life. Their internal voice will tell them something like this:

- "I can't take it anymore. Anything is better than this."
- "Everybody [or everything] would be better off if I weren't around anymore."
- "They will all be sorry."
- "I don't care about anything anymore."
- "I just want to go to sleep and not wake up."
- "I deserve to die."
- "I just want the pain to stop."

Don't wait another minute. Talk to someone, *anyone*, who cares about you. Call a friend, call a family member, call your doctor, call your minister, or go to the nearest ER. If you believe no one cares or no one is available, please call or text 988 for the Suicide and Crisis Lifeline. The lifeline is available twenty-four hours a day. They understand emotional fatigue. Talk or text with them and let them help you step back from the danger.

*Never tell yourself or let anyone tell you, or treat you, as if you are crazy, weak, or a waste of time.* Realize that no matter what has happened, no matter what the circumstances, no matter what anyone else may think or say, *every* human being is unique, priceless, and deserving of respect, including *you*. Fight for the incredible gift that God gave you: *your life.*

Finally, there are three treatments for emotional fatigue, a.k.a. major depression. All focus on the same end point: *changing our brain chemistry* back to normal.

1. Medications.

Modern anti-depressant medications began with Prozac in the 1980s. These prescription drugs all increase the levels of neurotransmitters, serotonin or norepinephrine or both, by blocking their "reuptake" and subsequent breakdown by our neurons. In other words, the drugs don't cause our brains to manufacture more. Instead, they make our neurotransmitters last longer. The medications do help, although they can take two to three weeks to "kick in" and make people feel better. However, anti-depressants are *not a cure*. They are a crutch to help people until the underlying cause (stressors) are eliminated. Only then will the emotional fatigue and brain dysfunction be cured.

2. Professional counselling and therapy.

Therapy helps by identifying a person's specific stressors and emphasizing that many, many people face the same or similar stressors. The exact details may be slightly different, but the roots of stress in our civilized society are all the same: money, family, relationships, our health, and jobs. Counsellors, both medical and religious, can then identify what strategies and community resources are available to help knock the stressors out.

3. *Eliminate the stress yourself.*

*This is the only cure.* Medications and counselling can help. But unless you want to take medication and see a therapist for the rest of your life, *you* must make the necessary changes in your life to eliminate, or at least control, your stressors. Taking control requires you to say no, and saying no requires unwavering self-respect. The central theme of this book is to solidify your self-respect so that you can do the following:

- Feel grateful for every day of your life (chapter 1).

- Avoid other people's problems while still helping them (chapter 2).
- Ask for help and allow others to run interference for you (chapter 3).
- Care less about what other people think of you (chapter 4).
- Recognize the manipulative three Bs (chapters 5 and 6).
- Develop the courage to effectively say no (chapter 7).
- Prune your tree of unwanted obligations (chapter 8).
- Expect the best by finding your important purpose in life (chapter 9).
- Realize that luck is the result of planning, preparation, and hard work (chapter 10).
- Understand that nothing is impossible with determination and other people's help (chapter 11).
- Stand up for yourself and others and refuse to be bullied (chapter 12 and 13).
- Recognize a con and avoid their trap (chapter 14).
- Understand emotional fatigue and protect and help yourself when you recognize it (chapter 15).

# 16

# Respect Yourself

> To thine own self be true. And it must follow, as the night
> the day. Thou canst not then be false to any man.
> —William Shakespeare

All the chapters in this book contain a common thread that ties them together, self-respect. As William Shakespeare wrote, "To thine own self be true. And it must follow, as the night the day. Thou canst not then be false to any man." It's an eloquent way of saying, "Respect yourself, then you will enjoy peace of mind." Whether we realize it or not, everyone is seeking the same thing: a life with no hassles, no anxiety, and no worries. Such a life doesn't come from being rich, or retired, or living off the grid. Peace of mind can only be obtained by *respecting yourself above everything and everyone else*. If you are fortunate enough to be part of a loving and supportive family, then self-respect is a given, and often taken for granted. But if you are not blessed to have a Mrs. Brown or her Papa in your life either as a mother, father, grandfather, grandmother, neighbor, or friend, then you must build your own self-respect. But how?

Focus on *four universal truths* over and over, again and again, until they become ingrained into your core:

*First*, realize that your very existence is a *miracle*. In 1850, the odds of you *ever being born* were trillions to one. *Even one year before your birth*, the odds of you *ever existing* were billions to one. Why?

Because each of us was formed from one of a dozen eggs that began maturing in our mother's ovaries during the month we were conceived. Only one of those eggs won the race to maturity and was released by one of her ovaries that month. *Your* egg had roughly twenty-four hours to then be fertilized by one, and only one, of hundreds of millions of sperm from your father. *Your* one lucky sperm won that race. Therefore, statistically, each of us is a super mega lottery winner. All of us are *so incredibly fortunate* to have ever been born.

*Second*, each of us is *unique* in our genetics, personalities, and experiences. Only identical twins will have the same genetics but their personalities and experiences will be different. No one else in history is exactly like you. Your abilities, physical, mental, and emotional, are one of a kind. It is a ridiculous comedy that societies *rank* men and women according to *desirable* traits. Were you born with the best skin color, hair color, eye color, height, weight, race, breast size, and physique? How well do you perform regurgitating the correct answers on standardized tests? How skilled are you at throwing, kicking, or shooting balls of various sizes and shapes in man-made sports? How well can you sing or play a brass or wood instrument? The list is nearly endless, and it changes over time. None of these artificial criteria have *any bearing* on your importance as a human being.

*Third*, some people will attempt to destroy your self-respect. They will treat you unfairly or with contempt for any of a thousand reasons. You are different from them, or you don't possess certain *acceptable* traits or you don't allow them to manipulate you. Their prejudice only shows their ignorance of the strength of your self-respect.

*Fourth*, you are never alone. Remember the words of Mrs. Brown. "There's someone who will *always* love you and boost you up and never die. That's our Lord Savior, Jesus Christ. So we *all got good reason* to be full of self-respect and happiness, no matter what." Remind yourself continuously that you are important, unique, and worthy of respect, no matter what you've done in the past or how you've been treated or where you are at this moment in time.

Never forget that your level of self-respect determines the quality of *every aspect of your life*. Self-respect gives you the courage to stand up, not just for yourself but for others as well. It helps you stare down the three *B*s and say no to the people who try to suppress you. It gives you the courage to demand the freedom to make your own choices and live the happy life you want and not what society or someone else wants. It gives you the confidence to realize the incredible power you possess to find your purpose, raise your expectations, shape your world, and achieve the seemingly impossible. And finally, self-respect grants you the peace of mind to never worry about what others may think of you because you know exactly who you are: a unique, priceless human being and child of God.

# About the Author

Tim Jones is a family physician practicing in rural Texas. The characters and lessons in *Mentors and Tormentors: On the Journey to Self-Respect* are drawn from his colorful childhood growing up on the Great Plains. After thirty years of telling these stories to help patients one-on-one, he has finally placed them in print for the benefit of a wider audience. Please enjoy, and remember to always pay attention and ask questions.

CPSIA information can be obtained
at www.ICGtesting.com
Printed in the USA
JSHW061115221222
35292JS00002B/8